THE BEST OF Chinese Cooking

BETTY YEW

TIMES BOOKS INTERNATIONAL
Singapore • Kuala Lumpur

The Publisher wishes to thank Takashimaya Singapore Ltd, Corning (Singapore) Pte Ltd and C K Tang Ltd for the loan of their crockery and utensils; Shang Antiques & Crafts for the lovely antiques; and HEALTHY Ginseng Birdnest Centre for the Chinese herbal ingredients.

Photographs by Peter Chua of Caesar Commercial Photo
Food Styling by Eddy Koh

Published by
Times Editions Pte Ltd
Times Centre, 1 New Industrial Road
Singapore 536196

Times Subang
Lot 46, Subang Hi-Tech Industrial Park
Batu Tiga
40000 Shah Alam
Selangor Darul Ehsan, Malaysia

Printed in Singapore

ISBN: 981 204 692 5

Dedicated with love
to
Choobs

"Food is the nearest thing to heaven"

– ancient Chinese saying

Contents

Preface

The Chinese have always been very serious about their eating, as serious as to be almost obsessed by food. This one great passion for food has contributed to Chinese cuisine being developed into a refined art. With the ease of international travel and the migration of Chinese to all the corners of the world, this superb cuisine is today enjoyed not only by the Chinese, but has gathered many ardent admirers.

Chinese cooking takes more things into consideration than just simply putting together a mass of ingredients. Obviously, the first consideration, as in many other cuisines, is the freshness of the main ingredients. Then there is the correct combination of main ingredients in order for the various flavours to complement each other. The seasoning and sauce are also very important. Finally, the right cooking technique, or combination of techniques, must be employed to enhance the texture, flavour and appearance of the food.

All these may seem to be very complicated, especially for those uninitiated into the art of Chinese cooking, or cooking at all. But, contrary to popular belief, Chinese cooking can be very simple if the basic techniques are understood and applied correctly. It is for this reason that I have decided to write a book focusing on the different methods of Chinese cooking. In this way, one does not only learn a recipe, one also acquires the skills to employ that particular method of cooking. This will make Chinese cooking simple to learn and master. Having learned the basic methods, one can also experiment with one's own different combinations using these methods.

Another reason that has prompted me to write this book are my experiences during a stay in Europe. I met numerous Europeans who enjoy authentic Chinese cooking tremendously. Some of them have even tried their hand at Chinese cooking but have expressed their frustration at the difficulties involved. Despite the presence of so many Chinese restaurants, most of them still cater to what they believe to be the 'European taste', i.e. dishes with thick, sweet sauces. Therefore, I hope that my European friends who are 'dying' for authentic Chinese food can prepare it any time they wish using this book.

I have concentrated mostly on home cooking because I want to capture on paper all the fantastic food that our mothers and grandmothers cooked for us. Some of the dishes may be simple but they taste great. In fact, the ultimate skill in cooking is the ability to make a simple dish taste divine. With life getting busier, and less and less people having the time to cook at home, I fear we may lose this wonderful home cooking one day if it is not recorded.

Throughout this book I have given the equivalent Cantonese word for the cooking methods, some of the main ingredients and popular dishes. I have chosen to use Cantonese because the Cantonese kitchen is the most widespread of all the Chinese kitchens.

Finally, my greatest wish is for anyone who wants to cook great Chinese food to be able to satisfy this desire by just picking up this book.

The Different Methods of Chinese Cooking

STIR-FRYING *(Chao)*

One of the most significant, famous and fastest methods of Chinese cooking is stir-frying, known as *chao* in Cantonese. In fact, it can be said that this cooking technique is one of the important contributions of the Chinese to international cuisine. It is probably the most difficult of the techniques too because speed and control are essential for success.

The emphasis of stir-frying is fast cooking at high temperatures to retain the natural colour and goodness of food and to give them a crisp texture, especially vegetables. It is also used to bring out the fragrance of ingredients and to seal in the juices of meat before further cooking. Very small amounts of oil are required, making it one of the least oily of the cooking methods.

A good source of heat which can be easily controlled is essential. The practice of stir-frying, like all other methods of Chinese cooking, evolved from the use of open charcoal burners which can be controlled to emit intense or low heat. The gas cooker used today is more versatile and practical. It is also cleaner and control is superior. The poor control of the electric hot plate makes it impractical for stir-frying.

An infinite variety of dishes, ranging from simple vegetable dishes to exotic meat dishes, can be prepared by stir-frying. In fact, in most complicated preparations which require several methods of cooking, stir-frying is often the initial stage.

Important points to bear in mind for stir-frying are:

a) All ingredients must be prepared, measured and at hand before starting to cook.
b) Ingredients should be cut into small cubes or slices of similar size to facilitate quick and even cooking.
c) Ensure that the wok is heated before adding oil and the oil is really hot before adding the ingredients. The correct temperature is important for successful stir-frying and intense heat must be used.
d) When frying garlic and shallots to flavour the oil, ensure they are fragrant and lightly brown in colour before adding other ingredients.
e) Stir constantly to ensure that all ingredients are cooked to the same degree.
f) Careful timing must be exercised to ensure food is not overfried or overcooked.
g) Garnish stir-fried dishes simply so as not to conceal the appetising appearance of the dish.

BOILING *(Poh, Sap, Luk)*

The term "boiling" is really a misnomer when applied to Chinese cooking. With the exception of boiling meat bones for stocks, Chinese food is rarely boiled for a lengthy period.

Boiling appears to be the simplest form of cooking. However, overboiling of meats and seafood, whatever their cuts and whether whole, in pieces or shredded, can toughen and spoil the texture, just as overcooking of vegetables can render them soft and unappetising. Boiling may also seem dull and uninteresting but in Chinese cooking it is done methodically and meticulously, which explains the different expressions for the different degrees of boiling. The end result is a wide range of excellent dishes with appealing smooth textures and flavours.

The most common method of boiling in Chinese cooking is known as *poh* in Cantonese. Poh is done in plenty of liquid, such as stock or water, at a rapid boil for a brief period. The heat is then reduced to emit gentle bubbling on the surface, often for a couple of hours. A considerable amount of the liquid is retained, as opposed to braising and stewing where the liquid or gravy is greatly reduced. The method is applied to make porridge and soups. Rice is also cooked this way except all the liquid is absorbed by the rice.

A variance of boiling is known as *sap* in Cantonese. Meat is put into rapidly boiling water for a brief period. The meat is immediately taken out of the boiling water or sometimes further cooking is applied by turning off the heat and leaving the meat in the hot water for a further period. The cooked meat is marinated, or covered with a sauce, or eaten as it is with a sauce dip. Timing is of the essence in this method of cooking. Simple as it may seem, anyone who has tried their hand at making the famous "White Cut Chicken" *(Pak Cham Kai)* of the ever popular "Hainanese Chicken Rice" dish will know how difficult it is to obtain the succulent, tender and silky smooth texture of the chicken meat. This simple dish, which may appear bland and unappetising to those who have never sampled it, makes a delightfully tasty and wholesome meal for lunch or dinner.

Another type of boiling, called *luk* in Cantonese, literally means quick blanching or scalding in boiling water or stock. It is mainly applied to cooking green leafy vegetables and noodles.

Many varieties of green leafy vegetables can be simply and quickly blanched, and then mixed with oil and sauces for crisp and crunchy vegetable dishes (known as *yau choy* in Cantonese, which literally means "oiled vegetable") with no compromise to taste. Noodles can also be prepared in this manner. When mixed with sauce and topped with meat, it is known as "*wantan mee.*" Another variation is to serve the noodles in soups. Luk is also used to soften dried and fresh egg noodles, and rid them of excess starch in preparation for stir-frying.

Meat can also be cooked in this manner. A good example is the "Chinese Steam Boat," familiar to most people. But the meat must be cut into small pieces or shredded so that it can be adequately scalded to seal in the flavour and marinade. This method is also used to prepare meat for soups so that scum will not form on the surface of the soups.

Some important points to remember when cooking in this manner are:

a) Use a good size wok or deep pot to hold enough water to immerse the food. Ensure that the water is at boiling point before putting in the food. Scum has to be skimmed off constantly if the stock is to be retained for soups so that the liquid will be clear.
b) Time the cooking period carefully and regulate heat as required so as not to overcook the food.
c) If boiling for a longer period on low heat, check that there is enough liquid in the pot. If too much liquid is boiled down, top with boiling water or stock as required.
d) To remove vegetables or noodles quickly from the boiling water to prevent overcooking, either use a large-sized wire mesh ladle or place the food in a perforated basket which can be easily lifted from the boiling pot.
e) To retain the crisp green colour of vegetables and to prevent noodles from being overcooked, plunge into a basin of cold water after scalding and drain well.
f) Garnishing of boiled dishes, especially soups, should be very simple such as a good sprinkling of chopped spring onions, coriander leaves and chillies.

SHALLOW AND DEEP-FRYING *(Cheen and Chau)*

In addition to stir-frying, there are two other variations of frying in Chinese cooking—shallow-frying (*cheen*) and deep-frying (*chau*).

Shallow-frying is cooking food in a small amount of oil like stir-frying. However the food is not tossed around and there is very little movement except to turn the food to ensure that the entire portion is cooked. Cooking in this manner results in a fragrant and slightly crispy outer layer, while the inside is moist and the natural flavour is retained. This method, which takes very little time, is mainly used for food that cooks easily, such as fish, eggs, dumplings, stuffed vegetables and thin slices of meat. Many types of fish, some of the best grades and qualities, are simply seasoned with salt and pepper and cooked this way. Most dishes prepared in this manner are served without a sauce but eaten with an interesting variety of dips. A good selection of garnishes, such as carved vegetables and fruits, is essential to liven up the plain fried dish.

A wok may be used for shallow-frying but a flat pan is more practical as it ensures that the oil is evenly spread on the surface. The oil must be well distributed in the pan and heated before adding the food. This will prevent the food from sticking to the pan. The correct temperature and timing are important to prevent overcooking. After cooking on high heat for a few seconds, regulate the flame to medium or low, depending on the thickness of the food. The pan may be covered during cooking to shorten cooking time and to prevent splattering of oil.

Deep-frying (*chau*) involves cooking food by immersing it in very hot oil. This method is mainly used for poultry and seafood when a very crispy outer layer is desired. Food cooked in this manner can either be marinated or coated with batter. It is then served with a dip or covered with a cooked sauce.

The important points to note for deep-frying are similar to those for shallow-frying except a wok is more suitable. In a wok the food can be totally immersed in oil or half immersed with adequate room for basting.

STEAMING *(Cheng)*

Steaming, known as *cheng* in Cantonese, is one of the most delightful Chinese methods of cooking. By placing food above boiling water, the heat from the steam cooks the food. It is simple, quick and nicest of all, it is easy to keep the kitchen free from oil splatters and the clutter of utensils. Even the most disorganised cook will be able to keep the kitchen reasonably neat and tidy since steamed food is usually prepared, steamed and served in the same dish.

Although the method is simple, a lot of effort is put into choosing the correct marinade to produce the desired flavour and texture. Very little oil is required which makes it one of the least oily preparation methods. For meat, either in pieces or minced, some oil and fat are essential to produce a smoother texture. Fish and prawns come out particularly well, and the Chinese prefer to steam the most expensive types of fish.

Garnishing is important for steamed dishes not only to improve the flavour but also the appearance. An imaginative choice of garnishing, such as shredded fresh red chillies and spring onions soaked in cold water to make them curl, a good sprinkling of chopped spring onion, or a bunch of coriander leaves or parsley adds colour and brightens up any steamed dish. Garnishing should only be concentrated on the surface of the food after it is cooked.

Important points to bear in mind when steaming are:

a) Use a proper steamer of an adequate size with a tight-fitting lid. A metal steamer is preferred (see notes on steamers on pages 14–15). The amount of water depends on the period of steaming required. As a general guide, fill the bottom pan up to the halfway mark. If the water should boil down before cooking is finished, top up

with boiling water to continue steaming.

b) Ensure that the water is at a rapid boil before putting food into the steamer.

c) If the cover is removed during cooking for inspection of food, wipe it dry before replacing to prevent condensed water from dripping onto the food.

d) To prevent too much water from dripping into the dish, a dry towel can be placed under the lid. Ensure that the ends of the towel are securely wrapped around the lid so they do not trail into the fire.

e) All meat and seafood should be marinated for at least 15 minutes before steaming. If a thickening, such as cornflour and tapioca flour is used, always stir the food again just before steaming to prevent starchy lumps from forming in the sauce.

f) The correct steaming time is very important to obtain a smooth texture for meat and seafood. Oversteaming of egg dishes will result in the dish being watery, coarse and pockmarked.

A variation of the simple steaming process is the 'double steaming' or 'closed steaming' process known as *tarn* in Cantonese. Instead of an open dish, steaming is carried out in a closed ceramic or stoneware receptacle or a bowl with a cover.

This method is mainly used to prepare what the Chinese would consider to be nutritious and health rendering soups. Ingredients ranging from the common chicken to exotic game and fowl, such as turtles, pigeons and flying foxes, are combined with various mixtures of herbs and spices to produce delectable dishes. Often the most expensive ingredients and herbs are used.

The imaginative and creative Chinese cook has even used the whole coconut, winter melon and pumpkin not only as essential ingredients but also as receptacles for this type of cooking. The flavour and fragrance of these soups must be tasted to be believed.

BRAISING AND STEWING (*Mun*)

Amongst the Chinese, the Cantonese are the most famous for their braised and stewed dishes, In this long cooking process, which sometimes takes several hours, meat, seafood and vegetables are simmered with a multitude of sauces and spices. Even less expensive cuts of meat, such as the shin and brisket, pig trotters and entrails, chicken feet and fish heads, are transformed into appetising Chinese dishes with rich, brown-coloured sauces and tantalising aromas.

A good combination of sauces, ingredients and spices is essential in braising and stewing. Light and thick soya sauces are major components. Flavouring ingredients include ginger, garlic and shallots. Popular spices are five spice powder, cinnamon, clove, star anise and Szechuan and white peppercorns. The mixture of spices is often wrapped in a muslin bag so the spices will not cloud the sauce and can be removed as required.

Meat should be seasoned and given time to marinate and absorb the seasonings before braising. Sometimes meat and even vegetables are first quickly fried in oil or blanched in boiling water to seal in the flavour and juices. Braised dishes require only very simple garnishing, such as a sprinkling of chopped spring onion or a topping of coriander leaves or parsley.

Choice of cooking utensils is important for better control over the slow cooking. The earthen pot or clay pot is popularly used. The wok is also used especially for whole fowls, fish and large cuts of meat. In this case, special care must be taken not to apply too much heat, which will ruin the dish. A practical utensil without too much attention required is the electric crock pot.

ROASTING, GRILLING AND SMOKING (*Siew, Wui* and *Yeen*)

Roasting (*siew*) in Chinese cooking is normally carried out either on an open or closed spit. In keeping with modern times, the conventional oven is also used. The Chinese are famous for their roasted pig, duck and goose with crispy skin and succulent meat. The best results can only be obtained by roasting on a closed turning spit shaped like a drum and fired by charcoal (for that special fragrant flavour).

An ingenious method of roasting is dry-roasting in a wok filled with coarse salt. This is normally done with chicken to produce the famous *yim koke kai,* literally known as "Salt Baked Chicken." It has a simple seasoning but the end result is delicious.

The Chinese are also famous for their grilled (*wui*) meat; mainly *char siew* and *siew pai kuat,* grilled pork and spareribs. Again, the best results are obtained from grilling on an open spit fired by charcoal. The electric grill or turbo broiler can also be used.

Important points to bear in mind when roasting or grilling are:

a) Select the correct cut of meat.
b) Prepare a good marinade and seasoning. Ensure that sufficient time is given for marinating. With large chunks of meat, prick the meat with a fork to enable the marinade to penetrate.
c) Ensure that the oven, grill or broiler is preheated to the required temperature before putting in the meat. This allows the high heat to cook the outside of the meat very quickly and seal in the juices and flavour of the meat. Careful timing will prevent overcooking or charring of meat.
d) Brush the meat with some melted fat to prevent it from drying out. Place a pan at the bottom of the oven or grill to catch any drippings which can be used for basting or as sauce.

As in other types of cuisine, the Chinese also employ the method of smoking (*yeen*) to prepare some dishes. Smoking will add fragrance and flavour to the meat. Tea leaves, camphor wood, pine needles, dried orange peel, flour or rice grains can be used for smoking in a pot or wok. The meat is often cooked by steaming, either before or after smoking. Poultry is usually deep-fried after smoking to obtain the crispy skin, well-liked by the Chinese.

Cooking Utensils

Chinese cooking does not require a large variety of utensils as most of them are very versatile. Moreover, most Chinese kitchens are usually small and therefore equipment has to be kept to a minimum.

THE WOK AND COVER

The wok, which is usually made of black cast iron or steel, quickly absorbs varying degrees of heat. Today, woks coated internally with non-stick material (teflon) and brightly coloured on the outside are available. These colourful woks not only brighten the kitchen but also reduce oil splatter from cooking and are much easier to clean. Flat bottomed woks are also available for electric plate cooking.

The size of the wok should be chosen to hold the amount of food that you would normally prepare for the family. I prefer a medium-sized wok with a long single handle as it is easier to hold and keep steady when cooking over intense heat. A wok cover to fit the wok is essential to reduce cooking time and to prevent too much reduction of liquid before the ingredients are cooked.

A wok should be well seasoned before use. Wash and dry it well and rub the surface with a little cooking oil. Heat the wok and allow it to cool. Repeat this process two to three times, then wipe with kitchen paper or cloth. Harsh detergents should not be used to clean a wok. The wok should be cleaned by placing it under running water while it is still hot and brushing it off. For non-stick woks, soft sponges should be used instead of a brush. After cleaning, towel dry or heat the wok to ensure that it is completely dry.

THE LADLE OR SPATULA

A long ladle or spatula with a wooden handle is ideal for cooking with the wok. The metal base is suitable for iron woks while non-stick woks require wooden ones to prevent scratching.

THE CHINESE CLEAVER

The Chinese cleaver is absolutely essential in the Chinese kitchen as it is used for chopping, cutting, slicing, mincing and shredding. A good heavy cleaver made of carbon steel is best for most purposes. It is easily sharpened with a whetstone.

THE CHOPPING BLOCK

The Chinese chopping block is usually round and a few inches thick. A heavy wooden chopping block is far better than the plastic blocks as ingredients will not slip while using the heavy cleaver. After use, it should be scraped with the cleaver, brushed with a wire mesh, washed and wiped dry. It should never be soaked in water. Once in a while, it should be sunned to prevent a board odour from developing.

STEAMERS

Metal steamers consist of a bottom section for holding the water and a top section to place trays (1 or 2) with holes for the steam to pass through. Finally a cover is placed on the top tray section. These are available at most Chinese provision stores. A wok with a tall cover can also be used for steaming. A steamer stand or tray is placed in the boiling water to hold the food above the water.

When steaming food, always allow the water to boil before putting in the food. Bamboo baskets are used for steaming breads and dumplings to prevent collection of water. Water drips onto the bread and dumplings can be prevented by placing a tea towel under the lid of the steamer. Ensure that the ends of the towel do not trail near the flame.

WOODEN CHOPSTICKS

A pair of long wooden chopsticks, although not essential, is useful as a beater and for picking up fried foods. If one is not adept at working with chopsticks, a flat perforated ladle might be more helpful.

WIRE MESH LADLE

The Chinese wire mesh ladle with a wooden handle is useful for scooping up deep-fried foods and scalding noodles. They are available in various types. A 15 cm (6 in) diameter size will suffice for the average kitchen.

EARTHEN OR CLAYPOT

Earthen pots or claypots are good for slow cooking, such as braising and stewing. Heat is absorbed and spread evenly and there is a lower rate of evaporation compared to other types of cooking pots and saucepans. Earthen pots are excellent for cooking meat, and rice and porridge turn out with more flavour. Cooked foods can be served directly in the claypots, and because these pots retain heat well, the food can be kept warm for a long time. Claypots come in a wide range of shapes and sizes to serve every need.

ELECTRIC RICE COOKER

For cooking rice, an automatic electric rice cooker is recommended. Provided the right amount of water is used, fluffy cooked rice will turn out every time. It is easy to use and clean.

ELECTRIC CROCK POT

An electric crock pot is a slow cooker, very useful for braising and stewing. Food can be set to cook very slowly for hours without any attendance, e.g. set to cook in the morning before you leave for work and ready to eat when you come home in the evening.

Meat, Seafood and Vegetables

BEEF

Beef is not the prime meat in Chinese cuisine. In the olden days, oxen and buffaloes were used to plough and till Chinese farmlands and fields. These animals were thought of as faithful servants and thus were not slaughtered for the table. Most Chinese today do not eat beef for religious reasons, and some, even though not bound by religion, rarely eat beef because of its strong flavour. Chinese cooks often use ginger roots, spices and strong flavourings to minimise and camouflage the strong taste of beef.

Beef is fibrous and thus it is generally sliced or shredded in Chinese cuisine. The fillet of beef is most favoured because it is excellent for quick stir-frying. Minced meat is usually used to prepare *Dim Sum* dishes.

Cutting: In order to cut meat correctly and neatly, use a good cutting knife or cleaver. Place the meat on a proper chopping board or firm surface. Beef should be cut across the grain. It is easier to slice beef when it is half frozen.

Tenderising: Beef can be tenderised by breaking the fibres, making it easier to chew. To do this, beat the meat firmly with a rolling pin or use the back of a cleaver and make firm chops. Meat can be tenderised using a marinade containing a small amount of acid, for example, vinegar, wine or fruit juice, such as pineapple, lemon or lime.

Freezing: Beef should be packed in freezer bags or wrapped in cling wrap before freezing. Unwanted fat should be removed before storing. Large amounts of meat should be portioned and packaged separately according to the amount required for cooking. Remove as much air as possible by pressing the bag or wrapping it tightly round the meat. Meat should never be frozen again after it has been defrosted.

Defrosting: When defrosting meat, it is best to do it slowly in the refrigerator. Frozen beef should be put into the refrigerator for defrosting the night before cooking.

CHICKEN

Chicken meat, like pork, is well-liked by the Chinese. The meat has no particular smell and a fine texture. The Chinese regard chicken as easy to digest and very nutritious, especially when cooked with Chinese herbs. My grandmother insists that double steamed chicken soup with ginseng and a mixture of Chinese herbs cooked in a double boiler (an electric crock-pot will not do!) has kept her in excellent health to the age of 90.

Chicken meat is so versatile in Chinese cooking that there are countless ways of preparing it; from dishes with exotic sauces to the simple boiling of a whole chicken to prepare the famous "White-Cut Chicken" (*Pak Cham Kai*) or also known as "Chicken Rice" (*Kai Fun*). The boiled chicken is so easy to prepare and it tastes good too. Chicken meat cut into small pieces, with or without the bones, blends well with other meats and seafood, vegetables and noodles in all manner of sauces. The bones make an excellent stock which is the basis of Chinese cuisine.

Everybody has their favourite cut of meat. Most Chinese prefer the wings and drumsticks for their smooth texture. For the adventurous gourmets, the bishop's nose is highly valued as the smoothest and the tastiest. Breast meat is usually preferred by Westerners.

One variety of chicken popular with the Chinese for health reasons is the black chicken (*hark kai*). The name is derived from the black

skin colour of the chicken. It is commonly used in herbal brews and serves as an excellent tonic for anaemics by restoring vitality and improving blood circulation. When double boiled with ginseng, it is supposed to boost the immune system.

PORK

Pork is a popular meat in Chinese cuisine. The meat is not strongly flavoured, it has a smooth texture and it is not too fibrous. Pork also blends well with vegetables, seafood, herbs and all seasonings.

Pork should always be well cooked. Unlike beef, this is possible without the meat becoming dry. Always cut pork across the grain and buy the cut of meat specified in the recipe.

Pork bones make a good basic stock for pork dishes and soups. To make a good stock, bring the water to the boil before dropping in the bones. Allow to boil for 5 minutes and then reduce the heat and let it simmer for 30 minutes to an hour, depending on the amount of stock. All traces of scum on the surface should be skimmed off during simmering. Be sure to strain the stock. Pork stock keeps well in the refrigerator for a couple of days and can be frozen for a period of 4 weeks.

SEAFOOD

Seafood also features very prominently in Chinese cuisine and the types that are well-liked will be sought after with very little consideration for cost. The Chinese are very particular about the freshness of seafood. With the advances in aqua-culture, fresh seafood in tanks is now available at most restaurants.

Fish favoured by the Chinese are carp, garoupa, pomfret, sea bass and threadfin. Their firm and smooth flesh cook well with steaming and retain their freshness without the 'fishy' smell and taste. The Chinese cook camouflages strong 'fishy' tasting and smelling fish with flavouring agents such as ginger, garlic, wine and sesame oil. Fish available in temperate climates which are suitable for Chinese cooking are cod, salmon and sole.

Fish can be steamed, deep-fried, stir-fried or braised. Even the head of a fish, although some may feel squeamish about eating it, makes a very tasty dishes, such as the famous *Hoong Siew Yee Tau* and the "Claypot Fish Head." Similarly, fish lips, considered by many as unpalatable, are a delicacy enjoyed by Chinese gourmets.

Prawns and crabs are also firm favourites. If they are fresh, they are preferably steamed in order to bring out their natural sweetness, although they are also cooked with a variety of sauces. Small-sized prawns are normally used to sweeten and flavour vegetable, noodle and rice dishes.

Cuttlefish is not an esteemed seafood and would not normally be served at banquets. Nevertheless, it is served at daily meals and used in combination with other meats and seafood. Cleaning cuttlefish is not too much of a chore if it is done systematically. The head and the soft bone in the open end of the cuttlefish should be removed first, the dark skin rubbed off and the ink sacs and eyes removed. To make the cuttlefish look appealing when cooked, cut it lengthwise. Spread the pieces with the inside facing up and make criss-cross patterns by cutting at an angle on the surface. This will make it curl when cooked. Dried cuttlefish is used as a flavouring in soup.

VEGETABLES

The Chinese are renowned for their vegetable preparation. Simple cooking methods such as stir-frying and blanching preserve the natural goodness, flavour and colour of vegetables.

Stir-frying produces a multitude of vegetables dishes consisting of single varieties of vegetables or careful combinations with special attention to complimentary colours and tastes. The end result is always a crunchy and nourishing feast. The simple quick blanching of green leafy vegetables in boiling water and

served mixed with oyster sauce and oil, literally known as *Luk Yau Choy* in Cantonese, is equally appetising.

Chinese vegetarian fare is amazingly versatile. With adept use of a vast variety of vegetables and different forms of soya bean, dishes which taste and look like meat can be prepared.

Despite the love for fresh food, many types of preserved vegetables also feature prominently as main ingredients in Chinese cooking. This probably originated in the days when good harvests had to be preserved for the winter. Nevertheless, preserved vegetables can be used to make amazing dishes that whet the appetite of even the most discriminating gourmet. The more common types are "Salted Cabbage," "Preserved Mustard Green," "Chinese Dried Radish," "Preserved Shanghai Vegetable" and "Preserved Szechuan Vegetable." The last type is made from radish or turnip salted with chilli and is used mainly in Szechuan cooking. It goes well with meat and seafood and is also used to prepare the famous "Hot and Sour Soup," available in most Chinese restaurants.

The best place to store fresh vegetables to retain their freshness as long as possible is in the bottom compartment of the refrigerator. Yellow and damaged parts should be removed before wrapping in absorbent paper (e.g. newspaper) and sealing in plastic bags. The paper helps to keep the vegetables dry by absorbing any condensed water, which hastens rotting.

ASPARAGUS

The green variety is available all the year round. Look for fresh young firm stalks. Old woody looking stalks should be avoided as they are more fibrous. The harder part of the stems must be skinned before slicing.

BAMBOO SHOOTS *(Chuk Soon)*

Canned bamboo shoots are convenient and should be well rinsed before use. If using fresh bamboo shoots, first peel the outer skin and cut off the tough fibrous layer. Boil the shoots with a little salt and half a tablespoon of sugar for approximately 30 minutes. Then boil again for 15 minutes in fresh water. Bamboo shoots keep well frozen for as long as 2 weeks.

BROCCOLI *(Kai Lan Fah)*

Fresh broccoli should have a firm dark green head that is closely packed. The harder parts of the stems can be pared and then sliced. For use in stir-frying dishes, broccoli should be prepared by blanching in boiling salted water with a little oil, or tossed in a little hot oil for a minute or two.

BITTERGOURD *(Fu Kwa)*

To reduce the bitter taste of bittergourd, scrape off the white seed portions and soak cut pieces in salt water.

CABBAGE

There are a variety of cabbages used in Chinese cuisine.

The Tientsin cabbage (*wong nga pak*) is a long whitish-green leaf cabbage with broad white stems. It is very popular in Chinese cooking and can be braised, stir-fried with meat and seafood, or boiled in soups. It is also great with fried noodles.

The white cabbage (*pau choy*) is the round variety with closely packed leaves. Look for the light weight ones as they are less watery.

The Chinese white cabbage (*pak choy*) is also a long leaf cabbage which is not so tightly packed as the Tientsin cabbage. The leaves are much greener and it is more watery with a bland taste. There is also a shorter variety called the Shanghai white cabbage (*siew pak choy*). The stems are light green in colour.

CELERY

Celery is available all year round. Choose crisp light green celery with young stalks. Very large stalks may be fibrous and the fibres have to be removed before slicing.

CHICORY

Chicory is grown in temperate countries, but it is available in major supermarkets. Look for white compact heads with yellow-green edges. Those with green tips can be bitter. Blanching in hot water with a little salt helps to remove the bitter taste.

CHINESE BROCCOLI OR KALE *(Kai Lan Choy)*

This is a dark green leafy vegetable with firm succulent stems. The Chinese prefer the stems, especially if they are young. Old stems should be skinned.

CHINESE CHIVES *(Kow Choy)*

This slightly pungent vegetable looks like spring onion except that it is flat and not hollow. The white head section has to be carefully washed to remove the fine sand particles. The vegetable can be eaten raw or cooked briefly to retain its crunchy texture. It is popularly added to stir-fried rice noodles and rice noodle soups. It is also delicious chopped and fried with eggs and prawns as an omelette.

CUCUMBER

Young green cucumbers are used mainly for garnishing. Old cucumbers with brown hard skin are used in soups, cut into large pieces with the skin on.

FENNEL

This is a bulb vegetable, white or pale green in colour and grown in temperate countries. It is imported and sold in major supermarkets. The root ends and stalks are trimmed before use.

GREEN STEMS *(Kai Choy)*

The green stem has broad stems and leaves and is slightly bitter. The stems are preferred and the leaves are sometimes discarded. Green stems pickled with salt is called *harm choy*. The stems should be soaked and washed in water before use to reduce the saltiness.

HAIRY MARROW *(Mou Kwa)*

This vegetable derives its name from the fine hairs on the skin. A versatile and popular vegetable with the Chinese, it can be steamed, braised or used in soups. It can also be shredded and stir-fried with meat.

MUSHROOMS *(Tung Ku)*

The types of mushrooms that can be used in Chinese cooking are champignons or button mushrooms, abalone or oyster mushrooms, straw mushrooms and dried Chinese mushrooms.

Fresh champignons or canned button mushrooms (*mou ku*) are available in supermarkets. Look for white unblemished ones. Do not peel the skin unless it is bruised or blemished. They cook quickly, usually in about 5 minutes, and combine well with meats and other vegetables. They can also be used in soups.

Oyster mushrooms (*kwan ku*) are also known as abalone mushrooms. They are flat and fan-shaped with a soft greyish or beige colour. They have a smooth texture with a subtle aroma and delicate taste. They are widely available fresh and are commonly used in stir-fried, braised, stewed and boiled dishes.

Straw mushrooms (*tsin cho ku*) are cultivated in straw, hence the name. They are sold either fresh or canned. Fresh ones have to be scalded before use. They can be stored in the refrigerator for only a few days.

There are two varieties of dried Chinese mushrooms. The *tung ku* (winter mushroom) is thick and greyish black and the *fah ku* (flower mushroom) is paler in colour and more expensive. For cooking, they have to be softened by soaking in water for at least 30 minutes. The stems should not be discarded but used for flavouring stocks, especially for strict vegetarian cooking. Remove the stems from the dried mushrooms, wash, dry and blend finely for the stock. A pepper mill can be used to grind the stems instead of an electric

blender. For longer storage, they should be well dried before blending and then stored in the refrigerator in an air-tight container.

MUSTARD GREEN *(Choy Sum)*

Choy sum is a green leafy vegetable with light green stems. Crunchy and juicy, it is a favourite for frying with noodles but it is equally delicious fried on its own or made into a soup.

Pickled mustard green, partially dried, is available in two forms: salty (*harm mui choy*) and slightly sweet (*tim mui choy*). To prepare for use, wash carefully in several changes of water to remove fine sand particles.

Dried mustard green (*choy korn*) is used for making soups. It has to be soaked to soften and washed carefully before use.

SNOW PEAS *(Hor Lan Tow)*

Snow peas are regarded as one of the classier vegetables. They are flat light green pea pods. To prepare for cooking, wash and soak in water to prevent the peas from splitting when cooked. Then break the ends slightly to remove the fibre from the side edges of the pea pods.

SPINACH (*Yeen Choy and Por Choy*)

Yeen choy is a small leaf variety of spinach made famous by the cartoon character Popeye. *Por choy* is the big leaf variety with long stems. It is quick to cook and its smooth texture makes it ideal for blanching and stir-frying. It is also a favourite vegetable for steam boats.

SZECHUAN VEGETABLE *(Char Choy)*

The Szechuan vegetable is preserved Chinese radish pickled in salt and chillies. You can see the chilli powder coating the olive green colour of the vegetable. It should be washed well and soaked in water to reduce the saltiness before use.

WINTER MELON *(Tung Kwa)*

This is a light green melon with a soft white pulpy flesh. It is excellent for soups but can also be steamed, braised or stir-fried. Although bland in taste, it absorbs flavours from meat and vegetables.

ANCHOVY, DRIED

Dried anchovies are small dried fish anywhere from 2½–5 cm (1–2 in) in length. They are often fried until crispy, mixed with fried peanuts and served with rice porridge. They are also used to make stock. The head and entrails should be removed and rinsed before use. To make stock, lightly brown 90 gms (3 oz) of anchovies in ½ tablespoon of hot oil. This will remove the 'fishy' smell. Put in 2½ cups water and bring to the boil. Simmer over low heat for approximately 30 minutes. Strain and use as required.

Ingredients

BEANCURD

Beancurd, made from soya beans, is a cheap protein-rich food which comes in various forms and shapes.

Soft beancurd is usually sold in squares or rectangles immersed in water. It should keep for a few days in the refrigerator. The circular soft beancurd, popularly known as Japanese taufu, is sold in plastic tubes. When unopened, it keeps well in the refrigerator for at least a week. Beancurd cubes fried in oil, called *taufu pok* are also available.

Beancurd made into yellowish translucent sheets is known as beancurd skin (*foo pei*). It is used for wrapping meat and vegetable fillings, especially for vegetarian dishes. Look for soft, flexible sheets. The brittle ones break easily on wrapping.

Dried soya bean sticks (*foo chok*), yellow in colour, are used in mixed vegetable dishes especially for vegetarian cooking. They have to be soaked in warm water before use.

Soft salted beancurd cubes (*lam yee*) are preserved in brine and wine solution with chillies. They have a strong and distinctive flavour and are popularly served with porridge.

BIRD'S NEST *(Yin Wor)*

Bird's nest is the gelatinous regurgitated saliva that swifts use to construct their nests. These swifts are mainly found in Borneo, Sarawak, Indonesia and China. When collected, the nests are entangled with grit, feathers, twigs and other construction materials. Cleaning is laboriously done by hand and this together with their scarcity contribute to their high cost.

They are usually made into an herbal soup with chicken or pigeon, or into a sweet clear soup taken hot or cold. The Chinese believe bird's nests cleanse the blood, nourish the lungs and throat, and ensure general good health.

CASHEW NUTS

The cashew is a sweet and kidney-shaped nut available either roasted or raw. Roasted nuts are also salted or non-salted, which must be taken into consideration when cooking. Raw nuts can be roasted in a moderate oven for 10–15 minutes, turning occasionally. They can also be dry-roasted in a wok until golden brown.

CHILLI OIL

Chilli oil is used a lot in Szechuan cooking. To make chilli oil, soak about 20 dried chillies in hot water until they are soft. Remove the stems. If a less pungent oil is preferred, cut the dried chillies in two and remove some of the seeds. Place the soaked chillies in a blender with 8 tablespoons of cooking oil. Blend mixture coarsely and pour into a saucepan. Cook over low heat for 3 minutes. Strain the oil and keep in an air-tight jar.

The residue can be stored for use in curries. It can also be made into a chilli sauce with preserved soya bean paste. Heat 5 tablespoons of cooking oil until hot and stir-fry 1 tablespoon of preserved soya bean paste over low heat until fragrant. Add 1/4 teaspoon of sugar and the chilli residue, and mix well. Cool and store in an air-tight container. It can be used as a dip for meat, seafood and noodle dishes.

CHINESE HERBS

Chinese herbs are important cooking ingredients for the Chinese, who believe that the consumption of food cooked with certain

herbs will keep the body's life forces in balance and harmony. There are thousands of Chinese herbs but here I will describe some of the more common and popular ones which I have used in my recipes.

Kei Chi (boxthorn fruit) are little red berries important for improving vision or eye ailments. They aid blood circulation and are also good for the liver and kidney. They impart a sweetish flavour to rich stews and soups.

Pak Hup are dried magnolia petals, native to China and Vietnam. They reduce 'heatiness,' help to restore and improve energy, and are good for those suffering from tuberculosis or ulcers.

Pak Kee is a pale yellow root, usually sold in paper thin slices. It is used in treatment of lung problems, poor blood circulation and fatigue.

Tong Kwai is a knobby root highly valued as an effective tonic for blood and gynaecological problems. Most Chinese women take this herb after childbirth to restore energy and strength, and during menstruation to relieve cramps and regulate the cycle. It is bitter in taste and has a strong pleasant fragrance after brewing. It is sold in 3 sections—the head (*tong kwai tow*), which is most expensive, the body (*tong kwai sum*), and the tail (*tong kwai mei*), which is the cheapest.

Tung Sam, regarded as the poor man's ginseng, is a thin brownish root. It is used as a tonic for problems with regard to the chest, digestion, blood circulation, body metabolism, and mental and physical fatigue.

Wai Sun, a root which looks like the sweet potato, is sold in thick slices. Literally translated, wai sun means mountain herb. It is a good tonic for the stomach, liver and kidneys. It is also supposed to improve the appetite.

Yan Sum (ginseng root) is highly priced and esteemed as a panacea for its curative powers in restoring energy and strength. In soups or drinks, ginseng will renew vigour and boost blood circulation, thus strengthening the body and keeping the body cells regenerated. Literally translated, yan sum means 'man root' because of its resemblance to the figure of a man with head, body, arms and legs. Collected from the wild in the past, today it is cultivated in many places. But the best quality is still believed to grow in the wild. There are two general grades of quality. *Pow sum* is the superior grade which comes from China. *Yong sum*, the cheaper grade, is mainly grown in the USA and Canada. It is available as *yong sum tow* (head) and *yong sum sow* (hair roots), which is the cheapest ginseng available.

Yok Chok is a rhizome that is usually sold in thin slices. It is believed to be excellent for lung and throat ailments.

CHINESE RICE WINE

Chinese rice wine is an important ingredient in Chinese cooking. It enhances the fragrance and flavour of dishes. A better quality brand to use is Shao Hsing Hua Tiau Wine. It is light brown in colour and a small amount will enhance the flavour of many dishes.

CINNAMON *(Kwai Peh)*

This is a rich aromatic spice obtained from the bark of the cinnamon tree and is imported from Sri Lanka. In the West, it is used mainly in sweets while in the East it is used in savoury dishes, mainly to reduce the strong flavour of meat. The Chinese cassia is very similar to cinnamon except it has a more delicate flavour. It comes in thicker pieces and is one of the spices used in five spice powder.

CLOVE *(Teng Heong)*

The clove is a rich deep brown spice that closely resembles a small nail tack in shape. It is indigenous to Moluccas or the "Spice Islands" of Indonesia. Its sweet and pungent aroma is used to in Chinese cooking to minimise the strong flavour of meat and to enhance the aroma of a blend of spices, e.g. that used in the popular "Pork Rib Soup" (*Bak Kut Teh*).

CORIANDER LEAVES *(Yim Sai)*

Also known as Chinese parsley, the leaves have a strong flavour and are used for flavouring and garnishing food. The flavour is different from English parsley which should not be used as a substitute, except for garnishing.

COOKING OIL

In the past, lard was preferred in Chinese cooking. With growing concern for cholesterol levels, most cooks now use natural vegetable oils. Groundnut oil is commonly used, but I prefer polyunsaturated oils, such as corn oil and sunflower seed oil. Lard is still used in certain dishes, especially to make light, flaky and crumbly pastries.

DATES

There are two types of Chinese dates—red dates and black dates. Red dates (*hoong chou*) are dark reddish in colour and sweet. They are commonly added to sweeten soups and stews. Before use they should be slit to release their full flavour. They are believed to be good for anaemics. Black dates (*hark chou*) are jet black in colour like prunes, and less sweet. Also used in soups and stews, they are believed to be a booster for the lungs and spleen, and also to restore energy in the fatigued.

DRIED RADISH *(Choy Poh)*

This is radish salted and dried in small pieces. It is light brown in colour and is used in minced meat dishes and omelettes.

DRIED SCALLOP *(Kong Yee Chee)*

Dried scallop is very expensive but fortunately it is very potent and only a small piece is enough to add flavour and sweetness to dishes. To prepare for use, rinse and shred after steaming for 15 minutes or soaking in water.

DRIED SOLE *(Peen Yee)*

Dried sole is sold in small plastic packets. To prepare for use, rinse quickly, then dry by towelling or sunning before deep-frying until light golden and crisp. Crumble into small pieces or blend in an electric blender until fine. It should be stored in an air-tight container and will keep well in the refrigerator.

EAR FUNGUS *(Wan Yee and Mok Yee)*

There are two varieties of black ear fungus which grow on the bark of trees—a larger one known as cloud ear fungus (*wan yee*) and a smaller one known wood ear fungus (*mok yee*). They have very little taste or aroma, but they readily absorb the flavours of other ingredients. The larger variety is crunchier and more expensive, but in general it is not an expensive ingredient. Sold in dried form, the fungus can be easily obtained from wet markets, Chinese provision stores and supermarkets. It has to be soaked to soften and rinsed before use.

FERMENTED BLACK BEANS *(Hak Tau See)*

Fermented black beans or black bean sauce is sold mainly in small plastic packets. It is made from salted and fermented black soya beans. They have a very strong flavour and are used sparingly in meat and seafood dishes. They have to be soaked in water for 5–10 minutes, rinsed and drained thoroughly before use.

FIVE SPICE POWDER *(Ng Heong Fun)*

This is a combination of star anise, cinnamon, clove, fennel and Szechuan peppercorn. It is sold ready-mixed at Chinese provision or medical stores. Only a small amount is required to spice roasted and braised poultry or meat. It is essentially used to reduce the strong flavour of beef, lamb and fish.

FISH SAUCE

Fish sauce is liquid extracted from salted fish and fermented. The sauce is light brown in colour and sold in bottles. It is used as a seasoning.

FRESH CHICKEN STOCK

Fresh chicken stock is the base of all good Chinese sauces and soups. Chicken cubes can be used as a substitute, but the salt content in the recipe should be reduced according to taste.

The stock is obtained from boiling chicken bones, meat scraps, feet and giblets over low heat for 30 minutes to one hour depending on the amount. The stock should be strained before use. Excess oil can be skimmed off with a ladle. An easier way is to refrigerate the stock until the fat has set on the surface and can then be scooped off.

FRIED GLUTEN BALLS

Fried gluten balls are sold in wet markets. You can also make them at home with the following recipe:

600 gms (21 oz) plain flour
1 teaspoon salt
1¾ cups water

Put flour and salt into a large bowl. Add water and form into a stiff dough. Leave to rest for at least 30 minutes. Fill a basin with water and 'wash' by kneading and pressing dough until spongy. Repeat 'washings' (about 3–4) until water is no longer milky. This takes approximately 12–15 minutes. The end result should be a mass of spongy dough slightly larger than a tennis ball and approximately 300 gms (10½ oz) in weight. Leave the dough to rest for 15–20 minutes to allow some water to seep out before frying.

Pinch small marble-sized pieces from the gluten dough and drop into deep hot oil. Deep-fry until golden brown in two or three batches to prevent balls from sticking together. Stir often to get even browning. Drain and cool. Store in an air-tight container. They keep well in the refrigerator for at least a month.

The milky white flour liquid from 'washing' the gluten dough can be saved to obtain non-glutinous flour (*tang meen fun*) used for making a transparent pastry for making *Dim Sum* dishes, such as "Prawn Dumplings" (*Kow Chee*). To obtain non-glutinous flour, pour the milky flour liquid into a large pot. Leave overnight, undisturbed in the refrigerator to settle. The next day, carefully pour off the clear water on top. The non-glutinous flour that settles at the bottom is used to make dumpling pastry.

GINGKO NUT *(Pak Kor)*

A yellow almond-shaped nut used as a savoury stuffing or in sweet soups. When cooked it becomes soft and tender. It is available shelled or unshelled. The centre vein is very bitter and should be removed. Native to Japan and the Chinese provinces of Guangxi, Sichuan and Hunan, it is believed to be good for asthma, coughs, weak bladders and urinary disorders.

GARLIC CRISPS

To prepare garlic crisps, slice garlic thinly lengthwise. Heat enough cooking oil for deep-frying and stir garlic over low heat until pale brown and crisp. Remove with a perforated ladle and drain on absorbent paper. Garlic crisps keep well in an air-tight container stored in the refrigerator.

GALANGAL (*Lam Keong*)

The galangal belongs to the same family as ginger but cannot be used as a substitute for ginger. The plant is native to Southern China. It is used in medicinal herbal mixtures and to camouflage the pronounced flavour of meats, such as duck or lamb.

GINGER *(Keong)*

The ginger root is very pungent and is used in Chinese cooking to reduce strong flavours in meat and 'fishy' smells in fish. Young tender ginger, which has a paler skin than normal old ginger, is juicier and less pungent. To prepare ginger, scrape off the skin with a sharp knife and slice, shred or chop according to the recipe

instructions. Dried or powdered ginger should not be used as a substitute for fresh ginger. It is better to omit ginger from the dish if fresh ginger cannot be obtained.

GARLIC

Garlic is used in most stir-frying dishes to flavour oil. Always use fresh garlic in Chinese cooking. Garlic power or flakes should not be used as substitutes for fresh garlic.

HAIR VEGETABLE *(Fatt Choy)*

Hair vegetable, also known as Black Moss, is a seaweed. It resembles a mass of black fine hair and is usually sold in plastic wrappers. *Fatt Choy* literally means prosperity vegetable and is normally a must during auspicious occasions, such as the Chinese New Year, to ensure luck and prosperity.

HASMA *(Shuet Kap)*

Dried glands of a snow frog found in Beijing, they are consumed as nourishment for the lungs, post-illness recovery and chronic coughs. Hasma is purported to balance the body system and produces a lovely smooth complexion. It is usually cooked with herbs and rock sugar in a clear sweet soup.

HOISIN SAUCE

This seasoning sauce is made from red beans, soya beans, plum, sesame seeds, chilli and five spice powder. It has a sweet, spicy and tangy flavour.

HOT BEAN SAUCE

Hot bean sauce is a mixture of fermented soya beans and chillies. It is also known by other names, such as chilli bean sauce or hot soya bean sauce.

LILY BUDS, DRIED *(Kam Cham)*

Dried lily buds are also known as lotus buds or golden needles. They are long thin dried buds from the water lily plant and are used as an ingredient in vegetable dishes. They have to be soaked for at least 30 minutes in hot water to soften before use. Very often, each strand is tied into a knot for vegetarian dishes, an old practice, the reason for which is not clear, but likely it is for appearance and to give a more 'chewy' bite.

LONG NGAN, DRIED

Long ngan is a sweet fruit which literally means "dragon's eye." Dried long ngan is brownish black in colour with a lovely fragrance. It is added to soups to give a sweet a taste. It is also used to make a popular Chinese sweet drink called *long ngan char*.

MALTOSE OR MALT SUGAR *(Mak Nga Tong)*

Maltose is a thick sweet syrup produced from germinating barley. It is sold in jars and is available at Chinese provision stores.

MUSHROOM SAUCE

This is soya sauce flavoured with mushrooms sold in bottles.

NON-GLUTINOUS FLOUR *(Tang Meen Fun)*

See recipe for **friedgluten balls** on page 24. When cooked, the flour becomes quite transparent and is used as the pastry for *Dim Sum* dumplings, such as *kow chee*.

NOODLES

To the Chinese, the noodle is a sign of longevity. Noodles come in many forms from thin strands to thick broad ribbons. They are sold fresh or dried and can be very different in taste and texture from variety to variety. The type of noodle specified in a recipe therefore should not be substituted with another variety. Fresh yellow noodles are made from flour, alkaline water and yellow colouring. Egg noodles (*wantan meen*) contain an additional ingredient of eggs. They can be fresh or dried. The dried variety are usually sold in round cakes.

OYSTER SAUCE

Oyster sauce is a versatile sauce used in Chinese cooking for flavouring. It is a dark brown thick sauce produced from oysters and soya sauce. It is sold in bottles and should be refrigerated once opened.

PICKLED GARLIC STEMS *(Tung Choy)*

Small chopped brown pieces of pickled garlic stems. Usually sold in rounded brown or black earthen jars, or in plastic packs. A Teochew favourite, it is mainly used in soups. To prepare for use, rinse in several changes of water and squeeze dry.

PLUM SAUCE

This is a sweet and sour sauce made from Chinese sour plums. It is used as a base for numerous sweet and sour dishes.

RICE NOODLES *(Sar Hor Fun)*

These are wide flat rice noodles made from steaming rice flour. They are available from local wet markets and supermarkets. They have to be refrigerated and will keep for up to about 5 days.

ROCK SUGAR

Rock sugar is crystallised sugar sold in lumps. It is not as sweet as granulated sugar.

ROSE WINE *(Mei-Kuei-Lu)*

Rose wine is a strong Chinese liquor with a unique flavour made from a blend of kao-liang spirit and the petals of a special species of rose. There is no substitute for this wine.

RICE

Rice is an important staple food in the daily diet of the Chinese. Good rice should be long grained. Old rice is preferred to new rice because when cooked it will not stick together.

RICE VERMICELLI *(Mai Fun)*

Rice vermicelli is a white dried noodle made from rice in the shape of long thin strands. For stir-frying, it should be soaked in water to soften before use. For soups, it is scalded briefly.

SALTED CABBAGE *(Harm Choy)*

Salted cabbage is salted and pickled from green stem vegetable. It should be washed and soaked to reduce the salt content before use. It can be fried with meat or used in soups, especially with duck.

SEA CUCUMBER *(Hoi Sum)*

Also known as sea slug or beche-de-mer, sea cucumber can be bought cleaned and ready for use. It has a jelly-like texture with no particular flavour. It is normally braised with meat, mushrooms and abalone for a very tasty dish.

SESAME SEEDS

White sesame seeds are commonly used roasted or raw to make Chinese sweets and fillings, or as a garnish in many savoury dishes. Sesame seeds are also ground into a creamy paste sold in cans or jars.

The oil extracted from the seed is strongly fragrant and is used only in small amounts for flavouring.

SHARKSFIN

This is a very expensive Chinese delicacy and is normally sold in its dried form. It can be bought processed and ready cleaned in frozen packets which saves you the tedious chore of preparing it.

SHRIMPS, DRIED

Small dried shelled shrimps are very strong in flavour and used for enhancing the taste of vegetable and soup dishes. They should be soaked in water to soften and rinsed before use.

SHALLOT CRISPS

To make shallot crisps, slice shallots thinly crosswise. Heat enough oil for deep-frying and stir shallots over low heat until pale brown.

Remove with a perforated ladle and drain on absorbent paper. When cool, store in an air-tight container. Shallot crisps keep well for several weeks in the refrigerator. (Garlic crisps are prepared the same way.)

SOUR PLUMS *(Sheen Mui)*

These are plums pickled in vinegar and salt. The marble-sized plums, light brown in colour, are used to add a sour tang to fish and meat dishes.

SOYA SAUCE

Soya sauce is liquid extracted from fermented soya beans and comes in two varieties; light and thick. Light soya sauce is diluted and light brown in colour. It is salty and an excellent flavouring or marinating agent. In fact, it is the most basic flavouring ingredient in Chinese cooking. Always use a good quality sauce extracted from the first infusion of the fermented soya beans. Thick soya sauce is like treacle and dark black in colour. It is made from fermented soya beans and caramel. It is slightly sweet and is used mainly for colouring, although it does add a bit of flavour.

PRESERVED SOYA BEAN *(Tau Cheong)*

This is available as whole soya beans or in purée form. It is light brown in colour and is sold in cans or jars.

SQUID, DRIED

Dried squid is sold in Chinese provision shops. It has a strong distinctive flavour and is used in soups and stews. It is also roasted, pressed and eaten with chilli sauce.

STAR ANISE *(Pat Kok)*

A brown eight-pointed star-shaped spice with a strong smell. It is the fruit of the oriental evergreen of the magnolia family which is native to China and Japan. It is used in small quantities to flavour meat, poultry and duck dishes.

SWEET BEAN PASTE

This paste is made from fermented soya beans, flour, sugar and spices.

SWEET POTATO FLOUR

This flour made from sweet potato is used as a thickening agent for sauces and soups. It gives a clearer and less starchy result than cornflour.

SZECHUAN PEPPERCORN *(Far Chew)*

These are brownish red peppercorns with an aromatic smell. They are used commonly in Szechuan cooking to season meat and poultry and can be obtained from Chinese medical or provision stores.

TRANSPARENT VERMICELLI *(Toong Fun)*

Transparent vermicelli is a thin strand noodle made from mung beans, also known as bean thread noodle. It is used as an ingredient in vegetarian dishes or in soups. It should be soaked in water to soften before use.

VINEGAR

Chinese vinegar is distilled from fermented rice. There are four varieties; white, red, black and sweet black.White vinegar is clear and mild in flavour and used in dishes with a sweet and sour sauce. White cider vinegar can be used as a substitute. Red vinegar is amber red in colour and used as a dip by itself or flavoured with ginger strips. It is particularly good served with seafood. Black vinegar is strongly flavoured and used only in small amounts. The sweet variety has a strong pungent sweet and sour taste used in braising dishes.

WHITE FUNGUS *(Suet Yee)*

White fungus can be white to yellowish, or creamy in colour. The white ones are the best quality. They are used in vegetarian dishes and sweet soups. The fungus is crunchy and has no particular taste. Like other dried fungus, it

has to be soaked in water to soften before use. The Chinese believe that white fungus is good for the complexion.

WILD SUGAR CANE (*Chook Cheh*)

Wild sugar cane has a narrower stem than normal sugar cane. It is used to sweeten sauces in stews. It is also boiled with rock sugar and taken as a "cooling" drink.

WATER CHESTNUT *(Mah Tai)*

The water chestnut is very crunchy and sweet and can be obtained fresh or in canned form. It is also available as a powder used for thickening, especially for soups.

YELLOW BEAN SAUCE

This is a paste made from fermented yellow soya beans sold in jars. Soya bean paste, which is saltier, can be used as a substitute.

How Much and What to Serve

One dish alone does not make a Chinese meal. The complete Chinese meal must have variety and be balanced. A one dish meal is only acceptable if it contains rice or noodles as the main ingredient. Even then, it is only served as a light meal.

The normal Chinese meal consists of several dishes (3 or 4) eaten with rice. The dishes are shared, which Westerners find most appealing and interesting compared to their usual practice of confining each person to one dish. On special occasions a dinner consisting of several courses (up to 10) will be served. The dishes are generally not the normal fare and are served one at a time. The last 3 courses are usually fried rice or noodles, soup and a sweet dessert.

Planning a Chinese meal is not as confusing as it may seem. It is merely putting together a balanced meal, which, like any other balanced meal, will consist of a vegetable dish, 1 or 2meat and/or seafood dishes, and a soup. The soup is served with the meal instead of as a starter before the main course. Thick soups such as "Shark's Fin" or "Hot and Sour" can be exceptions.

Each of the recipes in this book, unless stated otherwise, is sufficient for 2–3 persons when served with 1 other dish and rice, for 4–6 persons with 2 other dishes.

1. Winter Melon
2. Broccoli
3. Shanghai White Cabbage
4. Bittergourd
5. Ginger
6. Galangal
7. Garlic
8. Cucumber
9. Dried Chinese Mushrooms
10. Asparagus
11. Hairy Marrow
12. Chillies
13. Water Chestnuts
14. Wild Sugar Cane
15. Salted Cabbage
16. Dried Radish
17. Szechuan Vegetable
18. Kale
19. Coriander Leaves
20. Mustard Green
21. Celery
22. Spring Onion
23. Flying Dragon
24. Yam
25. Bamboo Shoots

1. Cooking Oil
2. Fish Sauce
3. Oyster Sauce
4. Vegetarian Oyster Sauce
5. Light Soya Sauce
6. Thick Soya Sauce
7. Preserved Soya Bean Paste
8. Salted Soya Beans
9. Salted Plums
10. Plum Sauce
11. Hot Bean Sauce
12. Hoisin Sauce
13. Rice Vinegar
14. Rice Wine
15. Chilli Oil
16. Noodles
17. Rice Vermicelli
18. Rice Flour
19. Shallot Crisps
20. Rice Noodles
21. Transparent Vermicelli
22. Cloves
23. Cinammon Sticks
24. Five Spice Powder

25. Star Anise
26. Dried Lily Buds
27. Dried Lotus Seeds
28. Gingko Nuts
29. Long Ngan
30. Hasma
31. Dried Scallops
32. Dried Shrimps
33. Cashew Nuts
34. Soft Beancurd
35. Fried Gluten Balls
36. Beancurd Skin
37. Boxthorn Fruit (*kei chi*)
38. Dried Anchovy
39. Dates
40. White Fungus
41. Fresh Sharksfin
42. Processed Sharksfin
43. Bird's Nest
44. Dried Sole
45. *Tung Kwai*
46. Fermented Black Beans
47. Cloud Ear Fungus
48. *Yong Sam Soe*
49. Hair Vegetable
50. *Yok Chok*
51. *Tung Sam*
52. *Pak Kei*
53. *Yong sum*

1. Bamboo Steamers
2. Electric Crock Pot
3. Wok
4. Earthen Pot
5. Electric Rice Cooker
6. Wire Mesh Ladle
7. Chopping Block
8. Cleaver
9. Ladle
10. Spatula

STIR-FRIED

DISHES

Oyster Sauce Beef with Leek

250 gms (8³/4 oz) fillet or tender cut of beef, sliced thickly across grain
4 tablespoons cooking oil
4 slices ginger
2 cloves garlic, minced
1 leek, discard some of the fibrous green part and cut slantingly into 2¹/2 cm (1 in) sections
1 red chilli, seeded, cut into strips and soaked in cold water

Seasoning Ingredients

1 dessertspoon light soya sauce
1 dessertspoon rice wine
Pinch of bicarbonate of soda, use only for cuts other than fillet
1 teaspoon cornflour
1 tablespoon cooking oil, to be added just before cooking

Sauce Ingredients (combined)

1 dessertspoon oyster sauce
1 teaspoon sesame oil
1 teaspoon rice wine
¹/4 teaspoon pepper
¹/4 teaspoon salt
¹/2 teaspoon sugar

Marinate sliced beef with seasoning ingredients for 1 hour.

Heat wok with 1 tablespoon of oil until hot and stir-fry beef until it changes colour. Remove and leave aside.

Put in remaining 3 tablespoons oil, and fry ginger and garlic until fragrant. Add leek and stir-fry for 1–2 minutes. Sprinkle 1–2 tablespoons of water and cover wok for a few seconds. Remove the cover, return beef and add sauce ingredients.

Stir well to mix for 1–2 minutes until beef is cooked. Dish onto a serving dish and garnish with red chilli.

For variation, use 2 stalks celery (cut slantingly) instead of leek, 1–2 red chillies (sliced) and 2 stalks spring onion cut into 2 ¹/2 cm (1 in) pieces. Add chillies and spring onion just before dishing out from the wok.

Stir-Fried Beef with Spring Onions

250 gms (8³/4 oz) fillet or tender cut of beef, shredded
3 tablespoons cooking oil
3 slices ginger, shredded
4 stalks spring onion, cut into 2¹/2 cm (1 in) lengths

Seasoning Ingredients

¹/2 tablespoon light soya sauce
1 teaspoon rice wine
¹/2 tablespoon cornflour
2 tablespoons water
1 tablespoon cooking oil, to be added just before frying beef

Sauce Ingredients (combined)

3 tablespoons fresh chicken stock or water
¹/2 tablespoon light soya sauce
¹/2 teaspoon thick soya sauce
1 teaspoon rice wine
1 teaspoon sesame oil
¹/2 teaspoon sugar
¹/4 teaspoon pepper
1 teaspoon cornflour

Marinate beef with seasoning ingredients for at least 1 hour.

Heat wok with 1 tablespoon of oil until hot. Stir-fry the beef until it changes colour using a pair of chopsticks to separate the meat, approximately 20–30 seconds. Drain and set aside.

Reheat a clean wok with remaining 2 tablespoons oil until hot and stir-fry ginger for a few seconds. Add spring onions and stir-fry for 10–15 seconds. Return beef to the wok and stir well to mix.

Add the sauce ingredients and when it starts to boil, dish out onto a serving dish.

For variation, use 1 large onion, cut into wedges, instead of spring onions.

Stir-Fried Capsicum and Chilli Beef

200 gms (7 oz) fillet or tender cut of beef, shredded
1 cup cooking oil
1 tablespoon chopped garlic
2 tablespoons fermented black beans (*hak tau see*), rinsed and chopped
1 red chilli, seeded and chopped
1 small red capsicum, cut into 2 cm (3/4 in) squares
1 small green capsicum, cut into 2 cm (3/4 in) squares
2 teaspoons cornflour mixed with 3/4 cup water

Seasoning Ingredients

1 tablespoon light soya sauce
1 teaspoon sugar
1 tablespoon cornflour
1 tablespoon cooking oil, to be added just before cooking beef

Sauce Ingredients (combined)

1 tablespoon light soya sauce
1 teaspoon thick soya sauce
1/2 tablespoon Chinese rice wine

Marinate beef in seasoning ingredients for 15 minutes. Just before cooking mix in 1 tablespoon of oil.

Heat 1 cup of oil in a medium saucepan. Add beef and stir-fry for 5–6 seconds, stirring constantly to prevent sticking.

Reheat clean frying pan with 1 1/2 tablespoons of the oil. Add garlic and fermented black beans and stir-fry until aromatic. Put in the chilli, and red and green capsicum and stir-fry for 10 seconds.

Add combined sauce ingredients and bring to the boil. Return beef to pan and toss to mix well.

Thicken with cornflour mixture and transfer to serving dish.

Illustrated on page 41.

Shredded Pork with Preserved Szechuan Vegetable

250 gms (8 3/4 oz) lean pork, shredded
3 tablespoons cooking oil
2 cloves garlic, minced
1 large piece Szechuan vegetable (125 gms, 4 1/3 oz), rinsed, shredded and soaked for 2 hours
1 tablespoon fresh chicken stock or water

Seasoning Ingredients

2 teaspoons Chinese rice wine
1 teaspoon light soya sauce
1/4 teaspoon sugar
1/4 teaspoon salt
2 teaspoons cornflour

Sauce Ingredients (combined)

1 teaspoon rice wine
1 teaspoon thick soya sauce
1 teaspoon light soya sauce
1 teaspoon vinegar
1 teaspoon sugar
1/4 teaspoon salt

Marinate pork with seasoning ingredients for 30 minutes.

Heat wok with oil until hot and lightly brown garlic. Put in pork and toss for 2–3 minutes.

Add the drained Szechuan vegetables and stir-fry briskly for 2 minutes. Put in 1 tablespoon stock or water and continue to stir-fry for 1–2 minutes longer.

Add combined sauce ingredients and stir-fry over high heat for a few more seconds before transferring to serving dish.

Chicken breast can be used instead of pork. If a spicy flavour is preferred, add 1 chopped red chilli while frying shredded Szechuan vegetable.

Fried Garlic Pork

500 gms (17½ oz) pork fillet or tender cut, thinly sliced
Oil for deep-frying
1 tablespoon chilli oil
10–12 cloves garlic, sliced
2 sprigs coriander leaves, for garnishing

Seasoning Ingredients

½ tablespoon light soya sauce
Pinch of five spice powder
1 teaspoon black peppercorns, lightly crushed
2 teaspoons cornflour
1 tablespoon oil, to be added just before cooking

Sauce Ingredients (combined)

½ tablespoon light soya sauce
1 teaspoon oyster sauce
½ teaspoon thick soya sauce
½ teaspoon sugar

Marinate pork with seasoning ingredients for 30 minutes. Just before cooking pork stir in 1 tablespoon oil to prevent sticking.

Heat oil for deep-frying until hot. Put in pork pieces, stirring lightly to separate the meat for 1 minute. Drain well and set aside.

Remove oil and add the chilli oil. Heat until hot and lightly brown the garlic.

Pour in combined sauce ingredients and then add the fried pork and stir-fry for 2 minutes until sauce is quite dry.

Dish onto a serving plate and garnish with coriander leaves.

If you prefer less garlic flavour, use whole cloves of garlic instead of slicing them.

Sweet and Sour Pork with Pineapple

360 gms (12⅔ oz) lean pork, cut into 2½ cm (1 in) cubes
Oil for deep-frying
1 onion, cut into wedges
1 cucumber, pared, cut into 4 long strips, remove soft centre and roll cut
4 slices pineapple, canned or fresh, cut into wedges
2 tomatoes, cut into wedges
1 red chilli, sliced
3 stalks spring onion
1 tablespoon custard powder mixed with 2 tablespoons chicken stock or water

Seasoning Ingredients

¼ teaspoon bicarbonate of soda
½ teaspoon salt
½ teaspoon sugar
1 egg white, lightly beaten
2 teaspoons custard powder or cornflour
1 tablespoon water

Sauce Ingredients (combined)

1 cup fresh chicken stock or water
2 tablespoons tomato sauce
½ tablespoon Worcestershire sauce
1 tablespoon light soya sauce
1¼ tablespoons white vinegar
½ tablespoon A1 sauce
½ tablespoon chilli sauce
½ tablespoon sugar
½ teaspoon sesame oil

Marinate pork with seasoning ingredients for 20–30 minutes. Deep-fry in hot oil for 2 minutes. Drain and leave aside.

Remove oil, leaving 3 tablespoons in wok. Add onion and stir-fry until transparent. Add cucumber, pineapple, tomatoes, chilli and spring onion and briskly stir for 1 minute.

Pour in combined sauce ingredients. When it begins to boil, thicken with custard powder mixture, and transfer to serving dish.

Be sure not to overcook the vegetables, especially the cucumbers. Soak the cucumbers in ice cold water mixed with 1 teaspoon of sugar for about 30 minutes. This will keep them firm after cooking. Illustrated on page 42.

Shredded Pork with Cloud Ear Fungus

250 gms (8¾ oz) lean pork, shredded
Oil for deep-frying
3 slices ginger, minced
2 cloves garlic, minced
2 shallots, sliced
2 teaspoons hot bean paste
120 gms (4¼ oz) celery, approximately 1 stick, thinly sliced diagonally
90 gms (3 oz) cloud ear fungus, soaked to soften and shredded
2 fresh chillies, cut into strips
1 teaspoon cornflour mixed with 1 tablespoon water

Seasoning Ingredients
¼ teaspoon salt
¼ teaspoon pepper
1 teaspoon Chinese rice wine
½ egg white
1 teaspoon cornflour

Sauce Ingredients (combined)
½ cup chicken stock
1 teaspoon sugar
¼ teaspoon pepper
1 teaspoon Chinese rice wine
1 teaspoon light soya sauce
½ teaspoon thick soya sauce

Marinate shredded pork with seasoning ingredients for 20 minutes.

Heat the wok with enough oil for deep-frying. When hot, deep-fry the pork for 1 minute until just cooked, stirring to separate the meat. Drain and leave aside.

Reheat the wok with 3 tablespoons of the oil and stir-fry ginger, garlic and shallots, and then the hot bean paste until fragrant. Add the celery, cloud ear fungus and chilli strips and stir-fry for 1½–2 minutes.

Return pork to wok and stir-fry briskly over high heat. Add the combined sauce ingredients.

When it begins to boil, thicken with cornflour mixture and transfer to serving dish.

Chicken can be used instead of pork.

Stir-Fried Liver with Spring Onion

150 gms (5¼ oz) pork liver, sliced
2 tablespoons cooking oil
6–8 slices ginger, shredded
2 cloves garlic, minced
3 stalks spring onions
1 teaspoon sesame oil

Seasoning Ingredients
1 teaspoon ginger juice
¼ teaspoon salt
¼ teaspoon pepper
1 teaspoon cornflour

Sauce Ingredients (combined)
1 tablespoon fresh chicken stock or water
1 teaspoon light soya sauce
2 teaspoons thick soya sauce
1 teaspoon Chinese rice wine
½ teaspoon sugar
¼ teaspoon salt
¼ teaspoon pepper
½ teaspoon cornflour

Marinate liver with seasoning ingredients for 20 minutes. Blanch seasoned liver in boiling water for 30 seconds. (Note: Blanching ensures a smoother texture.)

Heat wok with 2 tablespoons oil until moderately hot and stir-fry ginger and garlic until fragrant. Add spring onions and stir-fry briskly. Put in the liver and continue frying for 2 minutes.

Add sauce ingredients and when the sauce thickens, stir in the sesame oil and transfer to serving dish.

Use very fresh liver and be sure not to overcook. Liver contains twice the cholesterol of beef, but it is also richer in iron, zinc, niacin and vitamins A and B12.

Sweet and Sour Pork (*Koo Loo Yok*)

600 gms (21 oz) belly pork, cut into 2½ cm (1 in) pieces
Oil for deep-frying
2 tablespoons cooking oil
1 onion, cut into wedges
1 tomato, cut into wedges
1 red chilli, cut into strips
1 cucumber, remove centre portion and cut into wedges
1 sprig coriander leaves

Seasoning Ingredients
1 tablespoon sugar
1 teaspoon salt
½ teaspoon five spice powder
1 egg, beaten, to be added later
1½ tablespoons plain flour

Sauce Ingredients (combined)
1¼ cups fresh chicken stock or water
4 tablespoons tomato sauce
1½ teaspoons sugar
1 teaspoon salt
2 teaspoons cornflour

Season pork with seasoning ingredients and leave overnight in the refrigerator. Just before frying pork, stir in egg and flour.

Heat wok with oil for deep-frying and fry pork until golden brown. Drain pork from oil and leave aside.

Reheat wok with 2 tablespoons oil. Put in onion, then tomato and stir-fry for 1 minute. Pour in sauce ingredients and add chilli and cucumber.

When sauce comes to the boil, put in the fried pork, stirring quickly to mix the sauce.

Dish onto serving dish and garnish with coriander leaves.

The secret to this recipe is to season the meat overnight.

Hoisin Sauce Chicken

350 gms (12⅓ oz) fillet of chicken, trimmed and sliced in 2 lengthwise (approximately 1 cm, ⅓ in thick)
2 tablespoons cooking oil
6 cloves garlic, cut into thin slices
5 white parts of spring onion, cut into 3 cm (1¼ in) lengths
3 red chillies, seeded and cut in 4 lengthwise
3 green chillies, seeded and cut in 4 lengthwise
3 tablespoons Hoisin sauce
2 teaspoons sesame oil

Seasoning Ingredients
½ teaspoon salt
¼ teaspoon pepper
1 teaspoon light soya sauce
½ an egg white, beaten
1 teaspoon cornflour
2 teaspoons shallot oil, to be added just before cooking

Season chicken with seasoning ingredients. Just before cooking stir in shallot oil.

Heat a wok with 1 tablespoon oil and lightly brown ⅔ of garlic. Add chicken, put in the spring onion and stir-fry for 2 minutes until chicken is ¾ cooked. Remove and set aside.

Reheat wok with remaining 1 tablespoon oil and add the rest of the garlic. As it sizzles, add the chillies and Hoisin sauce and stir well. Return chicken to wok and toss in the sauce.

Finally stir in sesame oil and transfer to serving dish.

Chicken Feet with Hoisin Sauce

4 dried Chinese mushrooms,
soaked until soft and halved
16 chicken feet
2 tablespoons cooking oil
3 cloves garlic, minced
4 slices ginger
1 small red capsicum, diced
into 2 cm (3/4 in) squares
1 red chilli, seeded and diced
into 2 cm (3/4 in) squares
1 teaspoon cornflour mixed
with 1 tablespoon water
2 sprigs coriander leaves, chopped

Seasoning Ingredients
1 teaspoon shallot oil
1/4 teaspoon sugar
1/4 teaspoon pepper
1/4 teaspoon salt

Sauce Ingredients (combined)
3/4 cup fresh chicken stock
1 tablespoon Hoisin sauce
1 tablespoon oyster sauce
1/2 teaspoon salt
1/4 teaspoon pepper
1 teaspoon sugar

Marinate the mushrooms with seasoning ingredients for 15 minutes.

Trim claws of chicken feet. Cut off the upper portion of the feet. Put chicken feet into a deep saucepan and add water to cover them.

Bring to the boil, reduce heat and boil for 45–60 minutes or until feet are tender. Drain.

Heat oil in a saucepan and stir-fry garlic and ginger until aromatic. Pour in combined sauce ingredients and bring to the boil.

Add chicken feet, capsicum and chilli. Thicken with cornflour mixture. Serve garnished with coriander leaves.

Chicken with Dried Chillies

500 gms (17 1/2 oz) chicken meat from thighs
or breast
1/4 cup cooking oil
3 cloves garlic, minced
30 gms (1 oz) dried chillies,
cut in 2, washed and drained
1 teaspoon cornflour mixed
with 2 tablespoons water

Seasoning Ingredients
1 dessertspoon light soya sauce
1 dessertspoon oyster sauce
1 teaspoon ginger juice
1/2 teaspoon sesame oil
1/4 teaspoon salt
2 tablespoons water
2 teaspoons cornflour

Sauce Ingredients (combined)
1 dessertspoon light soya sauce
1 dessertspoon oyster sauce
1 teaspoon ginger juice
1 teaspoon Worcestershire sauce
1 teaspoon sesame oil
1/2 teaspoon thick soya sauce
2 teaspoons sugar

Pound the chicken meat lightly with the blunt edge of a cleaver. Cut into 2 1/2 cm (1 in) cubes and marinate with seasoning ingredients for at least 20 minutes.

Heat wok with oil and stir-fry garlic until fragrant. Add dried chillies and stir-fry over medium heat for 30 seconds.

Put in chicken and fry until chicken changes colour. Add combined sauce ingredients and stir-fry for 2 more minutes.

Stir in cornflour thickening and transfer to serving dish.

Stir-Fried Chicken with Mixed Mushrooms

250 gms (8¾ oz) chicken, cut into strips
180 gms (6⅓ oz) fresh champignons
or ½ of 385 gms (13½ oz) can button mushrooms, halved
180 gms (6⅓ oz) fresh straw mushrooms
or ½ of 425 gms (15 oz) can straw mushrooms, halved
180 gms fresh oyster mushrooms
or ½ of 425 gms (15 oz) can oyster mushrooms, halved
7 dried Chinese mushrooms, soaked and halved
5 tablespoons oil
3 cloves garlic, minced
1 stalk spring onion, chopped
1 sprig coriander leaves, chopped
1 red chilli, chopped

Seasoning Ingredients

2 teaspoons light soya sauce
1 teaspoon salt
1 teaspoon sugar
¼ teaspoon pepper
1 teaspoon sesame oil
2 teaspoons cornflour

Sauce Ingredients (combined)

1 cup fresh chicken stock or water
3 teaspoons oyster sauce
2 teaspoons light soya sauce
1 teaspoon sugar
½ teaspoon sesame oil
¼ teaspoon salt
¼ teaspoon pepper
3 teaspoons cornflour

Season chicken with seasoning ingredients for 15 minutes. Wash and blanch straw, button and oyster mushrooms in boiling water and drain.

Heat 1 tablespoon of the oil in a wok and stir-fry the Chinese mushrooms until fragrant. Remove and leave aside.

Reheat wok with 2 tablespoons of oil. Lightly brown the garlic. Add chicken and fry for 2 minutes. Remove and leave aside.

Heat remaining 2 tablespoons oil in wok, add the champignons, then straw and oyster mushrooms and stir-fry for 2 minutes. Add fried Chinese mushrooms and chicken and mix well.

Pour in combined sauce ingredients and bring to boil until the sauce thickens.

Mix in chopped spring onion, coriander leaves and chilli, and transfer to serving dish.

A clever combination of fresh, dried and canned mushrooms creates an interesting mix in this quick stir-fry dish.

Ginger and Sesame Chicken

3 whole chicken thighs,
cut into 2½ cm (1 in) thick pieces
2 tablespoons sesame oil
180 gms (6⅓ oz) old ginger, shredded
1 tablespoon brandy
½ tablespoon thick soya sauce
½ tablespoon light soya sauce
½ cup water

Seasoning Ingredients

1 teaspoon salt
½ teaspoon pepper
1 teaspoon sesame oil

Season chicken with seasoning ingredients for at least 30 minutes.

Heat wok with sesame oil and stir-fry ginger until lightly browned and fragrant. Put in chicken and continue cooking for 6–8 minutes. Add brandy and toss well. Stir in thick and light soya sauce. Continue stirring until sauce coats chicken.

Pour in the water and bring to the boil. Lower the heat and simmer chicken, covered, for approximately 15 minutes until chicken is tender and very little gravy remains.

A common chicken dish for ladies in confinement. The ginger is to help clear 'winds' from the stomach. Some Chinese believe that consuming large amounts of ginger during confinement will help to maintain good health in later years. Brandy is also a good tonic for health.

Stir-Fried Capsicum and Chilli Beef
Page 35

Sweet and Sour Pork with Pineapple
Page 36

Black Pepper Chicken with Mixed Vegetables
Page 49

Stir-Fried Mussels with Black Bean Sauce
Page 53

Stir-Fried Prawns with Cloud Ear Fungus and Snow Peas
Page 54

Hot Tangy Cuttlefish
Page 57

Chilli Oyster Crabs
Page 58

Stir-Fried Brinjals with Minced Meat
Page 60

Diced Chicken with Cashew Nuts

1 whole chicken breast, cut into 1 1/4 cm (1/2 in) cubes
4 tablespoons cooking oil
6 dried Chinese mushrooms, soaked and diced
1 onion, diced
1 can (425 gms, 15 oz) young corn, diced
2 green peppers, diced
1 medium-sized carrot, diced and parboiled
90 gms (3 oz) roasted cashew nuts
2 sprigs coriander leaves

Seasoning Ingredients

1 teaspoon sugar
1 teaspoon sesame oil
1 teaspoon salt
1 teaspoon Chinese rice wine
1 teaspoon cornflour
1/2 tablespoon oil

Sauce Ingredients (combined)

1 cup fresh chicken stock or water
2 dessertspoons oyster sauce
1 teaspoon light soya sauce
1 teaspoon sesame oil
1 teaspoon Chinese rice wine
1/2 teaspoon sugar
1/2 teaspoon salt
1 tablespoon cornflour

Marinate chicken cubes with seasoning ingredients for at least 30 minutes.

Heat 1 tablespoon oil in a wok. Stir-fry mushrooms for 1 minute and dish out. Stir-fry marinated chicken until cooked. Remove and wash wok.

Heat 3 tablespoons oil in clean wok. Fry onion until transparent and fragrant. Put in fried chicken, mushrooms and young corn, and stir-fry for 1–2 minutes. Add green peppers, carrot and lastly cashew nuts.

Stir in combined sauce ingredients and bring to the boil.

When the sauce thickens, dish out and serve garnished with coriander leaves.

This is one of the dishes I prepared when I entertained for the first time in my life, more than 30 years ago. Even non-cooks can rely on this one for guests.

Black Pepper Chicken with Mixed Vegetables

400 gms (14 oz) chicken meat, cut into 2 1/2 cm (1 in) pieces
Oil for deep-frying
1 1/2 tablespoons cooking oil
1 teaspoon cornflour mixed with 1 tablespoon water

Seasoning Ingredients

1 teaspoon black peppercorns, coarsely crushed
1 teaspoon light soya sauce
1/2 teaspoon salt
1/2 teaspoon sugar
1 tablespoon cornflour, to be added just before cooking
1 tablespoon cooking oil

Diced Ingredients (cut into 1 1/2 cm, 2/3 in squares)

1 large onion
1/2 red pepper
1/2 green pepper
6 young corns
1 red chilli, seeded

Sauce Ingredients (combined)

4 tablespoons fresh chicken stock
1/4 teaspoon salt
1 tablespoon oyster sauce
1/2 tablespoon light soya sauce
1 teaspoon sugar

Marinate chicken with seasoning ingredients for 15–30 minutes.

Just before deep-frying the chicken, mix in the cornflour followed by the oil. Deep-fry chicken in hot oil until light golden brown. Drain from oil and set aside.

Reheat a clean wok with 1 1/2 tablespoons oil and fry onion until soft. Add vegetables and toss for a few seconds.

Add sauce ingredients. When the sauce begins to boil, return chicken to wok.

Stir in cornflour mixture and transfer to a serving dish.

This is a peppery chicken dish with a good combination of colourful vegetables. Use the aromatic Sarawak black peppercorns and crush them only when ready to use. *Illustrated on page 43.*

Chicken Wings with Oyster Sauce

8 chicken wings, cut into 2 at the joint
6 stalks mustard green (*choy sum*), cut into 10 cm (4 in) sections
4 tablespoons cooking oil
1/4 teaspoon salt
6 slices ginger, shredded
4 stalks spring onion, cut into 2 1/2 cm (1 in) sections
1 tablespoon Chinese rice wine
1/2 tablespoon cornflour mixed with 1 tablespoon chicken stock or water
1 teaspoon sesame oil
1 red chilli, cut into strips and soaked in cold water

Seasoning Ingredients

1 tablespoon light soya sauce
1/2 teaspoon thick soya sauce
1/4 teaspoon pepper

Sauce Ingredients (combined)

1/2 cup fresh chicken stock or water
1 tablespoon oyster sauce
1/2 teaspoon thick soya sauce
1/4 teaspoon salt
1/2 teaspoon sugar
1/4 teaspoon black pepper

Marinate chicken wings with seasoning ingredients for 30 minutes. Blanch mustard green in boiling water for 1 minute and drain well.

Heat wok with 2 tablespoons oil and stir-fry blanched vegetables for a few seconds, adding 1/4 teaspoon of salt. Remove and arrange vegetables on a serving dish.

Reheat wok with 2 tablespoons oil and stir-fry ginger and spring onion until fragrant. Add the chicken wings, then the rice wine and stir-fry briskly.

Pour in sauce ingredients, cover the wok and allow to cook over moderate heat for 10 minutes. Remove the cover and thicken with cornflour mixture.

Add the sesame oil and dish out onto the plate of vegetables. Serve garnished with red chilli.

Mustard green can be substituted with endives (curly green leaf lettuce). With endives, omit blanching and proceed with stir-frying, adding 1 clove of garlic.

Chicken with Walnuts

300 gms (10 1/2 oz) chicken meat, cut into 2 cm (3/4 in) cubes
Oil for deep-frying
100 gms (3 1/2 oz) walnuts
4 slices ginger, shredded
2 shallots, sliced
16 slices of carrot, blanched in boiling water
1 red chilli, seeded and cut into wedges

Seasoning Ingredients

1 teaspoon light soya sauce
1 teaspoon oyster sauce
1 teaspoon Chinese rice wine
1/4 teaspoon salt
1/4 teaspoon pepper
2 teaspoons cornflour
1 tablespoon water

Sauce Ingredients (combined)

4 tablespoons fresh chicken stock
1 teaspoon Chinese rice wine
1/2 teaspoon light soya sauce
1/2 teaspoon sugar
1/4 teaspoon pepper
1 teaspoon cornflour

Marinate chicken with seasoning ingredients for 20 minutes. Heat oil in a wok and deep-fry chicken for 1 minute or until just cooked through. Drain and set aside.

Boil walnuts for 5 minutes or until they are soft. Deep-fry walnuts in hot oil for 1–2 minutes until lightly browned. Drain and set aside.

Reheat a clean wok with 2 tablespoons oil and stir-fry ginger and shallots until fragrant. Add carrots and fry for 1 minute. Return chicken to wok and stir-fry briskly.

Pour in combined sauce ingredients and when it boils, put in chillies and walnuts.

Toss well and transfer to serving dish.

The addition of crunchy walnuts gives a unique flavour to this otherwise common homestyle dish. To complete the meal, serve with a vegetable dish, like Stir-Fried Lettuce with Oyster Sauce, and a steamed fish.

Cencaluk Chicken

250 gms (8³/₄ oz) de-boned chicken thighs, cut into strips
1 teaspoon sugar
2 tablespoons salted baby shrimps *(cencaluk)*
2 tablespoons cooking oil
2 stems lemon grass, crushed
2 onions, cut into wedges
2 cloves garlic, minced
¹/₂ cup water
1 teaspoon thick soya sauce
2 red chillies, sliced
2 green chillies, sliced

Marinate chicken with sugar and *cencaluk* for 15 minutes.

Heat 2 tablespoons oil in a wok and fry crushed lemon grass, onions and garlic until fragrant. Put in chicken and fry for another 2 minutes.

Add water, soya sauce and chillies. Stir-fry until chicken is cooked and sauce is thickened.

Cencaluk chicken is not truly Chinese, in fact it is "Nonya." Cencaluk are salted baby shrimps sold in jars or bottles. They can be seen displayed in roadside stalls on the main trunk roads approaching Melaka (Malacca), and of course you can buy them from major supermarkets all over Malaysia. The tiny shrimps, called geragau, are found in abundance off the coast of Melaka. It is hard to imagine that these preserved pink soggy shrimps could be appetising, but to Nonyas they are a delicacy. Cencaluk has a strong fishy flavour. I had never acquired a taste for it until a Nonya friend of mine gave me this dish for lunch one day. Die-hard cencaluk lovers tell me that just a small dish of cencaluk alone with a squeeze of lime, minced shallots and chillies is enough to whet their appetite to polish off bowls of rice.

Stir-Fried Fish Fillet with Fresh Champignons

400 gms (14 oz) fish fillet (sea bass, garoupa or threadfin), cut into 4 x 2¹/₂ cm (1¹/₂ x 1 in) pieces
250 gms (8³/₄ oz) medium-sized fresh champignons, stems removed, caps wiped with kitchen paper
Oil for deep-frying
2 tablespoons cooking oil
3 cloves garlic
2¹/₂ cm (1 in) knob of ginger, chopped
³/₄ cup fresh anchovy or chicken stock
2 teaspoons cornflour
1¹/₂ teaspoons Chinese rice wine
1 tablespoon chopped spring onion
2 stalks spring onion, cut into 5 cm (2 in) lengths, shredded and soaked in cold water

Seasoning Ingredients

1 teaspoon sugar
1 teaspoon salt
¹/₄ teaspoon pepper
1 teaspoon sesame oil
2 teaspoons cornflour
1 tablespoon cooking oil, to be added just before cooking

Sauce Ingredients (combined)

1 tablespoon oyster sauce
¹/₂ teaspoon sesame oil
¹/₂ teaspoon thick soya sauce
¹/₄ teaspoon salt

Marinate fish slices with seasoning ingredients for at least 30 minutes. Stir in 1 tablespoon oil just before cooking. Blanch the champignons for 30 seconds, drain and set aside.

Heat oil for deep-frying. Deep-fry fish for 2 minutes or until golden. Drain from oil and set aside.

Heat a clean wok with 2 tablespoons oil and lightly brown garlic and ginger. Return mushrooms and fish to wok and stir-fry over high heat for 30 seconds. Stir in combined sauce ingredients.

Mix cornflour with a little of the stock. Pour remaining stock into wok and bring to the boil.

Stir in cornflour mixture and finally the wine and chopped spring onion. Transfer to serving dish and sprinkle shredded spring onion on top.

Use very fresh fish and choose white champignons. The tender fish slices compliment the smooth texture and earthy flavour of the mushrooms. A delightful dish ideal for entertaining.

Sliced Fish and Celery in Hot Sour Sauce

250 gms ($8\frac{3}{4}$ oz) fish fillet (threadfin or garoupa), cut into $1\frac{1}{2}$ x $1\frac{1}{2}$ x 5 cm ($\frac{3}{4}$ x $\frac{3}{4}$ x 2 in) slices
1 egg white, beaten
Cornflour for coating fish
Oil for deep-frying
2 tablespoons cooking oil
1 stalk young celery, sliced
90 gms (3 oz) carrots, sliced and parboiled
4 slices ginger, shredded
2 cloves garlic, minced
1 shallot, sliced
2 red chillies, cut into strips
1 stalk spring onion, cut into $2\frac{1}{2}$ cm (1 in) lengths
1 teaspoon sesame oil

Seasoning Ingredients
$\frac{1}{2}$ teaspoon salt
$\frac{1}{4}$ teaspoon sugar
1 teaspoon light soya sauce
2 teaspoons Chinese rice wine

Sauce Ingredients (combined)
$\frac{1}{2}$ cup fresh fish or chicken stock
$\frac{1}{2}$ teaspoon salt
1 teaspoon sugar
$\frac{1}{4}$ teaspoon pepper
1 teaspoon Chinese rice wine
1 teaspoon light soya sauce
$\frac{1}{2}$ tablespoon Chinese black vinegar
1 teaspoon cornflour

Marinate fish with seasoning ingredients for 20 minutes. Just before frying fish, stir in beaten egg white and coat thickly with cornflour.

Heat oil in a wok until hot and deep-fry fish slices until light golden brown. Drain.

Reheat a clean wok with 1 tablespoon oil and stir-fry celery and carrot for 1 minute. Remove and leave aside.

Heat another tablespoon of oil and lightly brown ginger, garlic and shallots. Put in chillies, carrots and celery and stir-fry briskly.

Add sauce ingredients and when it starts to boil, return fish to wok and stir gently, taking care not to break up the fish pieces.

When sauce thickens, put in spring onion and stir in sesame oil.

If the fish is not fresh, the fillet will fall apart when cooked. Fish from the garoupa and threadfin family have meaty, firm flesh making them ideal for stir-frying, steaming or braising.

Fish Slices with Leek and Cauliflower

600 gms (21 oz) fish fillet (threadfin or garoupa), cut into $1\frac{1}{4}$ x $2\frac{1}{2}$ x 4 cm ($\frac{1}{2}$ x 1 x $1\frac{1}{2}$ in) pieces
Oil for deep-frying
250 gms ($8\frac{3}{4}$ oz) cauliflower, cut into pieces
1 tablespoon cooking oil
6 cloves garlic, minced
10 slices carrot, parboiled
1 stalk leek, green portion discarded, cut into 5 cm (2 in) lengths diagonally
$\frac{1}{2}$ can button mushrooms, halved
$\frac{1}{4}$ teaspoon sesame oil
$\frac{1}{2}$ teaspoon salt
30 gms (1 oz) frozen peas
1 teaspoon cornflour mixed with 1 tablespoon water
1 stalk spring onion, chopped

Seasoning Ingredients
1 teaspoon salt
1 egg, lightly beaten
1 teaspoon cornflour

Sauce Ingredients (combined)
$\frac{3}{4}$ cup fresh chicken stock or water
1 teaspoon Chinese rice wine
1 tablespoon light soya sauce
$\frac{1}{2}$ tablespoon oyster sauce
1 teaspoon thick soya sauce
$\frac{1}{4}$ teaspoon pepper

Season fish slices with seasoning ingredients and leave for 10 minutes.

Heat oil for deep-frying until hot and deep-fry cauliflower for 10 seconds. Drain from oil and leave aside. Deep-fry fish slices for 1 minute. Drain well and set aside.

Heat wok with 1 tablespoon oil until hot and lightly brown garlic. Put in the cauliflower, carrot, leek and mushrooms and fry for another 2 minutes.

Add combined sauce and then fish. Add the sesame oil, salt to taste and peas.

Thicken with cornflour mixture and serve hot sprinkled with spring onion.

Fish and Cloud Ear Fungus in Wine Sauce

300 gms ($10\frac{1}{2}$ oz) fish fillet
(threadfin or garoupa),
cut into $1\frac{1}{2}$ x $1\frac{1}{2}$ x 4 cm ($\frac{3}{4}$ x $\frac{3}{4}$ x $1\frac{1}{2}$ oz) slices
Oil for deep-frying
30 gms (1 oz) cloud ear fungus, soaked for
30 minutes and cut into 2 or 3 pieces
2 tablespoons cooking oil
2 cloves garlic, chopped
6 slices ginger, shredded
1 red chilli, cut into strips, optional
2 stalks spring onion, chopped

Seasoning Ingredients
$\frac{1}{2}$ teaspoon salt
$\frac{1}{4}$ teaspoon pepper
$\frac{1}{4}$ teaspoon sugar
1 teaspoon ginger juice
1 teaspoon Chinese rice wine
1 teaspoon light soya sauce
1 tablespoon cornflour

Sauce Ingredients (combined)
$\frac{3}{4}$ cup fresh fish or chicken stock
1 teaspoon salt
$\frac{1}{2}$ teaspoon sugar
$\frac{1}{4}$ teaspoon pepper
1 tablespoon Chinese rice wine
1 teaspoon light soya sauce
1 teaspoon sesame oil
2 teaspoons cornflour

Marinate fish slices with the seasoning ingredients for 20 minutes. Deep-fry the fish in moderately hot oil for 1 minute. Remove with a perforated ladle and drain from oil.

Soak the cloud ear fungus for 30 minutes until soft. Trim off the hard centres and cut into 1 x 4 cm ($\frac{1}{3}$ x $1\frac{1}{2}$ in) slices.

Reheat a clean wok with 2 tablespoons oil and stir-fry garlic and ginger until lightly brown and fragrant. Add the chilli and cloud ear fungus and stir-fry for half a minute.

Add spring onions and combined sauce. When the sauce thickens, return fish to wok and carefully stir to coat fish with sauce until cooked.

Transfer to serving dish and serve hot.

The cloud ear fungus provides an interesting crunch and colour to this fish dish which contains just enough wine to stimulate the taste buds.

Stir-Fried Mussels with Black Bean Sauce

500 gms ($17\frac{1}{2}$ oz) frozen mussels in half shells,
thawed and rinsed
2 tablespoons chilli oil
5 cloves garlic, chopped
$1\frac{1}{2}$ cm ($\frac{3}{4}$ in) ginger, finely chopped
1 tablespoon fermented black beans, rinsed
1 red chilli, seeded and chopped
1 small red capsicum,
seeded and cut into $2\frac{1}{2}$ cm (1 in) squares
1 teaspoon Chinese rice wine
1 tablespoon chopped spring onion
Parsley or coriander leaves for garnishing

Sauce Ingredients (combined)
$\frac{1}{2}$ cup fresh chicken stock
1 tablespoon oyster sauce
$\frac{1}{2}$ teaspoon sugar
2 teaspoons cornflour

Heat chilli oil in a wok until hot and stir-fry garlic, ginger and fermented black beans until aromatic. Add chilli and mussels and stir-fry for 1 minute.

Pour in combined sauce ingredients. When it comes to the boil, add the capsicum, stir to mix, cover and let it simmer for 30 seconds. Remove cover and add rice wine and spring onion.

Transfer to serving dish and garnish with parsley or coriander leaves.

If fresh mussels are available, scald them for a minute or less and remove one shell for use. Clams are also suitable. Increase the weight to 600 gms (21 oz) and use them directly, without blanching. Illustrated on page 44.

Garlic Prawns

600 gms (21 oz) medium-sized prawns, in shells
1 small cucumber, sliced for garnishing
4 tablespoons cooking oil
8 cloves garlic, minced
1 1/2 tablespoons thick soya sauce

Seasoning Ingredients
1 teaspoon salt
1 teaspoon light soya sauce
1/2 teaspoon pepper

Trim the feelers of the prawns neatly with a pair of scissors. Season prawns with seasoning ingredients and leave for 15 minutes.

Arrange cucumber slices on a serving plate.

Heat wok with oil until hot and lightly brown garlic. Put in prawns and stir-fry for 1 minute. If the prawns are large, cover the wok for a minute or until prawns are cooked.

Dish onto the prepared serving dish and drizzle thick soya sauce over the prawns.

Stir-Fried Prawns with Garlic and Chilli

300 gms (10 1/2 oz) medium-sized prawns, in shell
1/2 teaspoon salt
1/4 teaspoon pepper
4 tablespoons cooking oil
6 cloves garlic, sliced
4 slices ginger
2 red chillies, sliced
2 stalks spring onion, chopped
1 tablespoon Chinese rice wine

Seasoning Ingredients (combined)
1/2 teaspoon salt
1/4 teaspoon white pepper
1/4 teaspoon black pepper

Wash the prawns and trim the feelers and whiskers. Drain and marinate with salt and pepper for 15 minutes.

Heat oil in a wok until hot and fry prawns for 1 minute until they turn a bright red colour. Remove prawns to a dish leaving the oil in the wok.

Lightly brown the garlic and ginger and then add the chillies and spring onion. Return prawns to the wok and stir-fry for half a minute. Add the combined seasonings and mix well.

Drizzle the wine over the sides of the wok. Stir-fry briskly for a few seconds and transfer to serving dish.

A lightly spiced prawn dish that takes only minutes to cook.

Stir-Fried Prawns with Cloud Ear Fungus and Snow Peas

250 gms (8 3/4 oz) peeled medium prawns, de-veined
Oil for deep-frying
2 tablespoons cooking oil
150 gms (5 1/4 oz) snow peas, cleaned
2 cloves garlic, finely chopped
2 cm (3/4 in) knob young ginger, finely chopped
10 large pieces cloud ear fungus (*wan yee*), soaked to soften

Seasoning Ingredients
1 teaspoon salt
1/2 teaspoon sugar
1/2 egg white, beaten

Sauce Ingredients (combined)
3/4 cup chicken stock
1 tablespoon light soya sauce
1/2 tablespoon oyster sauce
1/2 tablespoon Chinese rice wine
2 teaspoons cornflour

Marinate prawns with seasoning ingredients for 30 minutes. Heat oil for deep-frying in a saucepan and blanch prawns in hot oil for 10 seconds. Drain from oil and set aside.

Heat a wok with 2 tablespoons cooking oil and stir-fry snow peas for 15 seconds. Drain and set aside.

Put in garlic and ginger to brown, then add cloud ear fungus and the prawns and toss well.

Pour in combined sauce ingredients and bring to the boil. Return snow peas and mix well before transferring to serving dish.

Illustrated on page 45.

Sweet and Sour Plum Sauce Prawns

1 kg ($2^{1}/_{5}$ lbs) medium–large prawns, cleaned, eyes and feelers trimmed off
$^{1}/_{2}$ teaspoon salt
$^{1}/_{2}$ teaspoon pepper
Oil for deep-frying
3 tablespoons cooking oil
4 cloves garlic, finely chopped
3 shallots, finely chopped
2 cm ($^{3}/_{4}$ in) ginger, finely chopped
1 onion, chopped
3 tablespoons chilli sauce
3 tablespoons tomato sauce
1 tablespoon Hoisin sauce
2 teaspoons cornflour mixed with 2 tablespoons water
1 egg white, beaten
Cucumber and tomato slices, and coriander for garnishing

Sauce Ingredients (combined)

$1^{1}/_{2}$ cups fresh anchovy stock or water
1 tablespoon light soya sauce
2 tablespoons plum sauce
1 tablespoon sugar
$^{1}/_{2}$ teaspoon salt
$^{1}/_{2}$ teaspoon sesame oil
$^{1}/_{4}$ teaspoon pepper

Season prawns with pepper and salt for 15 minutes. Heat oil in a deep saucepan and deep-fry prawns for 30 seconds. Drain from oil and set aside.

Heat a clean wok with 3 tablespoons oil and sauté garlic, shallots and ginger until fragrant. Stir in combined chilli, tomato and Hoisin sauces.

Pour in combined sauce ingredients and bring to the boil. Add prawns and stir-fry until prawns are cooked through.

Thicken with cornflour mixture and stir in beaten egg white.

Transfer to serving dish and garnish with cucumber and tomato slices and coriander.

A refreshing change from the usual sweet and sour sauce. Be sure not to overcook the prawns so they keep their crispy texture.

Fruity Sauce Prawns

600 gms (21 oz) medium–large prawns, feelers trimmed
$^{1}/_{2}$ teaspoon pepper
1 teaspoon salt
6 tablespoons cooking oil
5 cm (2 in) piece ginger, chopped
5 cloves garlic, chopped
1 red chilli, seeded and chopped
2 tablespoons fruity ketchup
1 tablespoon coriander leaves
1 tablespoon chopped spring onion

Sauce Ingredients (combined)

$^{1}/_{2}$ tablespoon thick soya sauce
1 tablespoon light soya sauce
$^{1}/_{2}$ tablespoon sugar

Season prawns with salt and pepper.

Heat 3 tablespoons oil in deep saucepan until very hot. Put in prawns and fry for 2 minutes until prawns turn red. Drain from oil.

Heat 3 tablespoons oil in clean wok. Brown ginger and garlic. Stir in chilli and return prawns to saucepan.

Stir in combined sauce ingredients, followed by the fruity ketchup.

Place on serving dish and sprinkle on coriander leaves and spring onion.

Fruity ketchup is a tangy fruity sauce made with pineapple, tomato paste, vinegar and glucose syrup. It has the consistency and the reddish colour of tomato ketchup.

Stir-Fried Scallops with Chinese Mushrooms

250 gms (8¾ oz) shelled fresh scallops
½ teaspoon salt
¼ teaspoon pepper
30 gms (1 oz) Chinese dried mushroom, soaked and quartered
3 tablespoons cooking oil
2 cloves garlic, minced
2 shallots, sliced
4 slices ginger, shredded
8 pieces young corn, cut into 2
90 gms (3 oz) snow peas

Seasoning Ingredients
¼ teaspoon salt
¼ teaspoon pepper
½ teaspoon sugar
½ teaspoon sesame oil
½ teaspoon light soya sauce

Sauce Ingredients (combined)
½ cup fresh chicken stock or water
½ teaspoon salt
½ teaspoon sugar
1 teaspoon light soya sauce
1 teaspoon oyster sauce
1 teaspoon Chinese rice wine
1 teaspoon cornflour

Marinate the scallops with salt and pepper for 15 minutes. Marinate softened mushrooms with seasoning ingredients for 15 minutes.

Heat wok with oil and stir-fry garlic, shallots and ginger until fragrant. Put in mushrooms and stir-fry for 1 minute. Add the scallops, young corn and snow peas, and stir-fry briskly for another minute.

Pour in the sauce ingredients and allow to boil until sauce thickens before transferring to serving plate.

Transparent Cuttlefish with Dried Chillies

2 large soaked transparent cuttlefish
3 tablespoons cooking oil
12 dried chillies, cut into 2½ cm (1 in) pieces and rinsed
4 cloves garlic, minced
5 slices ginger, minced
1 teaspoon Szechuan peppercorns
1 tablespoon ground dried chillies (*chilli giling*), optional
2 tablespoons roasted cashew nuts

Sauce Ingredients (combined)
1½ tablespoons light soya sauce
½ tablespoon thick soya sauce
1 tablespoon sugar
2 teaspoons sesame oil
½ teaspoon salt
2 tablespoons water

Wash the cuttlefish. With a sharp knife at a slant, make shallow cuts across the inside surface of the cuttlefish in a criss-cross pattern. The cuttlefish will curl with an attractive pattern when cooked.

Cut the cuttlefish into bite-sized pieces and blanch in boiling water for 1 minute. Drain and set aside.

Heat oil in a wok until hot and stir-fry dried chillies for a few seconds. Dish out the dried chillies leaving the oil in the wok.

Heat up the oil again and lightly brown garlic, ginger and Szechuan peppercorns. Put in the cuttlefish and sauce ingredients and stir-fry for 1 minute.

Add the cashew nuts and dried chillies and toss until well-mixed. Transfer to serving dish.

Hot Tangy Cuttlefish

600 gms (21 oz) cuttlefish, score the inner body and cut into thick slices, about 2 x 5 cm (3/4 x 2 in)
1/2 teaspoon sugar
1/4 teaspoon pepper
2 tablespoons cooking oil
1 onion, sliced
4 cloves garlic, chopped
2 cm (3/4 in) knob young ginger, finely chopped
30 gms (1 oz) dried prawns, rinsed and ground
2 red chillies, seeded and chopped
4 leaves wrinkled lime (*limau purut*), finely shredded
Lemon slices for garnishing

Sauce Ingredients (combined)
1 1/2 tablespoons tomato sauce
1 1/2 tablespoons chilli sauce
1 tablespoon oyster sauce
1/2 tablespoon soya sauce
1/2 tablespoon cider vinegar
1 teaspoon sesame oil
3 tablespoons lemon juice
1 tablespoon sugar
1/2 teaspoon pepper

Season cuttlefish with sugar and pepper for 15–30 minutes. Boil saucepan of water and scald cuttlefish for a few seconds. Drain well and place on serving dish.

Heat wok with oil and cook onion and garlic until soft. Add ginger and dried prawns and stir-fry until fragrant. Add chillies, then pour in the combined sauce ingredients.

Finally stir in the *limau purut* leaves. As soon as it boils, remove from heat. Return cuttlefish to wok and mix well.

Transfer to serving dish and garnish with lemon slices.

This dish has a lovely sauce with a combination of all the tastes. Be sure not to overcook the cuttlefish as this will spoil the flavour of the dish. *Illustrated on page 46.*

Stir-Fried Szechuan Style Squid

600 gms (21 oz) fresh large squid, score the inner body and cut into thick slices, about 2 x 5 cm (3/4 x 2 in)
1/2 teaspoon salt
1/2 teaspoon pepper
3 tablespoons cooking oil, preferably lard
3 cloves garlic, minced
1 tablespoon hot bean paste
1 small tender young stalk celery, sliced
1 small leek, sliced
2 red chillies, sliced

Sauce Ingredients (combined)
3/4 cup fresh chicken stock or water
1 tablespoon light soya sauce
1 tablespoon Chinese wine
1 teaspoon sesame oil
1 teaspoon sugar
1/4 teaspoon pepper
1/4 teaspoon salt
2 teaspoons cornflour

Season the squids with salt and pepper for 15 minutes. Blanch the seasoned squids in boiling salted water for 30 seconds–1 minute. Drain well.

Heat wok with oil until hot and stir-fry garlic and hot bean paste until fragrant. Add celery and leek, and stir-fry for 1 1/2 minutes.

Stir in sauce ingredients and bring to the boil. When the sauce thickens, add the squid and chillies, and very briefly toss the mixture.

Transfer to serving dish and serve hot.

If squids are small to medium-sized, cut into 2 cm (3/4 in) rounds.

Spicy Squid with Onion

600 gms (21 oz) fresh large squids,
score the inner body and cut into thick slices,
about 2 x 5 cm (3/4 x 2 in)
1 teaspoon ginger juice
1/2 teaspoon salt
1/4 teaspoon pepper
3 tablespoons cooking oil
3 cloves garlic, minced
2 medium-sized onions, quartered
2–3 fresh red chillies, sliced
1 stalk spring onion, chopped
1 sprig coriander leaves, chopped

Sauce Ingredients (combined)
1/2 cup fresh chicken stock or water
1/2 tablespoon light soya sauce
1/2 tablespoon thick soya sauce
1 teaspoon sugar
1/4 teaspoon salt
1/4 teaspoon pepper
1 teaspoon cornflour

Marinate sliced squids with ginger juice, salt and pepper for 20 minutes.

Heat oil in a wok until hot and lightly brown garlic. Add the onion and stir-fry until soft. Add the red chillies and the squids, and stir-fry for 1–2 minutes.

Pour in sauce ingredients. When it boils and thickens, sprinkle in spring onion and coriander leaves and transfer to serving dish.

A tasty homestyle dish using nothing but ingredients regularly found in the kitchen.

Chilli Oyster Crabs

3 kg (6 2/3 lbs) crabs
1 cup cooking oil
60 gms (2 oz) ginger, cut into strips
7 cloves garlic, sliced
7 shallots, sliced
10 seeded red chillies,
machine blended with 1/2 cup water
5 eggs, beaten lightly
6 stalks spring onion, cut into 5 cm (2 in) lengths
2 sprigs coriander leaves, cut into 5 cm (2 in) lengths

Sauce Ingredients
3 tablespoons Chinese rice wine
3 tablespoons chilli sauce
4 tablespoons oyster sauce
4 dessertspoons sugar
1 teaspoon sesame oil
1/4 teaspoon pepper

Clean crabs and remove and crack pincers with a pestle. Trim legs and cut into 4 pieces.

Heat oil in a large wok and stir-fry ginger, garlic and shallots until fragrant. Put in chillies and fry for 2 minutes.

Add crabs and stir briskly. Cover wok for approximately 4–5 minutes. Uncover and stir briskly once again, then add sauce ingredients. When crabs are bright red and nearly cooked, pour in beaten eggs. Add spring onions, stirring to mix with sauce.

Dish out, garnish with coriander leaves and serve hot with rice or toasted bread.

My favourite crab dish. Crab lovers will cook this dish again and again. Illustrated on page 47.

Crabs in Black Bean Sauce

2 medium-sized crabs
2 tablespoons fermented black beans
4 tablespoons cooking oil
3 cloves garlic, minced
4 cm (1 1/2 in) piece ginger, shredded
7 shallots, sliced
2 red chillies, sliced
2 teaspoons cornflour mixed with 2 tablespoons water
2 stalks spring onion, cut into 3 cm (1 1/4 in) sections
2 sprigs coriander leaves, cut into 3 cm (1 1/4 in) sections

Sauce Ingredients (combined)

1/2 cup water
1 teaspoon light soya sauce
2 teaspoons Chinese rice wine
1 teaspoon sugar
1/2 teaspoon salt
1/4 teaspoon pepper

Clean crabs and remove and crack pincers with a pestle. Trim legs and cut into 4 pieces. Drain the cut crabs in a colander.

Immerse black beans in a bowl of water and leave for 10 minutes. Drain and rinse well under cold running water. Place black beans in a bowl and mash with a fork.

Heat wok until hot and add oil. When oil is hot, lightly brown garlic, ginger and shallots. Add black beans and stir-fry for 1 minute. Put in prepared crabs including the back shells and toss for 1 minute.

Add the sauce ingredients, mix well and cover the wok. Allow to boil for 4–5 minutes. Remove the lid and stir in chillies, cornflour mixture, spring onion and coriander leaves. Toss for 30 seconds or until sauce thickens.

Serve with toasted bread or rice.

Choose meaty live crabs for this dish.

Crabs in Hot Soya Bean Garlic Paste

1 1/2 kg (3 1/2 lbs) flower crabs, cleaned and cut into four
5 tablespoons cooking oil
5 shallots, sliced
3 cloves garlic, sliced
5 slices ginger, chopped
3 stalks lemon grass, crushed
3 tablespoons hot soya bean garlic paste
1 tablespoon sugar
4 tomatoes, diced
1/3 cup water
3 red chillies, seeded and cut in 2
3 green chillies, seeded and cut in 2
5 stalks spring onion, cut into 3 cm (1 1/4 in) lengths
Coriander leaves for garnishing

Ground Ingredients

6 red chillies
6 dried chillies, soaked
6 bird chillies (*chilli padi*)
6 shallots
3 cloves garlic
1 teaspoon anchovy stock granules

Heat oil in a wok and fry shallots, garlic, ginger and lemon grass until lightly browned. Add ground ingredients and cook over low heat until fragrant.

Stir in hot soya bean garlic paste and continue frying for 2–3 minutes until fragrant. Add sugar, tomatoes and water and allow to boil.

Put in crabs and continue frying for 3 minutes until crabs change colour. Cover the wok and let crabs cook for 6–7 minutes.

Remove the cover and stir-fry until gravy is thickened and crabs are cooked through. Add the chillies and spring onion.

Transfer to serving dish and garnish with coriander leaves.

Flower crabs, or sea crabs as they are often called, have to be fresh. The sauce of this dish is finger-licking good.

Scrambled Eggs Sharksfin

180 gms (6 1/3 oz) pre-prepared sharksfin
180 gms (6 1/3 oz) cooked crab meat
60 gms (2 oz) steamed or boiled chicken meat, cut into strips
6 eggs
1 tablespoon corn oil
1 teaspoon pepper
1 teaspoon salt
1 dessertspoon light soya sauce
1 dessertspoon rice wine
6 tablespoons cooking oil
60 gms (2 oz) beansprouts, heads and tails pinched off
1 stalk spring onion, cut into 2 1/2 cm (1 in) lengths
2 sprigs coriander leaves
1–2 heads lettuce

Wash sharksfin and drain well.

Put sharksfin, crab meat, chicken, eggs, corn oil, pepper, salt, light soya sauce and rice wine in a mixing bowl and mix well.

Heat 1 tablespoon of the cooking oil in a wok until very hot and fry beansprouts for a minute. Remove and leave aside.

Heat another tablespoon of the oil in the wok and pour in meat mixture. Scramble gently and at the same time add remaining oil, a tablespoon at a time. When mixture is almost cooked, put in beansprouts and spring onion. Stir-fry to mix well.

Garnish with coriander leaves and serve hot with fresh lettuce.

A very popular restaurant dish which can be easily prepared at home.

Stir-Fried Brinjals with Minced Meat

3 medium-sized brinjals, cut into 5 x 1 1/4 cm (2 x 1/2 in) pieces
4 tablespoons cooking oil
4 cloves garlic, minced
3 slices ginger
2 cloves garlic
1/2 tablespoon hot bean paste
120 gms (4 1/4 oz) lean pork with a little fat, or chicken, coarsely minced
1/2 cup fresh chicken stock
1/2 tablespoon cornflour mixed with 1 tablespoon water
2 stalks spring onion, chopped
1 sprig coriander leaves, chopped

Sauce Ingredients (combined)
1 tablespoon light soya sauce
1/4 teaspoon pepper
1/4 teaspoon salt
1/2 teaspoon sugar
1 teaspoon sesame oil

Soak cut brinjals in a little salt water.

Heat wok until hot with 3 tablespoons of cooking oil. Reduce heat a little to lightly brown garlic. Put in drained brinjals and stir-fry over high heat until soft. Remove and leave aside.

Reheat wok with 1 tablespoon cooking oil. Stir-fry ginger, garlic and hot bean paste until aromatic. Put in minced meat and when it changes colour, add combined sauce ingredients and stir-fry for 2 minutes.

Pour in chicken stock and when it begins to boil, return pre-fried brinjals to the wok and stir to mix well.

Thicken with cornflour mixture. Sprinkle in spring onion and coriander leaves, and transfer to serving dish.

Illustrated on page 48.

Szechuan Brinjals

450 gms ($15^3/_4$ oz) brinjals, quartered and cut into 2 cm ($^3/_4$ in) pieces
2 tablespoons chilli oil
2 tablespoons finely chopped garlic
1 tablespoon chopped ginger
2 tablespoons hot soya bean garlic paste
1 cup fresh chicken stock
2 red chillies, seeded and cut into diamond pieces
$^1/_2$ green pepper, seeded and cut into diamond pieces
2 stalks spring onion

Sauce Ingredients (combined)
1 tablespoon thick soya sauce
1 tablespoon Chinese black vinegar
1 teaspoon roasted ground Szechuan peppercorns
1 tablespoon sugar

Soak brinjal cubes in salted water. Drain well. Heat wok with chilli oil and lightly brown garlic and ginger. Add hot soya bean garlic paste and fry for 1 minute until fragrant.

Put in brinjals and stir-fry for another minute. Stir in combined sauce ingredients and toss until brinjals are well coated.

Pour in chicken stock and bring to the boil. Reduce heat and cook, uncovered, for 12–15 minutes until brinjals are soft and gravy is thick. Stir in chillies and green pepper.

Serve garnished with spring onion.

Soaking the brinjals in salt water prevents discolouring and extracts the bitterness. The long thin variety is preferred because it is softer and has a more delicate flavour.

Stir-Fried Bittergourd with Roast Pork

1 medium-sized bittergourd
$^1/_2$ teaspoon salt
2 tablespoons cooking oil
2 cloves garlic
180 gms ($6^1/_3$ oz) roast pork (*siew yok*), cut into $^1/_2$ cm ($^1/_4$ in) slices
1 red chilli, seeded and sliced, optional

Sauce Ingredients (combined)
2 tablespoons water
$^1/_4$ teaspoon salt
$^1/_2$ teaspoon sugar
$^1/_4$ teaspoon pepper
1 teaspoon light soya sauce
1 teaspoon Chinese rice wine

Halve the bittergourd and remove seeds. Cut into $^1/_2$ cm ($^1/_4$ in) slices at a slant. Rub salt into the bittergourd to lessen its bitter taste. Rinse and drain before cooking.

Heat oil in wok until hot and lightly brown garlic. Put in the roast pork and stir-fry briefly. Add the bittergourd and chilli, and stir-fry for 30 seconds.

Put in sauce ingredients and cover wok for 1 minute. Remove cover and toss mixture again. If a softer bittergourd is preferred, cook a little longer.

Bittergourd may not be everyone's idea of a great vegetable, but the bitter taste combines well with fragrant roast pork. Roast pork can be substituted with prawns, shredded pork or shredded chicken seasoned with $^1/_4$ teaspoon salt and pepper. If desired, 1 teaspoon preserved soya bean paste can be stir-fried with the garlic before adding bittergourd. Bittergourd is believed to improve the complexion.

Long Beans with Minced Pork and Prawns

250 gms (8¾ oz) long beans
2 tablespoons cooking oil
3 cloves garlic, minced
1 tablespoon hot bean paste
90 gms (3 oz) minced pork
90 gms (3 oz) shelled small prawns
1 teaspoon cornflour mixed in 1 tablespoon water

Sauce Ingredients (combined)
½ cup water
1 teaspoon oyster sauce
1 teaspoon light soya sauce
1 teaspoon sesame oil
1 teaspoon sugar
¼ teaspoon pepper

Wash and cut long beans into 5 cm (2 in) pieces.

Heat wok with 1 tablespoon of oil and stir-fry long beans for 1 minute. Leave aside.

Reheat a clean wok with 1 tablespoon oil and stir-fry garlic and hot bean paste until aromatic over low heat. Add the minced pork and prawns, and stir-fry over high flame.

Return pre-fried beans to wok and pour in sauce ingredients. Cover wok for 1 minute. When long beans are cooked and soft, thicken with cornflour mixture.

French beans can be used instead of long beans for this recipe. Pork can be substituted with chicken.

Stir-Fried Water Convolvulus with Shrimp Paste

480 gms (17 oz) water convolvulus, discard tough fibrous stems and cut into 10 cm (4 in) lengths
3 tablespoons cooking oil
1 tablespoon dried prawns, rinsed and coarsely ground
1 teaspoon sugar

Ground Ingredients
2 cloves garlic
3 red chillies
2½ cm (1 in) square dried shrimp paste

Wash the water convolvulus thoroughly and drain in a colander.

Heat wok with oil until hot. Reduce heat and stir-fry ground ingredients for 1 minute. Add the ground dried prawns and stir-fry until aromatic.

Add water convolvulus and sugar, and toss over high heat until limp and cooked before transferring to serving dish.

A very popular dish which is really a combination of Chinese and Malay cooking. French beans or long beans, sliced and cut into 5 cm (2 in) lengths, can also be used for this recipe.

Plain Stir-Fried Shanghai White Cabbage

300 gms (10½ oz)
Shanghai white cabbage *(siew pak choy)*
3 tablespoons cooking oil
4 cloves garlic, minced
1 teaspoon light soya sauce
½ teaspoon salt
Pinch of sugar

Cut off the ends of the cabbage, separate the stems and wash well to get rid of fine sand. Cut into 5 cm (2 in) lengths.

Heat oil in a wok until hot and lightly brown garlic. Put in cabbage and toss on high heat for 30 seconds. Cover the wok for another 30 seconds. Remove lid and add light soya sauce, salt and sugar. Toss quickly to mix well and dish onto serving plates.

High heat and speed is required to turn out a crunchy texture. Other green leafy vegetables like mustard green, lettuce and the bigger variety of green cabbage (pak choy) can also be used.

Stir-Fried Mustard Green with Prawns

600 gms (21 oz) mustard green (*choy sum*), discard tough fibrous stems and cut into 7 cm (2¾ in) lengths
120 gms (4¼ oz) shelled small prawns
¼ teaspoon salt
Pinch of pepper
Pinch of sugar
3 tablespoons cooking oil
3 cloves garlic, minced

Sauce Ingredients (combined)
½ cup of water
1 teaspoon light soya sauce
¼ teaspoon salt

Separate the mustard green stems from the leaves. Wash the leaves and stalks separately and drain well.

Season prawns with salt, pepper and sugar.

Heat wok with cooking oil until hot and lightly brown garlic. Add the seasoned prawns and stir-fry for 30 seconds. Put in stalks of mustard greens and continue to stir-fry until they change colour.

Add the leaves and then the sauce ingredients, and mix well. Cover the wok for 1 minute. Remove the cover and toss ingredients before dishing out.

Spinach or Chinese broccoli (kai lan) can be used instead of mustard green. If preferred, 2 slices of ginger minced with garlic can also be added.

Green Stems with Crab Meat

1 kg (2⅕ lbs) green stems (*kai choy*)
1 teaspoon bicarbonate of soda
2 tablespoons cooking oil
5 cloves garlic, minced
6 large button mushrooms, sliced
600 gms (21 oz) crabs, steamed, meat extracted
1 egg, beaten lightly

Sauce Ingredients (combined)
2 cups fresh chicken stock
1 teaspoon salt
½ teaspoon sugar
½ teaspoon sesame oil
¼ teaspoon pepper
1 tablespoon cornflour

Trim green stems, discarding leafy parts, and cut into 7½ cm (3 in) lengths. Boil half a wok of water and stir in bicarbonate of soda and 1 teaspoon oil. Put in green stems and boil for 3–4 minutes. Remove and immerse in a basin of cold water. Rinse and drain.

Heat 1 tablespoon oil in a wok and lightly brown garlic. Put in mushrooms, then green stems and stir-fry briskly for 1 minute.

Pour in combined sauce ingredients and bring to the boil. Add crab meat and when sauce thickens, gradually stir in beaten egg.

Place in a serving dish and serve immediately.

A popular banquet vegetable dish.

Stir-Fried Beansprouts with Chinese Chives and Prawns

300 gms (10½ oz) beansprouts
180 gms shelled small–medium-sized prawns
3 tablespoons cooking oil
2 cloves garlic, minced
2 red chillies, cut into strips
120 gms (4¼ oz) Chinese chives, cut into 4 cm (1½ in) lengths

Seasoning Ingredients
½ teaspoon salt
¼ teaspoon pepper
¼ teaspoon sugar
½ sesame oil

Sauce Ingredients (combined)
1 tablespoon water
½ teaspoon salt
½ teaspoon sugar
1 teaspoon light soya sauce
1 teaspoon Chinese rice wine
½ teaspoon sesame oil

Remove tails from beansprouts. Wash and drain. Marinate prawns with seasoning ingredients for 10 minutes.

Heat 2 tablespoons of oil in a wok until hot and toss beansprouts for 30 seconds. Remove and set aside.

Heat 1 tablespoon oil in the wok and lightly brown garlic. Add the prawns and stir-fry until prawns change colour. Add the chillies and Chinese chives, and toss for 30 seconds.

Add the sauce ingredients, and return beansprouts to wok. Toss ingredients quickly on high heat and dish onto serving plate.

There are two varieties of chives, the green flat blades and the pale yellow blades. Either one can be used for this recipe but the yellow ones generally have a richer flavour.

Shredded Cabbage and Carrots

2 tablespoons cooking oil
1 clove garlic, minced
2 shallots, sliced
1 large cloud ear fungus (*mok yee*), soaked, rinsed and cut into strips (discard hard centre)
120 gms (4¼ oz) carrot, sliced
250 gms (8¾ oz) cabbage or *spitskool*, washed and shredded

Sauce Ingredients (combined)
2½ tablespoons fresh chicken stock
2 teaspoons light soya sauce
1 teaspoon oyster sauce
1 teaspoon Chinese rice wine
½ teaspoon sugar
½ teaspoon salt
¼ teaspoon pepper
½ teaspoon cornflour

Heat 2 tablespoons oil in a wok until hot and lightly brown garlic and shallots.

Put in cloud ear fungus and stir-fry for 1 minute.

Add carrots, stir-fry for 30 seconds and then add cabbage. Toss well and cover the wok for 1–2 minutes.

Remove cover and stir in combined sauce ingredients.

Transfer to serving dish and serve hot.

The carrots and cabbage make this dish sweet and colourful. Unlike greens, this dish can be prepared early and is useful for entertaining. The light weight cabbage is ideal for stir-frying. The rugby ball-shaped cabbage common in Europe and known as spitskool in Dutch and spitzkohl in German is perfect for this recipe. *Illustrated on page 73.*

Leek and Cloud Ear Fungus

2 tablespoons cooking oil
2 cloves garlic, minced
12 pieces small variety cloud ear fungus (*wan yee*), soaked until soft
2 dried Chinese mushrooms, soaked until soft and shredded
1 leek, approximately 180 gms (6 1/3 oz), sliced at a slant
1 red chilli, seeded and sliced at a slant

Sauce Ingredients (combined)
1/4 cup fresh chicken stock
1 teaspoon light soya sauce
1 teaspoon oyster sauce
1 teaspoon Chinese rice wine
1/2 teaspoon sugar
1/2 teaspoon salt
1/4 teaspoon pepper
1 teaspoon cornflour

Heat wok with oil until hot. Lightly brown garlic and stir-fry cloud ear fungus and dried Chinese mushrooms until fragrant.

Add the leek and chillies and continue to stir-fry for 1 minute. Cover the wok for a few seconds.

Remove cover and add sauce ingredients. Toss well and when sauce thickens, transfer to serving dish and serve hot.

Leeks are widely used in stir-fry dishes with meats and seafood. They are so full of flavour that they even go well with fungus.

Leek with Champignons

300 gms (10 1/2 oz) leek, approximately 1 large leek
2 tablespoons cooking oil
2 cloves garlic, minced
150 gms (5 1/4 oz) fresh champignons, each sliced into 3
1/2 small red pepper, cut into diamond-shaped pieces

Sauce Ingredients (combined)
3 tablespoons fresh chicken stock
1/2 teaspoon salt
1/2 teaspoon sugar
1/4 teaspoon pepper
1 teaspoon light soya sauce
1 teaspoon Chinese rice wine
1 teaspoon oyster sauce
1/4 teaspoon sesame oil
1 teaspoon cornflour

Wash the leek, discard the fibrous sections and then cut into 1 cm (1/3 in) sections diagonally.

Heat oil in the wok until hot and lightly brown garlic. Put in leek and stir-fry for 1 minute.

Add champignons and cook for 30 seconds.

Put in the red pepper and stir in sauce ingredients.

When it boils and thickens, remove and place on a serving dish.

If you are tired of the common leafy vegetables, leeks provide a wonderful contrast with button mushrooms.

Fried Turnip and Cloud Ear Fungus

240 gms (8 1/2 oz) chicken or pork, cut into strips
3 tablespoons cooking oil
3 cloves garlic
240 gms (8 1/2 oz) turnip, cut into strips
4 pieces cloud ear fungus, soaked and cut into thin strips
3 teaspoons cornflour mixed with 1 tablespoon water
1 stalk spring onion, cut into 5 cm (2 in) lengths
2 sprigs coriander leaves, cut into 5 cm (2 in) lengths

Seasoning Ingredients
2 teaspoons light soya sauce
1/2 teaspoon sesame oil
1/2 teaspoon salt
1/2 teaspoon pepper
1/2 teaspoon sugar
2 teaspoons cornflour

Sauce Ingredients (combined)
1 cup fresh chicken stock
1 teaspoon thick soya sauce
1 teaspoon sesame oil
2 teaspoons light soya sauce
1 teaspoon sugar
1 teaspoon salt
1/4 teaspoon pepper

Marinate chicken or pork strips with seasoning ingredients and leave for 30 minutes.

Heat 1 tablespoon of oil in a wok and brown garlic. Add meat and fry over high heat for 1 minute. Dish out and leave aside.

Wash wok and heat 2 tablespoons oil until hot. Put in turnip, stir-fry and cover wok for 1 minute.

Remove cover, add cloud ear fungus and stir-fry quickly.

Add sauce ingredients and bring to the boil. Put in fried meat then stir in cornflour mixture.

Serve hot, garnished with spring onion and coriander leaves.

Mixed Four-Colour Vegetables

250 gms (8 3/4 oz) broccoli, cut into florets
1/2 of 425 gms (15 oz) can straw mushrooms
1 small carrot, sliced
2 tablespoons cooking oil
2 cloves garlic, minced
1 small red pepper, cut into 1 1/2 cm (3/4 in) cubes
2 sprigs coriander leaves

Sauce Ingredients (combined)
3 tablespoons fresh chicken stock
1/2 teaspoon salt
1/2 teaspoon sugar
1/4 teaspoon pepper
1 teaspoon light soya sauce
1 teaspoon Chinese rice wine
1 teaspoon oyster sauce
1/2 teaspoon sesame oil
1 teaspoon cornflour

Blanch broccoli and straw mushrooms in boiling water for 1 minute and drain. Put in carrots to boil for 2 minutes or until just soft and drain.

Heat oil in a wok until hot and lightly brown garlic. Add all the blanched vegetables and toss briefly. Put in red peppers and stir-fry for 30 seconds.

Add sauce ingredients and toss until sauce thickens.

Dish out and serve garnished with coriander leaves.

A classic Chinese vegetable dish. Prawns and meat can be added for variety. *Illustrated on page 74.*

Vegetarian Fried Gluten Balls with Mixed Vegetables

10–12 dried Chinese mushrooms, washed well and soaked until soft
2 tablespoons cooking oil
2 slices ginger, minced
2 cloves garlic, minced
18 pieces fried gluten balls, about 90 gms (3 oz), soaked (see page 24)
1 medium-sized carrot, sliced and parboiled
2 sticks celery, cut into 1/2 cm (1/4 in) slices diagonally
1 teaspoon cornflour mixed with 1 tablespoon water
1 red chilli, cut into strips

Seasoning Ingredients
1/2 teaspoon sugar
1/4 teaspoon salt
1/4 teaspoon pepper
1/2 teaspoon light soya sauce
1 teaspoon Chinese rice wine
1 teaspoon oyster sauce

Sauce Ingredients (combined)
1 cup fresh chicken stock
1/2 teaspoon sugar
1/4 teaspoon salt
1/4 teaspoon pepper
1 teaspoon sesame oil
1 teaspoon Chinese rice wine
1 teaspoon oyster sauce
1 teaspoon light soya sauce
1/4 teaspoon thick soya sauce

Drain and lightly squeeze the soaked Chinese mushrooms. If cooking strictly vegetarian, reserve the mushroom water for stock. Marinate mushrooms with seasoning ingredients for at least 30 minutes or overnight in the refrigerator.

Heat oil in a wok until hot and lightly brown ginger and garlic. Add mushrooms and stir-fry for 1 minute.

Squeeze out water from gluten balls and add to wok. Continue to stir-fry for another minute.

Put in carrots and celery, toss to mix well and pour in sauce ingredients. When it begins to boil, thicken with cornflour mixture and stir in chillies.

Transfer to serving dish and serve hot.

If cooking strictly vegetarian, use vegetarian oyster sauce instead of ordinary oyster sauce. Replace chicken stock with the same amount of water from the soaking of the mushrooms.

Vegetarian Four-Colour Vegetables

6 dried Chinese mushrooms, soaked until soft and halved
Pinch of salt and pepper
1/4 teaspoon sugar
1/2 teaspoon sesame oil
10 gms (1/3 oz) hair vegetable (*fatt choy*), soaked for at least 20 minutes until soft
8 small bunches Shanghai white cabbage (*siew pak choy*), kept whole and soaked in water
5 tablespoons cooking oil
1/4 teaspoon salt
2 slices ginger, minced
2 cloves garlic, minced
1 piece dried scallop, soaked in a little water and shredded
120 gms (4 1/4 oz) fried gluten balls, approximately 15 pieces, soaked (see page 24)
10–12 slices carrots, parboiled
1 teaspoon cornflour mixed with 1 tablespoon water

Sauce Ingredients (combined)
1 cup fresh chicken stock
1/2 teaspoon sugar
1/2 teaspoon salt
1/4 teaspoon pepper
1/2 teaspoon sesame oil
1 teaspoon Chinese rice wine
1 teaspoon light soya sauce
1 teaspoon oyster sauce

Marinate dried Chinese mushrooms with salt, pepper, sugar and sesame oil for 30 minutes.

Drain the hair vegetable and put to boil in a small saucepan of water with 1 tablespoon of cooking oil and 1/4 teaspoon salt. Cook for 1–2 minutes. Drain and leave aside.

Rinse Shanghai white cabbage under running water to remove fine sand particles wedged between the stems. Drain and blanch in boiling water with 1 tablespoon of cooking oil for 1 minute. Drain and immerse in cold water to stop vegetable from cooking further and to retain its crisp green colour. Drain and arrange vegetable in the centre of serving dish or around the sides of the dish as preferred.

Heat remaining 3 tablespoons of oil in a wok until hot and lightly brown ginger and garlic. Add the Chinese mushrooms and scallop and stir-fry until fragrant.

Put in fried gluten balls and toss for 1 minute. Add the hair vegetable and carrots and mix well.

Pour in combined sauce ingredients and when it begins to boil, thicken with cornflour mixture. Pour over the cabbage in the serving dish and serve hot.

If cooking strictly vegetarian, replace fresh chicken stock with water used to soak dried mushrooms, mixed with 1 tablespoon ground dried mushrooms stems.

Vegetarian Favourites

45 gms (1½ oz) dried beancurd sticks (*fu chok*), about 2
Oil for deep-frying
4 dried Chinese mushrooms, soaked until soft and halved
Pinch of salt, sugar and pepper
Dash of sesame oil
2 tablespoons cooking oil
2 cloves garlic, minced
30 gms (1 oz) cloud ear fungus (about 3 pieces), soaked, hard centres trimmed off and quartered
15 gms (½ oz) dried lily buds (*kam cham*), soaked in hot water until soft
240 gms (8½ oz) Tientsin cabbage (*wong nga pak*), washed, halved and cut into 5 cm (2 in) lengths
10 canned button mushrooms or fresh champignons, halved
10 slices carrot, parboiled
30 gms (1 oz) transparent vermicelli, soaked until soft
1 teaspoon cornflour mixed with 1 tablespoon water

Sauce Ingredients (combined)

½ cup fresh chicken stock
2 teaspoons oyster sauce
2 teaspoons light soya sauce
½ teaspoon sesame oil
½ teaspoon sugar
½ teaspoon salt
¼ teaspoon pepper

Rinse and drain the dried beancurd sticks. Break into 5 cm (2 in) pieces. Deep-fry in hot oil for 30–45 seconds. Drain and soak in water until soft.

Marinate Chinese mushrooms with salt, pepper, sugar and sesame oil for 15 minutes.

Heat oil in a wok until hot and lightly brown garlic. Put in Chinese mushrooms and stir-fry for 1 minute. Add the cloud ear fungus, lily buds and dried beancurd sticks, and continue to stir-fry for another minute. Put in Tientsin cabbage and toss briefly.

Cover the wok for 2 minutes. Remove cover and add button mushrooms, carrots and vermicelli.

Pour in combined sauce ingredients and allow to boil over low heat for 2 minutes.

Thicken with cornflour mixture, mix well and transfer to serving dish.

If strictly cooking vegetarian, use mushroom stock mixed with 1 tablespoon ground dried mushroom stems in place of chicken stock and mushroom sauce.

Mixed Mushrooms with Vegetables

3 green stems (*kai choy*), stems only cut into 2½ cm (1 in) diagonal pieces
½ teaspoon salt
½ teaspoon sugar
Pinch of bicarbonate of soda
4 tablespoons cooking oil
3 slices ginger
2 cloves garlic, minced
5 dried Chinese mushrooms, soaked until soft and halved
120 gms (4¼ oz) snow peas, blanched
10 slices carrots, parboiled
10 pieces fresh young corn
120 gms (4¼ oz) canned bamboo shoots, rinsed and sliced
½ of 454 gms (16 oz) can button mushrooms, rinsed and halved
½ of 454 gms (16 oz) can straw or abalone mushrooms, rinsed and halved
2 teaspoons cornflour mixed with 1 tablespoon water

Sauce Ingredients (combined)
1½ cups fresh chicken stock
1 tablespoon oyster sauce
1 tablespoon light soya sauce
½ teaspoon sesame oil
½ teaspoon salt
1 teaspoon sugar
¼ teaspoon pepper

Bring a saucepan of water with salt, sugar, bicarbonate of soda and 1 tablespoon of oil to the boil. Put in cut green stems and boil for 2–3 minutes. Remove and immerse in cold water for 2–3 minutes. Drain and set aside.

Heat wok with 1 tablespoon of oil and lightly brown ginger and garlic. Add Chinese mushrooms and stir-fry for 1 minute, then add snow peas and carrots, and toss for 30 seconds. Dish out and leave aside.

Reheat wok with remaining 2 tablespoons oil until hot and stir-fry young corn, bamboo shoots, button and straw mushrooms for 30 seconds.

Add combined sauce ingredients and bring to the boil. Return Chinese mushrooms, snow peas, carrots and green stems to the wok. Stir well and thicken with cornflour mixture.

If cooking strictly vegetarian, use fresh mushroom stock mixed with 1 tablespoon ground dried mushroom stems instead of chicken stock and vegetarian oyster sauce.

Straw Mushrooms with Seafood

300 gms (10½ oz) fresh mushrooms or 454 gms (16 oz) can of straw mushrooms
3–4 tablespoons cooking oil
¼ teaspoon each of salt and sugar
120 gms (4¼ oz) shelled small prawns
120 gms (4¼ oz) squid, cut with criss-cross patterns and sliced into bite-sized pieces
4 cloves garlic, minced
15 snow peas
1 teaspoon cornflour mixed with 1 tablespoon water
1 stalk spring onion, cut into 2½ cm (1 in) lengths
1 sprig coriander leaves, cut into 2½ cm (1 in) lengths

Seasoning Ingredients

¼ teaspoon salt
¼ teaspoon pepper
¼ teaspoon sugar
1 teaspoon light soya sauce

Sauce Ingredients (combined)

½ cup fresh chicken stock
2 teaspoon light soya sauce
1 teaspoon oyster sauce
1 teaspoon Chinese rice wine
1 teaspoon sesame oil
½ teaspoon sugar
½ teaspoon salt
¼ teaspoon pepper

If using fresh straw mushrooms, clean and wash well, then blanch in boiling water with 1 tablespoon oil and ¼ teaspoon salt and sugar added. Drain and set aside.

Heat 1 tablespoon oil in a wok until hot and stir-fry straw mushrooms for 30–45 seconds over high heat. Drain and set aside.

Marinate prawns and squid with seasoning ingredients for 15 minutes.

Reheat wok with 2 tablespoons oil and lightly brown garlic. Stir-fry snow peas for 1 minute. Add seafood and stir-fry for another minute or until it is just cooked. Return straw mushrooms to wok and toss well to mix.

Pour in sauce ingredients and when mixture boils, thicken with cornflour mixture. Sprinkle with spring onion and coriander leaves and serve.

Fried Beancurd with Chilli

90 gms (3 oz) chicken or pork, minced
3 tablespoons cooking oil
4 cloves garlic, minced
3 red chillies, seeded and minced
2 teaspoons preserved soya bean paste
1 stalk leek, sliced at a slant
2 pieces square soft beancurd, cut into 4 cm (1½ in) pieces
2 stalks spring onion, chopped

Seasoning Ingredients

½ teaspoon light soya sauce
½ teaspoon salt
¼ teaspoon sesame oil

Sauce Ingredients (combined)

½ cup fresh chicken stock or water
1 teaspoon oyster sauce
½ teaspoon sugar
½ teaspoon sesame oil
½ teaspoon salt
½ teaspoon thick soya sauce
¼ teaspoon pepper
2 teaspoons cornflour

Season meat with seasoning ingredients and leave for 15 minutes.

Heat 3 tablespoons oil in a wok and fry garlic and chillies until fragrant. Add preserved soya bean paste and fry until aromatic.

Put in minced meat, then leek and stir-fry for half a minute. Add beancurd, stir-fry for 2 minutes, breaking beancurd gently with frying spatula.

Pour in prepared sauce ingredients and boil until gravy thickens. Add spring onions and transfer to serving dish.

Preserved soya bean paste compliments the beancurd. This dish is delicious and goes well with rice.

Beancurd with Crab Meat Sauce

1 piece square soft beancurd (*tau fu*), cut into 2½ cm (1 in) cubes
1 egg, beaten
2 tablespoons plain flour
Oil for deep-frying
1 tablespoon cooking oil
2 slices ginger, finely shredded
1 shallot, sliced
1 tablespoon cooked crab meat
1 teaspoon cornflour mixed with 1 tablespoon fresh chicken stock or water
2 stalks spring onion, chopped

Seasoning Ingredients

¼ teaspoon salt
¼ teaspoon pepper
½ teaspoon Chinese rice wine
½ teaspoon sesame oil

Sauce Ingredients (combined)

½ cup fresh chicken stock
¼ teaspoon each of salt and sugar
Pinch of pepper
1 teaspoon light soya sauce
½ teaspoon sesame oil

Marinate beancurd cubes with seasoning ingredients for at least 15 minutes. Carefully mix in beaten egg. Coat each piece beancurd with plain flour and deep-fry until golden. Drain well and set aside.

Heat wok with 1 tablespoon oil until hot and stir-fry ginger and shallot until fragrant. Pour in the sauce ingredients and add crab meat.

Return beancurd to the wok, mix to coat with sauce and then add cornflour mixture.

Dish out and serve sprinkled with spring onion.

Finely shredded ham or boiled chicken can be used instead of crab meat.

Beancurd with Barbecued Pork and Mushroom Sauce

2 pieces square soft beancurd (*tau fu*)
Oil for deep-frying
2 tablespoons cooking oil
2 shallots, sliced
1 clove garlic, minced
3 dried Chinese mushrooms, soaked and diced
4 canned button mushrooms, diced
180 gms (6⅓ oz) barbecued pork (*char siew*), diced
1 tablespoon frozen green peas
2 teaspoons cornflour mixed with 1 tablespoon water
1 stalk spring onion, chopped

Seasoning Ingredients

¼ teaspoon salt
¼ teaspoon pepper
½ teaspoon Chinese rice wine
½ teaspoon sesame oil

Sauce Ingredients (combined)

¾ cup fresh chicken stock
¼ teaspoon salt
¼ teaspoon pepper
½ teaspoon sugar
1 teaspoon Chinese rice wine
1 teaspoon sesame oil
1 teaspoon light soya sauce
1 teaspoon oyster sauce

Cut beancurd cakes into 2½ cm (1 in) cubes and soak in cold water for 1 minute. Carefully drain beancurd cubes and season with seasoning ingredients for 15 minutes. Either deep-fry the seasoned beancurd in hot oil for 2 minutes or leave as they are.

Heat 2 tablespoons oil in a wok until hot and lightly brown shallots and garlic. Put in diced Chinese mushrooms and stir-fry for 30 seconds. Add the button mushrooms and barbecued pork and continue to stir-fry for 30–45 seconds.

Pour in combined sauce ingredients and when it starts to boil, add beancurd and then stir in green peas.

Thicken with cornflour mixture. Add spring onion and mix well. Transfer to serving dish and serve hot.

If you are trying to beat the clock simply steam the beancurd for 10 minutes, draw off the excess water, and drizzle with prepared sauce. *Illustrated on page 75.*

Shredded Cabbage and Carrots
Page 64

Mixed Four-Colour Vegetables
Page 66

Beancurd with Barbecued Pork and Mushroom Sauce
Page 72

Fried Yellow Noodles with Meat and Prawns
Page 81

Fried Rice with Chicken and Pineapple
Page 86

Spicy Sesame Seed Chicken
Page 88

Potato, Carrot and Onion Soup
Page 94

Chicken Corn Soup
Page 95

Fried Hokkien Mee

90 gms (3 oz) chicken or pork, shredded
Dash of salt and pepper
90 gms (3 oz) shelled small prawns
90 gms (3 oz) cleaned squid or cuttlefish, sliced
2 tablespoons cooking oil
3 shallots, sliced
120 gms (4¹/₄ oz) pork fat, diced
4 cloves garlic, minced
6 slices fish cake, optional
3–4 stalks mustard green (*choy sum*), washed and cut into 5 cm (2 in) lengths
480 gms (17 oz) fresh thick strand yellow noodles
Lettuce leaves, shredded

Seasoning Ingredients

¹/₂ teaspoon sesame oil
¹/₄ teaspoon pepper
¹/₂ tablespoon light soya sauce

Sauce Ingredients (combined)

2 cups fresh chicken or pork bone stock
1 tablespoon thick soya sauce

Season chicken with salt and pepper. Season prawns and cuttlefish with seasoning ingredients and leave for 15 minutes.

Heat oil in a wok until hot and stir-fry shallots until light brown and crisp. Drain and set aside.

Reheat wok and put in pork fat. Stir-fry until light brown and crisp. Drain and leave oil in the wok.

When the oil is hot, lightly brown garlic. Put in meat and stir-fry until it changes colour. Then add prawns, cuttlefish and fish cake (optional) and toss well for 30 seconds. Add the mustard green and stir-fry for a few seconds. Put in noodles and toss for 2 minutes.

Add combined sauce ingredients, stir and cover wok for 12–15 minutes. Remove cover and sprinkle in pork crisps and shallot crisps. Garnish with lettuce.

Serves 2 as a meal by itself.

Fried Yellow Noodles with Meat and Prawns

120 gms (4¹/₄ oz) small shelled prawns, de-veined and washed
¹/₄ teaspoon salt
¹/₄ teaspoon sugar
Dash of pepper and sesame oil
120 gms (4¹/₄ oz) chicken or pork meat, shredded
¹/₂ teaspoon light soya sauce
¹/₄ teaspoon sugar
¹/₂ teaspoon cornflour
3 tablespoons cooking oil
2 cloves garlic, minced
2 stalks mustard green (*choy sum*), washed and cut into 5 cm (2 in) lengths
4 shallots, sliced
300 gms (10¹/₂ oz) fresh yellow noodles
1 teaspoon cornflour mixed with 1 tablespoon water
1 tablespoon shallot crisps
1 stalk spring onion, chopped

Sauce Ingredients (combined)

¹/₂ cup fresh chicken or pork bone stock
1 tablespoon light soya sauce
¹/₂ teaspoon thick soya sauce
¹/₂ teaspoon sugar
¹/₄ teaspoon salt
¹/₄ teaspoon pepper

Marinate prawns with salt, sugar, pepper and sesame oil and meat with light soya sauce, sugar and cornflour and leave for 15 minutes.

Heat 1 tablespoon oil in a wok until hot and lightly brown garlic. Put in meat, then the prawns and toss until meat changes colour. Add the mustard green and stir-fry for 1 minute. Remove and leave aside.

Reheat wok with 2 tablespoons oil and lightly brown shallots. Put in noodles and stir-fry briskly for 1–2 minutes.

Stir in combined sauce ingredients and return fried meat mixture to the wok. Stir well and thicken with cornflour mixture. Garnish with shallot crisps and spring onion.

Serves 2 as a meal by itself.

A nutritious one-dish meal that's as quick as fast food. *Illustrated on page 76.*

Fried Flat Rice Noodles with Beef

120 gms (4¼ oz) beef, cut into thin slices
6 tablespoons cooking oil
½ teaspoon salt
5 small stalks mustard green, trim both ends with scissors
300 gms (10½ oz) fresh flat rice noodles, loosened with fingers to separate strands
1 tablespoon light soya sauce mixed with 1 tablespoon chicken stock or water
100 gms (3½ oz) beansprouts, tailed
1 stalk spring onion, cut into 2½ cm (1 in) lengths
1 sprig coriander leaves, cut into 2½ cm (1 in) lengths

Seasoning Ingredients

⅓ teaspoon bicarbonate of soda
1 dessertspoon ginger juice
½ teaspoon salt
¼ teaspoon sugar
2 teaspoons cornflour
1 tablespoon oil, add after all the above ingredients are well mixed with the meat

Sauce Ingredients (combined)

5 tablespoons fresh chicken stock
½ teaspoon light soya sauce
2 teaspoons thick soya sauce
3 teaspoons cornflour

Marinate beef with seasoning ingredients for at least 20 minutes.

Bring half a saucepan of water to the boil. Add 1 tablespoon oil and ½ teaspoon salt. Scald the mustard green until just cooked. Drain well and arrange on an oval dish. Turn off heat and scald beef. Allow to soak for 1 minute. Remove scum from the surface, then drain meat and leave aside.

Heat wok with 1 tablespoon of oil. Ensure that the whole wok is well greased, then pour off excess oil. Put in rice noodles and toss in hot wok for 2 minutes.

Add light soya sauce mixed with chicken stock, and stir-fry until well mixed. Remove and place noodles on mustard green.

Reheat wok with 1 tablespoon of oil and stir-fry beansprouts for 30 seconds. Remove and place over fried rice noodles.

Wash wok and reheat with 1 tablespoon of oil. Put in combined sauce ingredients. Add meat, then spring onion and coriander leaves. Toss quickly and then add 2 tablespoons of cooking oil and mix.

Pour meat mixture over noodles. Serve with cut red chillies and light soya sauce.

Serves 2 as a meal by itself.

A popular Cantonese style noodle dish. A red hot wok is required for the best results.

Fried Rice Vermicelli with Mixed Vegetables

1 packet (600 gms, 21 oz) rice vermicelli (*mai fun*), soaked for 15 minutes until soft and drained
½ cup oil
6 shallots, minced
4 cloves garlic, minced
6 large Tientsin cabbage (*wong nga pak*) leaves, washed and cut into strips
1 carrot, sliced
300 gms (10½ oz) beansprouts, tailed and rinsed
3 eggs, made into thin omelette and shredded
1 small head lettuce, cut into strips
2 red chillies, cut into strips
Chilli sauce

Sauce Ingredients (combined)
1 cup water
1 chicken stock cube
2 tablespoons oyster sauce
2 tablespoons light soya sauce
1 teaspoon sugar
½ teaspoon pepper
¼ teaspoon salt

Heat oil in wok and fry minced shallots and garlic until lightly brown. Put in vegetables by piling one on top of the other in the following order: cabbage, carrots, beansprouts. Put the vermicelli on the top. Pour in sauce ingredients. Do not stir. Cover wok for 10 minutes.

Remove cover and stir-fry until well-mixed. Dish out on serving plate and garnish with omelette, lettuce and chilli strips. Serve with chilli sauce.

Serves 4 as a meal by itself.

A simple noodle dish that is easy to prepare and tastes great. I have yet to come across anybody who does not like this dish.

Fried Transparent Vermicelli

120 gms (4¼ oz) transparent vermicelli (*toong fun*)
2 cups fresh chicken stock
1 chicken drumstick, de-boned and cut into strips
120 gms (4¼ oz) medium-sized prawns, shelled
½ teaspoon salt
¼ teaspoon pepper
1 teaspoon light soya sauce
1 teaspoon cornflour
4 tablespoons cooking oil
3 shallots, sliced
2 cloves garlic, sliced
2 cm (¾ in) ginger, cut into strips
4 Chinese dried mushrooms, soaked and cut into strips
2 fresh red chillies, cut into strips
2 stalks spring onion, cut into 2 cm (¾ in) lengths
2 sprigs coriander leaves

Seasoning Ingredients
1 teaspoon thick soya sauce
1 teaspoon light soya sauce
1 teaspoon sesame oil
1 teaspoon salt
½ teaspoon sugar

Wash and drain vermicelli. Combine seasoning ingredients and add to chicken stock. Soak noodles in seasonings for at least 30 minutes.

Season chicken and prawns with ½ teaspoon salt, ¼ teaspoon pepper, 1 teaspoon light soya sauce and 1 teaspoon cornflour.

Heat 4 tablespoons oil in wok and lightly brown shallots, garlic and ginger. Put in mushroom strips and stir-fry. Add chicken and prawns and fry for 2 minutes.

Pour in stock and vermicelli mixture and stir-fry until liquid evaporates and mixture is almost dry.

Sprinkle on chillies and spring onion and mix well. Garnish with coriander leaves.

Sufficient for 2 as a meal by itself.

The transparent vermicelli is very absorbent so the correct amount of liquid must be used. Be sure to use a good stock as it will be absorbed by the noodles during soaking.

Fried Crispy Noodles with Seafood

150 gms (5¼ oz) pork or chicken, shredded
120 gms (4¼ oz) small prawns, shelled
120 gms (4¼ oz) small–medium cuttlefish, cut into 1¼ cm (½ in) pieces
2 teaspoons salt
1½ teaspoons sesame oil
Dash of pepper
3 tablespoons cooking oil
1 packet dried egg noodles, approximately 200 gms (7 oz)
Oil for deep-frying
4 slices ginger, shredded
3 cloves garlic, minced
4 dried Chinese mushrooms, soaked and shredded
240 gms (8½ oz) mustard greens, cut into 3 cm (1¼ in) lengths
1½ tablespoons cornflour mixed with 3 tablespoons chicken or pork bone stock

Sauce Ingredients (combined)
2 cups fresh chicken or pork bone stock
½ tablespoon light soya sauce
½ tablespoon oyster sauce
½ teaspoon sesame oil
½ teaspoon salt
½ teaspoon sugar

Season meat, prawns and cuttlefish separately with ½ teaspoon each of the salt and sesame oil and a dash of pepper. Leave for 15 minutes.

Bring a large saucepan of water to the boil and stir in 1 tablespoon of oil and ½ teaspoon salt. Cook noodles for 3–4 minutes until they separate and become soft. Drain and immerse in cold water for 30 seconds. Drain in a colander and allow to dry for 30 minutes before deep-frying.

Heat wok with deep-frying oil until hot and put in the noodles, one third at a time, and fry until crispy and light brown. Remove with a wire mesh ladle and place on serving dish.

Pour off the oil, leaving 1 tablespoon oil in the wok and lightly brown ginger and garlic. Add meat and stir-fry until it changes colour. Add the prawns and cuttlefish and stir-fry until cooked. Dish out and leave aside.

Reheat wok with 2 tablespoons oil and stir-fry the Chinese mushrooms for 30 seconds until fragrant. Put in mustard green, stems first, and then the leaves, and toss briefly.

Pour in combined sauce ingredients and bring to the boil. Return meat mixture to the wok and mix well. When the sauce boils again, gradually stir in cornflour mixture.

Pour the boiling hot sauce over the noodles and serve immediately.

Sufficient for 2 as a meal by itself.

This Cantonese noodle dish requires some time to prepare, but it only takes a few minutes to cook. Ready fried noodles are available in stores and they are just as delicious.

Fried Fresh Egg Noodles

120 gms (4¼ oz) chicken or pork strips
120 gms (4¼ oz) small prawns, shelled
Dash of light soya sauce
Pinch of pepper and salt
4 small rolls fresh egg noodles (*wantan mee*)
4 tablespoons cooking oil
6 shallots, sliced
5 cloves garlic, sliced
5 dried Chinese mushrooms, soaked and cut into strips
1 carrot, shredded
4 leaves Tientsin cabbage (*wong nga pak*), cut into strips
300 gms (10½ oz) beansprouts, tailed and rinsed
1 stalk spring onion, chopped
1 sprig coriander leaves, chopped
1 tablespoon shallot crisps
1 red chilli, cut into strips

Sauce Ingredients (combined)

2 tablespoons oyster sauce
1 tablespoon light soya sauce
1 tablespoon water
1 teaspoon thick soya sauce
1 teaspoon salt

Season chicken or pork strips and prawns with light soya sauce, pepper and salt and keep aside.

Bring half a saucepan of water to a rapid boil. Scald noodles for approximately 30 seconds. Drain with a large wire mesh ladle and immediately plunge noodles into a basin of cold water for a few seconds. Drain well and place in a dish. Mix noodles with 1 tablespoon of oil.

Heat 3 tablespoons oil in a wok and lightly brown garlic and shallots. Put in dried mushroom strips and stir-fry for a minute.

Add seasoned meat and prawns and stir-fry briskly. Add carrots and cabbage and continue stir-frying for 1–2 minutes and then add the beansprouts.

Put in noodles and sauce ingredients. Toss well with a pair of chopsticks until noodles are well combined with sauce.

Throw in spring onion and coriander leaves and serve hot, garnished with shallot crisps and chilli strips. Serves 4 as a meal by itself.

Plunging the noodles in a large basin of cold water is a step that cannot be omitted. Rinsing the noodles not only prevents them from being overcooked, it also gets rid of the tapioca starch.

Dried Chinese Noodles with Minced Meat

300 gms (10½ oz) pork with a little fat or chicken, minced
5 tablespoons cooking oil
3 cloves garlic, minced
1 tablespoon hot bean paste
90 gms (3 oz) preserved Szechuan vegetable, washed, cut into strips and soaked for 30 minutes
300 gms (10½ oz) dried noodle sticks
2 stalks spring onions, chopped

Seasoning Ingredients

½ teaspoon each of salt, pepper and sugar
½ tablespoon light soya sauce
½ tablespoon chilli oil
1 teaspoon cornflour

Sauce Ingredients (combined)

¾ cup fresh chicken or pork bone stock
½ tablespoon light soya sauce
1 teaspoon thick soya sauce
1 tablespoon Chinese rice wine
1 teaspoon black vinegar
1 tablespoon chilli oil
1 teaspoon sesame oil
½ teaspoon sugar
½ teaspoon pepper
1 teaspoon cornflour

Marinate minced meat with seasoning ingredients for 30 minutes.

Heat 3 tablespoons oil in a wok until hot and lightly brown garlic. Add the hot bean paste and stir-fry over low heat until fragrant.

Add the Szechuan vegetables and stir-fry over high heat for 1 minute. Put in minced meat and toss for 1–2 minutes.

Pour in combined sauce ingredients and bring to the boil until sauce thickens. Leave aside.

Drop dried noodle sticks into a large saucepan of boiling water and boil for 8 minutes or until cooked. Drain in a colander and stir in 2 tablespoons oil to prevent noodles from sticking.

Place noodles in a serving dish and add minced pork sauce mixture. Toss well and serve sprinkled with spring onion.

Serves 2 as a meal by itself.

Soak the Szechuan vegetable ahead of time to get rid of some of the salt and shred it into thin, even strips.

Fried Rice with Chicken and Pineapple

120 gms (4¼ oz) chicken, diced
1 teaspoon salt
¾ teaspoon pepper
2 tablespoons cooking oil
1 clove garlic, minced
2 shallots, sliced
360 gms (12⅔ oz) cooked rice, preferably 1 day old
2 slices ham, sliced
60 gms (2 oz) carrot, diced and parboiled
1 tablespoon frozen green peas
90 gms (3 oz) fresh or canned pineapple, diced
1 tablespoon light soya sauce
1 red chilli, chopped
1 stalk spring onion, chopped
1 sprig coriander leaves, chopped

Marinate chicken with ½ teaspoon salt and ¼ teaspoon pepper for 15 minutes.

Heat wok with oil until hot and lightly brown garlic and shallots. Add the chicken and stir-fry until meat changes colour.

Put in the rice and toss briefly. Add ham, carrots, green peas and pineapple and mix well.

Put in 1 teaspoon light soya sauce, ½ teaspoon salt and ½ teaspoon pepper and stir-fry again for 1–2 minutes. Sprinkle in chopped chilli, spring onion and coriander leaves.

Serves 2 as a meal by itself.

This dish is a creation by the Thai Chinese. It goes especially well with any curry dish in place of plain rice. Illustrated on page 77.

BOILED DISHES

Drunken Chicken

600 gms (21 oz) whole chicken thighs and drumsticks, washed and drained
1/2 teaspoon each of salt and pepper
1 tablespoon cooked oil mixed with 1/2 teaspoon sesame oil
2 sprigs coriander leaves

Sauce Ingredients (combined)
3/4 cup Chinese rice wine
1 teaspoon sugar
1/3 teaspoon salt

Marinate chicken with salt and pepper for at least 20 minutes. Bring half a saucepan of water, or enough to cover chicken, to the boil. Just before the water starts to boil, put in the chicken.

When the water begins to boil rapidly, cover the saucepan and turn off the flame. Let the chicken steep in the covered saucepan for 20 minutes.

Remove chicken and place on a serving dish. Rub the chicken with combined cooking and sesame oil.

Place sauce ingredients into a small saucepan and allow to heat through without boiling. Pour over chicken and let it cool. Cover the bowl with plastic wrap and leave to marinate overnight in the refrigerator.

Just before serving, chop the chicken into bite-sized pieces and garnish with coriander leaves. Serve cold, at room temperature or warmed.

This dish can be served as an appetiser or a main dish. For a more "boozy" chicken, rub the chicken with 2 extra tablespoons of Chinese rice wine.

Spicy Sesame Seed Chicken

600 gms (21 oz) whole chicken thighs and drumsticks
1 teaspoon salt
1/2 teaspoon pepper
1 tablespoon sesame seed, toasted
1 tablespoon cooking oil or chilli oil
1 clove garlic, minced
5 thin slices ginger, minced
1 red chilli, minced
1 stalk spring onion, chopped

Sauce Ingredients (combined)
1 1/2 teaspoon sugar
1/4 teaspoon salt
1 teaspoon light soya sauce
1 teaspoon black vinegar
1 teaspoon chilli oil
1 tablespoon thick soya sauce

Marinate chicken with salt and pepper and leave for 20 minutes. Pound 3/4 of the sesame seed into a paste and set aside.

Bring 1/2 a saucepan of water to the boil. When the water is about to boil put in the whole chicken pieces. When the water begins to boil rapidly, turn off the fire, cover the saucepan tightly and allow chicken to steep for 20 minutes until cooked through.

Drain chicken from stock and de-bone. Cut into serving size pieces and arrange on a serving dish.

Heat 1 tablespoon cooking or chilli oil in a wok until hot. Turn off the fire and put in garlic, ginger and chilli. Stir-fry for 30 seconds. Stir ground sesame paste into combined sauce ingredients and pour into the wok.

Mix well and pour sauce over chicken. Sprinkle with remaining sesame seeds and spring onion.

A lovely Szechuan dish with the crunchy, nutty taste of sesame. Illustrated on page 78. To prepare chilli oil see page 20.

Pork Rib Soup (*Bak Kut Teh*)

600 gms (21 oz) meaty pork ribs, cut into 5 cm (2 in) pieces
600 gms (21 oz) pork trotters, cut into 5 cm (2 in) pieces
5 whole garlic bulbs, rinsed and unpeeled
7 cups water
4 tablespoons light soya sauce
1 tablespoon thick soya sauce
1/2 teaspoon salt
10 dried Chinese mushrooms, soaked to soften
8–10 pieces fried beancurd cubes (*taufu pok*), halved

Spices (tied in a muslin bag)
20 white peppercorns
2 whole star anise
5 cm (2 in) piece cinnamon
7 cloves
1 teaspoon Szechuan peppercorns
1 teaspoon cumin
2 teaspoons *kei chee*, approximately 10 gms (1/3 oz)
15 gms (1/2 oz) *yok chok*
30 gms (1 oz) *tong kwei*

Chilli Sauce Dip (combined)
2 red chillies, sliced
1 tablespoon thick soya sauce

Rinse pork and remove bone chips if any. Drain and set aside.

In a large saucepan, bring pork, whole garlic bulbs, water, soya sauces and salt to the boil. Add the muslin bag of spices and boil for 5 minutes before removing.

Reduce heat, put in mushrooms and simmer for 1 1/4 hours or until pork ribs are just tender. To keep the stock clear, skim off the scum and oil on the surface every 15 minutes.

Ten minutes before removing soup from heat add the beancurd cubes. Serve with rice and chilli sauce dip.

One version of the origin of this popular dish credits it to the early migrant workers (coolies) from China who came without their wives. They had to cook for themselves and they just threw all the meat into a pot and added soya sauce and lots of garlic which was supposed to combat stomach ailments. Herbs were later added to improve their general well being.

Watercress and Sparerib Soup

600 gms (21 oz) watercress
360 gms (12 2/3 oz) pork ribs, chopped into 4 cm (1 1/2 in) pieces
5 cups water
1 1/2 teaspoons salt
Dash of pepper
2 tablespoons light soya sauce

Wash the watercress and cut off the roots. Break off the older stems and tie them together into a bunch with a piece of string.

Put spareribs and water into a medium-sized pot and bring to the boil. Add the tied-up bunch of watercress stems and simmer, covered, over low heat for 30 minutes. Remove and discard the bunch of stems and skim off excess oil from the surface.

Put in the watercress and salt and simmer, covered, for another 10–15 minutes until spareribs and watercress are tender.

Add a dash of pepper and serve soup with a small dish of light soya sauce as a dip for the spareribs.

Salted green stems are often boiled with spareribs and will give the soup a sour tang. Follow the above recipe, substituting watercress with 180 gms (6 1/2 oz) salted green stems (harm choy), cut into 5 cm (2 in) pieces. Soak the stems in water for 20–30 minutes to reduce the salt content. Add the stems after simmering spareribs for 30 minutes. Simmer for another 20–30 minutes until spareribs are tender and the vegetable soft. Sour plums can be added to give the soup even more tang.

Duck and Harm Choy Soup

½ a duck
250 gms (8¾ oz) salted green stems (*harm choy*), cut into 5 cm (2 in) squares
1 tablespoon cooking oil
5 cm (2 in) piece ginger, crushed
10 cups water
2 pickled sour plums (*sheen mui*)
2 tomatoes, quartered
¼ teaspoon pepper

Cut the duck into 4 pieces and set aside.

Soak the salted stems for 1 hour. Drain and lightly squeeze out excess water.

Heat oil in a pot and sauté ginger for 1–2 minutes until aromatic. Add duck and stir-fry for 5 minutes until the duck changes colour.

Pour water into the pot and add salted stems and sour plums. Bring to the boil, reduce heat to low, cover and simmer for 2½ hours or until the duck is tender.

Add the tomatoes and pepper and simmer for a further 10 minutes.

A very popular and appetising soup. Duck can be replaced with other meats. Sometimes a chilli is added to give it a spicy taste. Ducks have a fatty layer under the skin. Skin the duck ahead of time to avoid extra oil. For extra flavour, add 1 small dried squid cut into pieces. The Nonyas add dried tamarind skin and chillies to make this soup sour and spicy.

Old Cucumber and Pork Soup

1 large old cucumber with skin
360 gms (12⅔ oz) whole piece lean pork with fat, uncut and rinsed
6 dried Chinese red dates, seeded and rinsed
5 cups water
1½ teaspoons salt
2 tablespoons light soya sauce

Cut the old cucumber in half lengthways. Scoop out the seeds with a spoon and cut each half into 5 cm (2 in) pieces.

Put cucumber, whole pork and water in a large pot. Add dates to the pot. Cover and bring to the boil.

Add salt, reduce heat and simmer for ¾–1 hour. Skim off the surface scum from time to time.

When the pork is tender, remove and cut into 2 cm (¾ in) thick slices. Return pork to soup.

Serve with a small dish of light soya sauce as a dip for the pork.

A famous Cantonese soup which is supposed to be 'cooling' for the body. For extra flavour add a small dried squid cut into pieces.

Pork Tripe and Peppercorn Soup

600 gms (21 oz) pork tripe
2 teaspoons salt
Juice of 1 lemon
8 cups fresh pork bone or chicken stock
½ tablespoon white peppercorns, tied in a muslin bag and lightly crushed
1½ teaspoons salt

Wash inside and outside of tripe thoroughly and remove fat, if any. Rub with ⅓ of the salt and lemon juice and rinse with cold water. Repeat this a couple of times until the tripe is no longer slimy. Rinse well and leave uncut.

Put tripe, strained stock, bag of peppercorns and salt into a pot and bring to the boil.

Reduce heat and simmer, covered, for at least 1½ hours or until tripe is tender. Discard the bag of peppercorns.

Cut the tripe into 2 x 5 cm (¾ x 2 in) pieces and return to the pot. Reheat and serve.

A hot, peppery soup famous with the Hokkiens. The pork tripe has to be cleaned several times with lemon to get rid of the smell, but the effort is well worth it.

Beef Soup with Vegetables

300 gms (10½ oz) lean tender cut of beef, cut into 1¼ cm (½ in) cubes
½ teaspoon pepper
1 teaspoon light soya sauce
1 beef bouillon cube dissolved in 5 cups water or 5 cups fresh beef stock
1 small carrot, diced
1 large onion, diced
1 stick celery, cut into 1 cm (⅓ in) slices
120 gms (4¼ oz) fresh champignons, quartered
1 teaspoon salt
2 stalks spring onion, chopped
2 sprigs coriander leaves, chopped

Marinate beef with pepper and light soya sauce and set aside.

Bring beef stock to the boil and put in beef. Reduce heat to a gentle boil and simmer for 30 minutes. Skim off the surface scum constantly.

Add carrots and onion and continue to cook for 30 minutes. When beef is tender add celery and fresh champignons. Simmer for 5–10 minutes. Add salt to taste.

Serve hot sprinkled with chopped spring onion and coriander leaves.

If you are preparing beef stock from bones and tough meat, strain through a muslin cloth first to obtain a clear stock.

Transparent Noodles and Fish Ball Soup

45 gms (1½ oz) transparent noodles (*toong fun*), cut into 10 cm (4 in) lengths and soaked for 10 minutes
2 tablespoons cooking oil
2 shallots, sliced
2 cloves garlic, minced
4 cups fresh anchovy or chicken stock
2 teaspoons preserved dried Chinese white cabbage (*tung choy*), rinsed
15 medium-sized fish balls, rinsed
Salt and pepper
2 stalks spring onions, chopped

Drain soft transparent noodles and set aside.

Heat oil in a pot until hot and stir-fry shallots and garlic until lightly browned. Remove the shallots and garlic crisps from the oil and set aside.

Pour in strained stock and bring to the boil. Add the transparent noodles and preserved dried Chinese white cabbage and boil for 5 minutes. Put in the fish balls and boil for 2–3 minutes longer. Add salt and pepper to taste.

Serve hot soup garnished with a sprinkling of shallot and garlic crisps and spring onions.

The Teochews are famous for this clear, savoury soup. The fish balls are white and bouncy with no fishy taste.

Dried Fish Bladder Soup

1 chicken drumstick, de-boned and shredded
6 cups fresh chicken stock
90 gms (3 oz) dried and pre-fried fish bladder, soaked until soft and cut into 2½ cm (1 in) pieces
3 dried Chinese mushrooms, soaked and shredded
1 small carrot, cut into strips
4 water chestnuts, shredded
90 gms (3 oz) crab meat
2 stalks spring onion, chopped
2 tablespoons sweet potato flour mixed with 3 tablespoons chicken stock or water and strained
1 egg, beaten
Salt and pepper to taste

Seasoning Ingredients

½ teaspoon pepper
½ teaspoon salt
½ teaspoon cornflour

Marinate chicken with seasoning ingredients and leave for 10 minutes.

Bring stock to the boil in a large saucepan. Add fish bladder, mushrooms, carrots and water chestnuts and when the soup begins to boil again, reduce heat and simmer for 10 minutes.

Add crab meat and spring onion and stir in sweet potato flour mixture. Drizzle in the beaten egg.

Add salt and pepper to taste. Serve hot.

A thick soup that requires a good stock. The spongy, soft fish maw is very bland by itself.

Fish Head and Rice Vermicelli Soup

1 fish head (garoupa, red snapper or threadfin), approximately 4/5–1 kg (1 3/4–2 1/5 lbs)
Oil for deep-frying
7 cups anchovy or fresh chicken stock
2 1/2 cm (1 in) ginger, crushed
90 gms (3 oz) salted cabbage, shredded and soaked for 15–20 minutes
1 1/4 teaspoon salt
1/2 teaspoon pepper
240 gms (8 1/2 oz) rice vermicelli (*mai fun*), soaked for 15 minutes to soften
2 stalks spring onion
1 tablespoon shallot crisps

Seasoning Ingredients
1 teaspoon salt
1/2 teaspoon pepper
1 teaspoon Chinese rice wine

Chilli Dip (combined)
2 tablespoons light soya sauce
2 red chillies, sliced

Chop fish head into 5 cm (2 in) pieces and season with seasoning ingredients for 30 minutes.

Deep-fry in hot oil for 5 minutes. Drain from oil and set aside.

Put strained stock, ginger, salted cabbage, salt and pepper into a pot and bring to the boil. Reduce heat and simmer for 10 minutes.

Add the fish and bring to the boil again for 10 minutes or until the fish head is cooked.

Scald vermicelli in boiling water for 3 minutes or until cooked. Drain and place in a deep serving bowl.

Pour the hot fish soup over the vermicelli and serve sprinkled with spring onion and shallot crisps and serve with a small dish of chilli dip.

This dish is often served in hawker stalls around Singapore and Malaysia.

Prawn Wantan Soup

150 gms (5 1/4 oz) small shelled prawn, minced
120 gms (4 1/4 oz) pork, minced
3 fresh water chestnuts, finely minced
2 dried Chinese mushrooms, soaked and finely minced
1/2 egg white, beaten
120 gms (4 1/4 oz) wantan skins
1 tablespoon cooking oil
2 bunches mustard green (*choy sum*), cut into 3 sections
2 stalks spring onions, chopped

Seasoning Ingredients
1 teaspoon light soya sauce
1/2 teaspoon salt
1/2 teaspoon sugar
1/4 teaspoon pepper
1 teaspoon cornflour

Stock Ingredients
6 cups fresh anchovy, chicken or pork bone stock
1 1/2 teaspoons salt
1 teaspoon sesame oil
1/2 teaspoon pepper

Mix prawns, pork, water chestnuts and mushrooms with egg white and seasoning ingredients and leave for 30 minutes.

Put 1 teaspoon of mixture in the centre of each wantan skin. Wrap around the filling and fold the edges to seal.

Boil a saucepan of water and add 1 tablespoon of oil. Drop wantans in boiling water and cook for 1 minute. Remove with a perforated ladle and place in a deep soup bowl. Scald the mustard green in the same boiling water for 1 minute. Drain and arrange around the sides of the bowl.

Bring stock ingredients to the boil. Pour over wantans and vegetables. Serve garnished with chopped spring onion.

This dish is widely available at restaurants and hawker stalls, but it is worth the effort to make it yourself. It is usually served with egg noodles. The freshest ingredients should be used and the texture of the filling can be made to your own liking.

Beancurd and Transparent Noodle Soup

120 gms (4¼ oz) pork or chicken, shredded
4 dried Chinese mushrooms, soaked and shredded
30 gms (1 oz) transparent noodles, cut into 10 cm (4 in) lengths, and soaked to soften
1 square piece soft beancurd, cut into ½ cm (¼ in) thick strips
1 tablespoon sweet potato flour mixed with 2 tablespoons chicken stock, strained
2 eggs, lightly beaten
2 stalks spring onion, chopped
2 sprigs coriander leaves, chopped
1 teaspoon sesame oil

Seasoning Ingredients

1 teaspoon Chinese rice wine
½ teaspoon sesame oil
¼ teaspoon salt
¼ teaspoon pepper

Stock Ingredients

4 cups fresh chicken stock, strained
1 teaspoon salt
¼ teaspoon pepper
¼ teaspoon sugar

Marinate meat with seasoning ingredients for 10 minutes. Blanch in boiling water for 1 minute to get rid of scum. Drain and set aside.

Put stock ingredients into a deep pot and bring to the boil. Put in mushrooms and transparent noodles and let boil for l minute. Reduce heat and let it boil for 5 more minutes. Add meat and beancurd and simmer for a 3–5 minutes.

Thicken with sweet potato mixture. Stir in beaten eggs and sprinkle in spring onion and coriander leaves. Finally, stir in sesame oil. Serve hot.

When reheating thick soup, heat it slowly on a low flame, stirring constantly.

Hot Sour Soup

1 chicken drumstick, de-boned and cut into small cubes
300 gms (10½ oz) shelled small prawns (optional), diced
9 cups fresh chicken stock
1 large piece Szechuan vegetable (*char choy*), unwashed and diced
1 carrot, diced
4 dried Chinese mushrooms, soaked and diced
½ can button mushrooms, quartered
½ can straw mushrooms, quartered
10 pieces fresh young corn, diced
3 red chillies, split to remove seeds
⅔ cup Chinese black vinegar
1 square piece soft beancurd (*taufu*), diced
100 gms (3½ oz) frozen green peas, rinsed
4 tablespoons sweet potato flour mixed with ½ cup chicken stock, strained
2 eggs, lightly beaten

Seasoning Ingredients

1 teaspoon pepper
1 teaspoon salt
1 teaspoon cornflour

Marinate chicken and prawns with seasoning ingredients for 15 minutes.

Pour strained stock into a deep cooking pot and bring to the boil. Add Szechuan vegetable, carrot, all the mushrooms, corn, chillies and black vinegar. Allow to simmer for 10 minutes.

Put in chicken and prawns and when mixture begins to boil, add beancurd and green peas. Simmer for another 5 minutes, then stir in strained sweet potato flour mixture and finally the beaten eggs.

Pungent, peppery and slightly sour, this is one of the most well-known Chinese soups. Originally it was said to be a peasant soup in Szechuan and Peking. There are many versions of this soup, but the main ingredients which cannot be substituted are Szechuan vegetable and vinegar.

Eight Treasure Beancurd Soup

60 gms (2 oz) chicken meat, diced
60 gms (2 oz) fresh shelled prawns, diced
30 gms (1 oz) chicken liver, diced
60 gms (2 oz) fresh champignons
or straw mushrooms, diced
5 cups fresh chicken stock, strained
60 gms (2 oz) barbecued pork (*char siew*), diced
4 sticks tender young asparagus,
tough stems discarded, diced
1 square soft beancurd, diced
30 gms (1 oz) frozen green peas, rinsed
1 1/2 teaspoons salt
1/2 teaspoon pepper
1 tablespoon sweet potato flour mixed
with 2 tablespoons chicken stock, strained

Seasoning Ingredients
1/2 teaspoon salt
1/2 teaspoon sesame oil
1/4 teaspoon pepper

Marinate chicken, prawns and chicken liver with seasoning ingredients and set aside.

Bring a large saucepan of water to the boil and blanch champignons or straw mushrooms for 30 seconds. Drain and set aside.

Blanch seasoned meats for 30 seconds. Drain and set aside.

Bring chicken stock to the boil and put in all the blanched ingredients. Bring to the boil again and add barbecued pork, asparagus, beancurd, peas and salt and pepper to taste. Reduce heat and simmer for 5 minutes.

Thicken with sweet potato flour mixture.

Tomato Egg Soup

5 cups fresh chicken stock
240 gms (8 1/2 oz) fresh ripe tomatoes, peeled,
seeded and diced
2 eggs, beaten with a fork
3 tablespoons finely chopped spring onion

Seasoning Ingredients
2 teaspoons sesame oil
1 teaspoon sugar
1 1/2 teaspoons salt
1/2 teaspoon chicken stock granules
1 tablespoon light soya sauce

Put the stock in a large saucepan and bring to the boil.

Add seasoning ingredients and tomatoes. Reduce heat and simmer for 2 minutes.

Stir in the egg gradually in a slow thin stream using a fork to pull the egg across the surface of the soup into strands.

Sprinkle in spring onions and serve hot.

A delicate, clear soup with the tangy taste of tomato. The method is straightforward and the ingredients are generally stocked in any kitchen. The egg should not form lumps, so a fork is used to make the egg appear strand-like. This step isused in many Chinese dishes.

Potato, Carrot and Onion Soup

3 cups chicken or anchovy stock, strained
1 medium-sized potato, diced
1/2 a medium-sized carrot, diced
1 onion, diced
5 fresh champignons or canned button
mushrooms, diced
1 tomato, diced
1/2 teaspoon salt
1/2 teaspoon pepper
1 stalk spring onion, chopped
2 sprigs coriander leaves, chopped

Bring chicken or anchovy stock to the boil. Put in potatoes, carrot, and onion and simmer over medium heat for 5 minutes.

Put in mushrooms, tomato, salt and pepper and continue to simmer for 8–10 minutes or until potatoes and carrots are soft.

Serve hot sprinkled with spring onion and coriander leaves.

A hearty and nutritious homestyle soup. Soups play an integral part in Chinese meals. The soup is consumed as the meal progresses, and acts as a palate cleanser. *Illustrated on page 79.*

Chicken Corn Soup

7½ cups fresh chicken stock
4 dried Chinese mushrooms, soaked and shredded
1 large boneless chicken breast, skinned and shredded
½ tablespoon oil
1 can sweet corn (325 gms, 11½ oz), drained
½ teaspoon pepper
1 teaspoon salt
4 tablespoons sweet potato flour mixed with 5 tablespoons water, strained
1 egg white, lightly beaten with a fork
2 stalks spring onion, chopped
2 tablespoons shallot crisps

Place chicken stock in a pot and bring to the boil. Add mushrooms, reduce heat and simmer for 5 minutes.

Mix oil with chicken to prevent sticking and add to soup. Put in sweet corn, pepper and salt to taste. Simmer for another 5–8 minutes.

Increase the heat to medium and stir in the potato flour mixture. Stir well to ensure that the mixture does not form lumps. When the soup boils again, drizzle in the beaten egg white and stir soup to distribute the egg.

Serve hot, topped with spring onion and shallot crisps.

Another well-known Chinese soup, popular with Westerners. Tender young corn is ideal for this soup. Illustrated on page 80.

Prawn Noodles (*Har Meen*)

Stock Ingredients
2 tablespoons cooking oil
150 gms (5¼ oz) dried anchovy, rinsed
8 cups water
500 gms (17½ oz) pork bones
1½ teaspoons salt
½ teaspoon pepper

150 gms (51/4 oz) lean pork with a little fat
250 gms (8¾ oz) medium-sized prawns, with shells on
4 tablespoons cooking oil
12 shallots, sliced
1 tablespoon ground dried chilli or dried chilli paste
600 gms (21 oz) fresh yellow noodles
300 gms (10½ oz) beansprouts, tailed and rinsed
150 gms (5¼ oz) water convolvulus, roots discarded and cut into 12½ cm (5 in) lengths
3 red chillies, sliced

To make stock, heat oil in a large pot and lightly brown anchovy. Add water and pork bones and bring to the boil. Add salt and pepper and simmer for 45 minutes over low heat. Strain stock and discard the anchovy and pork bones.

Pour strained stock into a clean pot and bring to the boil. Add lean pork, reduce heat and simmer for 10 minutes. Add the prawns and cook for another 5 minutes or until prawns are just cooked.

Remove pork and prawns. Slice the pork thinly and set aside. Shell the prawns, split into two halves and lift out the dark veins. Rinse and set aside.

Heat cooking oil in a saucepan and lightly brown shallots. Drain from the oil and set aside for garnishing. Put in chilli paste and stir-fry for 1 minute over low heat. Pour in strained stock and bring to the boil. Add salt to taste and keep gravy hot.

Boil a large saucepan of water and scald noodles for 1 minute. Drain and leave on a large dish.

Blanch the beansprouts and water convolvulus separately for 30 seconds in the same boiling water. Place next to the noodles.

Divide yellow noodles, beansprouts and water convolvulus and place in 3 or 4 serving bowls. Garnish with sliced pork and prawns. Pour in hot stock and serve immediately sprinkled with shallot crisps.

A hawker style noodle soup easy to prepare at home. Works as a meal for 3–4 people.

Long Bean Rice (*Tau Kok Farn*)

150 gms (5¼ oz) pork with a little fat, shredded
4 tablespoons cooking oil
4 shallots, sliced
3 cloves garlic, minced
90 gms (3 oz) small dried prawns, soaked, drained and diced
450 gms (15¾ oz, 3 rice measuring cups) rice, washed and drained in a colander
1 teaspoon salt
½ teaspoon pepper
4½ cups fresh chicken stock or pork bone stock
300 gms (10½ oz) long beans, diced

Seasoning Ingredients

½ teaspoon salt
½ teaspoon pepper
1 teaspoon light soya sauce

Marinate pork with seasoning ingredients for 15 minutes.

Heat wok with 1 tablespoon of oil until hot and lightly brown half the shallots and half the garlic. Put in dried prawns and stir-fry for 1 minute. Add pork and stir-fry until meat changes colour. Remove and set aside.

Reheat wok with 2 tablespoons of oil until hot and lightly brown remaining shallots and garlic. Put in rice, salt and pepper and stir-fry for 2–3 minutes. Transfer rice to an electric rice cooker and add enough stock to come up to 2½ cm (1 in) above the rice level.

Heat remaining tablespoon of oil in the wok and stir-fry long beans for 2 minutes. Remove and set aside.

When rice begins to boil, put in the pork and prawn mixture and the long beans. Cook until rice is done.

Complete with a simple, clear soup, such as Tomato Egg Soup (see page 94), for a wholesome meal the whole family will enjoy.

Fragrant Yam Rice

300 gms skinless, boneless chicken, cut into 2½ cm (1 in) pieces
Oil for deep-frying
350 gms (12⅓ oz) cleaned yam, cut into 1½ cm (¾ in) pieces
6 shallots, sliced
3 tablespoons cooking oil
60 gms (2 oz) dried prawns, soaked for 15 minutes and drained
300 gms rice (10½ oz, 2 rice measuring cups), washed and drained
2 teaspoons light soya sauce
3½ cups fresh chicken stock or water
2 tablespoons chopped spring onion
1 red chilli, sliced

Seasoning Ingredients

½ teaspoon salt
½ teaspoon sugar
¼ teaspoon pepper
1 teaspoon light soya sauce
½ teaspoon thick soya sauce
1 teaspoon sesame oil
1 teaspoon Chinese rice wine
1 teaspoon cornflour

Marinate chicken with seasoning ingredients and set aside.

Heat oil in deep saucepan and deep-fry yam pieces for 8–10 minutes or until just cooked. Drain from oil and set aside. Put in sliced shallots and fry until golden. Drain shallot crisps from oil and set aside for garnishing.

Reheat a clean saucepan with 3 tablespoons oil and stir-fry prawns until fragrant. Dish out and set aside. Put in rice and toss for 1–2 minutes. Stir in light soya sauce. Remove saucepan from the heat and place the fried rice in a rice cooker. Pour in chicken stock and switch the rice cooker on.

When the stock comes to the boil, add yam and chicken. Let the rice cook until done. Just before dishing out, sprinkle with shallot crisps, spring onion and red chilli.

Serves about 4 people as a meal by itself.

A welcome change from oily fried rice. Serve with a clear soup as a light meal for lunch or dinner. Illustrated on page 105.

Hainanese Chicken Rice

1 fat chicken, approximately 1½ kg (3⅓ lbs)
2½ teaspoons salt
4–5 cups chicken stock,
or enough to immerse chicken
450 gms (15¾ oz, 4 rice measuring cups)
long grain rice
2½ cm (1 in) piece ginger, crushed
4 cloves garlic, minced
1 teaspoon salt
3 screwpine leaves, knotted
1 tablespoon cooked oil mixed
with 1 teaspoon sesame oil
Cucumber slices
2–3 sprigs coriander leaves
180 gms (6⅓ oz) cabbage, shredded
Salt to taste

Chilli Sauce
10 red chillies
4 bird chillies (*chilli padi*), optional
2½cm (1 in) ginger
5 cloves garlic
1 teaspoon sugar
½ teaspoon salt
2 tablespoons melted chicken fat
from 1 large piece chicken fat
Juice of 1 small lime

Clean chicken removing all the entrails including pancreas. Remove chicken fat, rinse and chop into small pieces. Keep aside for cooking the rice. Rub inside and outside of the chicken with 1½ teaspoons salt and set aside.

In a large pot, put in stock and 1 teaspoon salt and bring to the boil. When the stock is just about to boil, put in the whole chicken and let it boil, covered, for 5 minutes. Keep the pot tightly covered, turn off the flame and let the chicken steep for 20 minutes.

Remove the chicken from the pot and immerse the whole chicken in ice-cold water until completely cold. Retain the chicken stock for cooking the rice and making soup.

Wash and drain rice in a colander.

Heat wok until hot and melt the chicken fat. Remove and discard the shrivelled chicken residue when all the oil has oozed out. Add ginger and fry for 1 minute. Then add garlic and fry until lightly browned.

Put in rice and stir-fry until well mixed with fat for approximately 2–3 minutes.

Transfer the rice to an electric rice cooker. Add the chicken stock from boiling the chicken to cover just 2 cm (¾ in) above the rice. Stir in salt and put in screwpine leaves.

When the rice is cooked, rub the cooled chicken with the combined oil and sesame oil. Chop into bite-sized pieces and arrange on a serving dish garnished with cucumber slices. Top with coriander leaves and serve with chilli sauce.

To prepare the chilli sauce. Blend all the ingredients except the chicken oil and lime juice in the blender until fine. Stir in chicken oil and lime juice. If more chicken fat is required for the chilli sauce, ask the butcher for extra pieces of fat.

To prepare the soup, add fresh chicken stock as required to the remaining stock from boiling the chicken. When it begins to boil, add shredded cabbage and simmer for 10 minutes. Add salt to taste.

Serves about 6 people as a meal by itself.

This dish calls for chicken that is just cooked. The texture of the meat should be very smooth. A great deal of precision is required in this dish, and a few minutes either way will result in an imperfect chicken. Herein lies the difficulty, and control and timing are essential.

Chicken Porridge

2 whole chicken thighs and drumsticks
1 1/2 teaspoons salt
3/4 teaspoon pepper
10 cups fresh chicken stock
300 gms (10 1/2 oz, 2 rice measuring cups) rice
2 stalks spring onion, chopped
2 tablespoons shallot crisps

Marinate chicken with 1 teaspoon salt and 1/4 teaspoon pepper for 15 minutes.

Put chicken and enough water to cover it, in a pot and bring to the boil. Simmer for 15 minutes. Remove chicken, shred and leave aside. Strain the stock and add to fresh chicken stock to make 10 cups.

Wash the rice and add stock, 1/2 teaspoon salt and 1/2 teaspoon pepper. Bring to the boil and simmer over low heat, partially covered for 1 1/2 hours, stirring occasionally to prevent porridge sticking to the bottom of the pot.

Serve hot, topped with a sprinkling of shredded chicken, spring onion, shallot crisps and a dash of pepper.

Serves about 8 people as a meal by itself.

This Cantonese congée has a thick, starchy consistency, and it is ideal as a simple, light meal. A humble dish like this one can be turned into a gastronomic delight with the addition of expensive ingredients like sharksfin, scallops, abalone, fish lips and slices of carp.

SHALLOW AND DEEP-FRIED

DISHES

Chinese Style Fillet Steak

250 gms (8¾ oz) fillet steak
2 tablespoons cooking oil
1 onion, sliced
½ tablespoon Chinese rice wine
1 teaspoon toasted sesame seeds

Seasoning Ingredients
¼ teaspoon bicarbonate of soda
¼ teaspoon salt
¼ teaspoon pepper
1 teaspoon sugar
1 teaspoon light soya sauce
1 teaspoon oyster sauce
2 teaspoons Chinese rice wine
1 teaspoon cornflour

Trim off all the fat from the meat. Slice into 5 mm (⅕ in) slices. Gently flatten meat with a meat mallet or rolling pin. Season with seasoning ingredients and leave for 3 hours or preferably overnight in the refrigerator.

Heat cooking oil in a large flat pan or wok until hot. Sauté onion until lightly browned. Dish out onto a serving dish.

Spread out meat slices on the heated pan and brown on both sides. Do not overlap the strips of meat or they will not brown evenly. When beef is browned, sprinkle with wine.

Arrange meat over the onions and sprinkle with toasted sesame seeds.

In Chinese cooking beef is often sliced thinly to ensure tenderness, so skill in wielding the cleaver is essential. Quality cuts of beef are always marinated with soya sauce, sugar and tenderiser.

Pork Chops with Onion and Mushroom Sauce

2 pieces 3 cm (1¼ in) thick boneless pork chops
8–10 dried Chinese mushrooms, soaked until soft
4 tablespoons cooking oil
150 gms (5¼ in) cream crackers, finely ground
2½ cm (1 in) cinnamon stick
1 onion, sliced
½ tablespoon plain flour
60 gms (2 oz) green peas

Seasoning Ingredients 'A'
¼ teaspoon salt
¼ teaspoon pepper
½ teaspoon sugar
1 egg, lightly beaten

Seasoning Ingredients 'B'
¼ teaspoon salt
¼ teaspoon pepper
¼ teaspoon sugar
½ teaspoon light soya sauce

Sauce Ingredients (combined)
1 cup fresh pork or chicken or bone stock
½ teaspoon sugar
½ teaspoon salt
1 teaspoon light soya sauce
1 teaspoon thick soya sauce

Slice each chop into 2 without cutting through. Spread out to make one large piece of chop. Using the blunt edge of a cleaver, bash lightly on both sides to tenderise meat. Marinate with seasoning ingredients 'A' for 30 minutes.

Season softened mushrooms with seasoning ingredients 'B' for 30 minutes.

Heat the oil in a pan or wok until hot. Coat chops thoroughly with cream cracker crumbs and cook chops on both sides over low heat until golden brown. Transfer chops onto a serving dish and keep warm. Strain the oil.

Reheat a clean pan or wok with 1½ tablespoons of the oil and stir-fry the cinnamon and onion over high heat until onion turns transparent. Add mushrooms and stir-fry for 2 minutes. Add the flour and fry for 30 seconds.

Pour in combined sauce ingredients and simmer until sauce is thick. Stir in peas and pour sauce over the chops.

This is the typical Hainanese pork chop with an English style sauce. Chicken breast meat or boneless thighs can also be used. This dish is usually served with chips and salad.

Fried Pork Chops

250 gms (8¾ oz) boneless pork chop meat or pork fillet, cut into 5 mm (⅕ in) slices
3 tablespoons cooking oil
1 tomato, sliced
½ a cucumber, sliced

Seasoning Ingredients

½ teaspoon salt
½ teaspoon pepper
1 teaspoon sugar
1 teaspoon light soya sauce
1 teaspoon oyster sauce
1 teaspoon Chinese rice wine
½ an egg white, lightly beaten

Pound meat slices lightly with the blunt edge of a cleaver to tenderise. Marinate with seasoning ingredients overnight in the refrigerator.

Heat a flat pan or wok with oil until hot, reduce heat to low and brown chops on both sides until cooked through.

Serve garnished with tomato and cucumber slices.

This dish is a perfect blend of East and West. Serve with rice and a stir-fried vegetable, or with chips and a salad.

Meat Patties in Sauce

300 gms (10½ oz) minced pork or chicken
4 eggs, lightly beaten
4 tablespoons cooking oil
2 onions, sliced
2 tomatoes, quartered
3–4 sprigs coriander leaves, chopped

Seasoning Ingredients

½ teaspoon salt
½ teaspoon pepper
1 teaspoon cornflour

Sauce Ingredients

¾ cup fresh pork bone or chicken stock
1 teaspoon light soya sauce
1 teaspoon thick soya sauce
½ teaspoon sugar
¼ teaspoon salt
1 teaspoon cornflour

Marinate minced meat with seasoning ingredients for 30 minutes. Just before cooking meat, mix in the beaten eggs.

Heat 3 tablespoons of the oil in a flat pan until hot. Reduce heat to medium and drop a heaping tablespoon of meat mixture onto pan. Fry 3 or 4 meat patties at one time, ensuring that they do not overlap. Cook each side for approximately 1–2 minutes until golden brown and cooked through. Remove, place on a dish and set aside.

Heat wok with remaining 1 tablespoon of oil and stir-fry onions until transparent and soft. Put in tomatoes and fry for 1 minute.

Pour in combined sauce ingredients and carefully return meat patties to the pan. Simmer for 1 minute until sauce thickens.

Sprinkle with coriander leaves and serve hot with rice.

Adding eggs to the meat makes the patties fluffy, soft and fragrant.

Fried Meat and Vegetable Dumplings

180 gms (6⅓ oz) minced pork with a little fat or chicken
2 leaves white cabbage (*pak choy*), approximately 120 gms (4¼ oz), finely chopped
30 gms (1 oz) Chinese chives, finely chopped
1 stalk spring onion, finely chopped
2 tablespoons cooking oil
¾ cup fresh chicken stock

Seasoning Ingredients

1 teaspoon sugar
¾ teaspoon salt
¼ teaspoon pepper
1 teaspoon light soya sauce
1 teaspoon Chinese rice wine
1 teaspoon sesame oil
1 tablespoon cooked or shallot oil

Pastry

120 gms (4¼ oz) plain flour
¼ teaspoon salt
⅔ cup boiling water

Vinegar and Ginger Dip

2 tablespoons vinegar
1 teaspoon sugar
30 gms (1 oz) thin slices ginger, shredded

Season minced meat with seasoning ingredients and set aside.

Place finely chopped cabbage in a muslin cloth and squeeze to remove excess vegetable liquid. Add to minced pork, chives and spring onion. Mix into a smooth paste.

Lift the mixture with the hand and slap it against a bowl or chopping board continuously for 1 minute to improve the texture of the meat.

Refrigerate meat mixture for 1 hour.

To make the pastry, sieve flour into a mixing bowl and add salt. Pour boiling water into the flour and quickly mix into a stiff dough with a spoon.

Form dough into a round ball and leave to rest, covered with a dry towel for 30 minutes.

Knead dough on a lightly floured board for 3–5 minutes until smooth. Shape into a long sausage roll and divide equally into 18 pieces.

Make each piece into a round ball and roll out into a thin circle (approximately 7 cm, 2¾ in diameter).

Put a teaspoon of meat mixture, slightly off centre into each circle. Pleat one half of the wrapper and press against the unpleated side to seal and form a half-moon shape dumpling.

Heat a flat pan with 2 tablespoons oil until hot, reduce heat and place the dumplings in a circle close together.

Fry for 1 minute until the bottom of the dumpling is golden brown. Do not disturb the dumpling while frying.

Pour the chicken stock into the pan, cover and simmer dumplings on low heat for 4–5 minutes until cooked through.

Drain off remaining liquid and transfer dumplings onto a serving dish.

Serve hot with vinegar and ginger dip or chilli sauce.

To prepare the vinegar and ginger dip, heat combined vinegar and sugar. Stir until sugar dissolves and pour immediately over ginger.

Leave, covered, for 1–2 hours before serving.

This is a version of the famous Shanghai dumplings (wor tip), also known as pan stickers. Perfect as a light lunch, especially when served with a pot of hot tea.

Deep-Fried Spareribs with Sweet and Sour Sauce

600 gms (21 oz) spareribs, cut into 4 cm (1 1/2 in) pieces
1 egg white, lightly beaten
Cornflour for coating
Oil for deep-frying
Cucumber slices
2 sprigs coriander leaves

Seasoning Ingredients
1/2 teaspoon salt
1/2 teaspoon pepper
1/2 teaspoon sugar
1/4 teaspoon five spice powder
1/2 tablespoon light soya sauce
1/2 tablespoon Chinese rice wine

Sauce Ingredients
1 tablespoon tomato sauce
1 teaspoon Chinese rice wine
1 teaspoon light soya sauce
2 teaspoons white or cider vinegar
2 teaspoons sugar
1/4 teaspoon salt
1/4 teaspoon pepper
1 tablespoon water
1 teaspoon cornflour

Marinate pork ribs with seasoning ingredients for 2 hours. Just before deep-frying spareribs, stir beaten egg white into marinade. Remove spareribs and coat evenly with cornflour.

Heat oil for deep-frying until hot and deep-fry spareribs until brown. Drain from oil and leave aside.

Reheat a clean wok with 1 tablespoon of the oil and add combined sauce ingredients. When it begins to boil, return spareribs to wok and stir-fry until sauce is thick and dry.

Serve garnished with cucumber and coriander leaves.

Chicken drumsticks can be used instead of pork ribs.

Deep-Fried Pork Rolls

250 gms (8 3/4 oz) boneless pork loin (*yok ngan*), half frozen to facilitate slicing
5 cm (2 in) piece carrot, cut into strips
5 cm (2 in) piece canned bamboo shoots, cut into strips
2 large pieces dried Chinese mushrooms, soaked and shredded
1/2 cup breadcrumbs
Oil for deep-frying
Pineapple or cucumber slices for garnishing

Seasoning Ingredients
1/2 teaspoon salt
1/2 teaspoon sugar
1/4 teaspoon pepper
2 teaspoons Chinese rice wine
1 egg, beaten
1 tablespoon cornflour

To double the size of the sliced meat so that it will be large enough to cover the vegetables, proceed in the following manner:

Cut a 1/4 cm (1/10 in) slice across the grain without cutting through. Cut the next slice completely through 1/4 cm (1/10 in) from the first cut. Continue to cut in double slices on the whole piece of meat.

Lightly bash each piece of meat with the blunt edge of a cleaver to tenderize. Marinate meat with seasoning ingredients for 30 minutes.

Open and spread out each piece of meat on a flat surface and place 2 strips each of carrot, bamboo shoots and dried mushrooms.

Roll up the meat, enclosing the vegetables. Coat well with breadcrumbs.

Heat a wok with deep-frying oil. Deep-fry pork rolls for approximately 5 minutes or until golden. Drain from oil.

Arrange on a serving dish and garnish with pineapple and cucumber slices.

A popular starter for Chinese meals. Stuffings can be varied using other vegetables. They can be served hot and crisp, or drizzled with sweet and sour sauce. Chicken breast meat can be used instead of pork.

Beancurd Wrapped Pork Roll (*Lor Bak*)

300 gms (10½ oz) pork with a little fat (*siong yok*), cut into finger size strips, approximately 2 x 11½ cm (¾ x 4½ in)
6 beancurd sheets, approximately 20 x 20 cm (8 x 8 in) each
½ an egg white, beaten
Oil for deep-frying
Chilli sauce

Seasoning Ingredients
1 onion, ground
1 dessertspoon oyster sauce
1 dessertspoon light soya sauce
1 teaspoon thick soya sauce
1 teaspoon sugar
1 teaspoon five spice powder
½ teaspoon salt
1 egg, beaten

Marinate pork strips with seasoning ingredients for two hours or preferably overnight in the refrigerator.

Spread out a beancurd sheet and place 2 strips of meat lengthwise. Wrap and roll up like a spring roll. Seal the edges with a little beaten egg white.

Prick the beancurd skin with a needle to prevent air bubbles forming when frying the beancurd rolls.

Heat oil in a wok for deep-frying until hot. Reduce heat and deep-fry beancurd rolls until golden brown. Drain from oil.

Cut into bite-sized pieces and serve with chilli sauce.

Penang is famous for this dish. Fresh five spice powder is important to obtain the special fragrance. The Penang blend is the most suitable for this dish.

Chicken Fingers with Walnuts

300 gms (10½ oz) chicken fillet, trimmed and cut into 2 lengthwise
100 gms (3½ oz) walnuts, boiled and chopped finely or blended in grinder
1 egg white, beaten
2 tablespoons cornflour
1 tablespoon sesame seeds
2 tablespoons cooking oil
Tomato ketchup and chilli sauce

Seasoning Ingredients
½ teaspoon chicken stock granules
1 teaspoon light soya sauce
1 teaspoon oyster sauce
½ tablespoon fruity ketchup
¼ teaspoon salt
¼ teaspoon pepper

Marinate chicken strips with seasoning ingredients for 1 hour.

Bring a saucepan of water to the boil and add walnuts. Turn off the heat and soak walnuts in the hot water for 10 minutes. Drain, chop or blend coarsely and set aside.

Just before deep-frying chicken, stir beaten egg white and cornflour into chicken marinade. Add sesame seeds to chopped walnuts. Dip chicken strips in walnut mixture and coat thoroughly.

Heat oil in electric fryer to 180°C (350°F) and fry chicken until golden brown (approximately 3–4 minutes).

Serve with tomato ketchup and chilli sauce.

The texture of chicken fillets is finer and smoother than breast meat. Fillets are ideal for stir-frying or deep-frying because they cook so quickly. This finger food is great for buffet entertaining.

Paper-Wrapped Chicken with Mushrooms

1 chicken, approximately 1–1¼ kg (½–⅔ lb), cut into 10 large pieces
1 stalk spring onion, chopped
2 sprigs coriander leaves, chopped
20 dried Chinese mushrooms, soaked until soft
1 tablespoon oyster sauce
½ teaspoon pepper
½ teaspoon sugar
½ teaspoon sesame oil
2 dried scallops, crushed
3 tablespoons cooking oil
2½ cm (1 in) ginger, crushed
½ cup water or fresh chicken stock
Grease-proof paper made into 10 x 15 cm (4 x 6 in) bags
1 tablespoon corn oil combined with 1 teaspoon sesame oil
Oil for deep-frying
Cucumber slices

Seasoning Ingredients

½ teaspoon salt
½ teaspoon pepper
½ teaspoon five spice powder
1 teaspoon sugar
2 tablespoons oyster sauce
1 tablespoon brandy
½ tablespoon ginger juice
½ tablespoon light soya sauce
½ tablespoon sesame oil
1 tablespoon cornflour

Marinate chicken pieces in a bowl with seasoning ingredients and chopped spring onion and coriander leaves. Leave for 3 hours or overnight in the refrigerator.

Marinate mushrooms with oyster sauce, sugar, pepper and sesame oil for at least 1 hour.

Steam the dried scallops for 15 minutes or until soft. Shred with fingers and set aside.

Heat cooking oil in a wok until hot and fry ginger for 30 seconds. Put in dried scallops and toss for a few seconds. Add dried mushrooms and stir-fry for 1 minute. Pour in chicken stock and simmer over low heat for 8–10 minutes. Remove and leave to cool.

Lightly grease the inside of each paper bag with combined corn oil and sesame oil. Put a piece of chicken and two pieces of dried mushroom into each bag. Fold and staple the opening with a stapler.

Heat oil for deep-frying in a wok until hot and deep-fry paper bag chicken for 7–8 minutes.

Arrange the bags on a serving dish and garnish with cucumber slices.

A popular dish with many variations. All types of ingredients, such as sausages and bamboo shoots, can be added but I prefer mushrooms, which add an earthy fragrance. The marinade is very important for this dish.

Crispy Skin Chicken

1 chicken, approximately ½ kg (¼ lb)
1 tablespoon salt
3 sticks cinnamon, 7½ cm (3 in) long
Juice of 10 small limes, strained
2 tablespoons maltose (*mak ngah tong*)
1 teaspoon salt
Oil for deep-frying
Cucumber slices
Tomato slices
Prawn crackers

Clean chicken thoroughly and remove pancreas. Cut off feet. Break the thigh bone joints and carefully remove thigh bones from the inside with the help of small knife. Leave drumstick bones intact. Rub the inside of chicken with salt and place cinnamon sticks horizontally across the stomach.

Making sure it is greaseless, bring half a wok of water to boil. Tie neck of chicken firmly with a piece of strong string. Hold chicken just above rapidly boiling water and, using a ladle, scald chicken several times with boiling water.

Throw water away and wash wok thoroughly—there should be no grease. Bring another half wok of water to boil, add strained lime juice and stir in maltose and salt until maltose dissolves completely.

Dip and scald chicken in boiling maltose water by turning chicken quickly in wok. Remove chicken and hang in the sun to dry for 5 hours.

Heat oil for deep-frying in a wok until hot and fry chicken for 15 minutes until golden brown. If chicken should brown too quickly, lower heat. Should air bubbles appear on chicken skin, prick with a skewer.

Cut chicken into serving size pieces and serve hot, garnished with cucumber and tomato slices and topped with prawn crackers.

Pick a chicken with perfect skin without a tear or slit for this recipe.

Crispy Spiced Chicken Wings

10 chicken wings, with wing tips removed
1 egg, lightly beaten
Cornflour for coating chicken
Oil for deep-frying
½ a cucumber, pared and sliced
1 tomato, sliced

Seasoning Ingredients

¼ teaspoon pepper
¼ teaspoon five spice powder
½ teaspoon salt
½ teaspoon sugar
1 tablespoon light soya sauce
1 tablespoon Chinese rice wine

Marinate chicken wings with seasoning ingredients for 2 hours.

Just before deep-frying, mix in the beaten egg and coat chicken with cornflour.

Deep-fry in hot oil until golden and crisp.

Arrange on a serving dish garnished with tomato and cucumber slices.

After frying the chicken wings the oil will be murky with a lot of residue. The oil can be reused after straining through a fine muslin cloth or a fine mesh strainer.

Five Spice Crispy Skin Chicken

1 kg chicken (1/2 lb) or 4 chicken thighs,
cut into large pieces
Oil for deep-frying
Lettuce and cucumber slices

Seasoning Ingredients
1 tablespoon sugar
1 teaspoon salt
1 teaspoon pepper
1/2 teaspoon five spice powder
1 egg, lightly beaten
2 tablespoons water
2 tablespoons self-raising flour

Flour Coating Mixture (combined)
60 gms (2 oz) corn flakes, finely ground
240 gms (8 1/2 oz) self-raising flour
1/2 teaspoon salt
1/2 teaspoon pepper
1/4 teaspoon bicarbonate of soda

Batter
60 gms (2 oz) self-raising flour
3/4 cup water or milk
1/4 teaspoon salt
1/4 teaspoon pepper

Marinate chicken pieces with seasoning ingredients for 1–2 hours.

Just before frying, coat chicken pieces with flour coating mixture. Dip into batter mixture and drop into hot oil. Fry over high heat for 1 minute, then reduce heat to moderate and cook until chicken is golden in colour.

Drain well and serve with lettuce or cucumber slices.

Illustrated on page 106. The recipe can be varied to make "Hot and Spicy Crispy Fried Chicken." Use the above recipe, omitting the five spice powder from the seasoning. Replace with 1 teaspoon of your favourite curry powder. Add another 1/2 tablespoon of curry powder to flour coating mixture.

Spicy Fried Chicken

1 kg (1/2 lb) chicken or 4 chicken thighs,
cut into serving size pieces
Flour for coating chicken
1 cup milk
Oil for deep-frying
Cucumber slices

Ground Ingredients
15–20 dried chillies, rinsed
and thoroughly dried in the sun
20 black peppercorns
2 teaspoons cumin
1 teaspoon fennel

Seasoning Ingredients
1 teaspoon turmeric powder
1 dessertspoon light soya sauce
1 teaspoon salt
1 teaspoon sugar

Place ground ingredients in an electric pepper or coffee mill and blend until fine. Store in an air-tight jar until required. This amount is enough to marinate two large chickens.

Drain excess water from chicken and towel dry. Marinate chicken with 1/2 of the ground ingredients and the seasoning ingredients. Leave for 5 hours or preferably overnight in the refrigerator.

Coat chicken pieces with flour, dip into the milk and re-coat with flour. Deep-fry in hot oil for 12–15 minutes or until cooked and golden brown in colour.

Serve hot with cucumber slices.

If you like spicy crispy fried chicken, it is well worth grinding your own fresh spices.

Five Spice Meat Roll

600 gms (21 oz) chicken with 2 pieces chicken fat or streaky pork, minced
300 gms (10½ oz) small prawns, minced
240 gms (8½ oz) crab meat
10 cm (4 in) piece carrot, minced coarsely
6 fresh water chestnuts, minced coarsely
5 dried Chinese mushrooms, soaked and minced coarsely
2–3 stalks spring onions, chopped
½ egg, beaten
1 tablespoon plain flour
1 large sheet dried beancurd sheet (*foo peh*), cut into 30 x 12½ cm (12 x 5 in) pieces
Flour paste
Oil-for deep-frying
Cucumber and tomato slices for garnishing

Seasoning Ingredients

½ teaspoon five spice powder
½ teaspoon salt
½ teaspoon pepper
½ tablespoon light soya sauce
½ tablespoon sesame oil

Combine chicken, prawns, crab meat, carrot, water chestnuts, mushrooms and spring onion and mix with seasoning ingredients, egg and flour. Leave for 1 hour.

Put some marinated meat mixture in the centre of each beancurd sheet and roll up into 4 cm (1½ in) diameter rolls. Seal edges with a little flour paste.

Place rolls in a steamer over rapidly boiling water and steam for 12 minutes. Cut rolls into 2½ cm (1 in) pieces with a sharp knife.

Heat oil for deep-frying in a wok until hot and fry five spice rolls until light golden brown.

Serve garnished with cucumber and tomato slices.

The five spice powder lends this dish its name as well as its distinctive aroma. This is a famous Teochew dish which my aunties cook to perfection during festivities.

Fish in Oyster Sauce

600 gms (21 oz) garoupa or threadfin
Oil for deep-frying
2 tablespoons cooking oil
6 cloves garlic
3 dried Chinese mushrooms, soaked and sliced
10 slices carrot, parboiled
1 stalk leek, cut into 5 cm (2 in) lengths
30 gms (1 oz) frozen green peas
1 red chilli, cut into strips
2 teaspoons cornflour mixed with 1 tablespoon water
1 stalk spring onion, chopped
1 sprig coriander leaves, chopped

Seasoning Ingredients

1½ teaspoons salt
1½ tablespoons cornflour
½ teaspoon pepper

Sauce Ingredients (combined)

1½ tablespoons oyster sauce
½ tablespoon light soya sauce
1 teaspoon Chinese rice wine
¼ teaspoon pepper
¼ teaspoon sesame oil
½ teaspoon salt
½ teaspoon thick soya sauce
¾ cup fresh chicken stock

Cut 2 diagonal slits across each side of the fish. Rub fish with seasoning ingredients.

Heat oil in a wok until very hot. Put in fish and deep-fry for 15 minutes until fish is cooked and golden. Drain and place on a serving dish.

Heat 2 tablespoons of oil in a clean wok and lightly brown garlic. Stir-fry mushrooms for 1 minute. Add carrot and leek and stir-fry for another minute.

Pour in combined sauce ingredients and bring to a quick boil. Put in peas and chilli strips.

Thicken with cornflour mixture and pour sauce over fish.

Serve hot garnished with spring onion and coriander leaves.

The Chinese prefer the fish cooked whole, rather than in parts and frozen fish simply won't do. Deep-frying in hot oil makes the crust crispy and delicious. Mixed vegetables and a simple sauce enhance the flavour of any fried fish.

Sea Bass with Spicy Black Vinegar Sauce

500–600 gms (17–21 oz) sea bass (*siakap*)
or any fresh water fish
1 teaspoon salt
1/2 teaspoon pepper
Cornflour for coating fish
3 tablespoons oil for deep-frying
2 tablespoons cooking oil
2 large cloves garlic
2 1/2 cm (1 in) piece fresh ginger root
1 red chilli
2 stalks spring onion
2 teaspoons cornflour mixed with 2 tablespoons
chicken stock or water

Sauce Ingredients (combined)
2/3 cup chicken stock
3/4 tablespoon light soya sauce
1/4 teaspoon thick soya sauce
60 gms sugar
2 tablespoons black vinegar
Pinch of salt

Use a sharp knife and deeply score both sides of the fish starting 4 cm (1 1/2 in) from the gill opening. Lightly cut a criss-cross pattern on the tail end.

Marinate fish with salt and pepper and set aside for 15 minutes. Coat fish with cornflour, making sure to coat the slits.

Heat 3 tablespoons of oil in a non-stick frying pan and fry fish on both sides, covered, until batter is crisp and golden brown (about 10 minutes). Place fish on serving dish.

Reheat pan with 2 tablespoons cooking oil. Add garlic and ginger and stir-fry for 20 seconds until fragrant. Stir in chilli and sauce ingredients and bring to a rapid boil.

Add the spring onions. Thicken with cornflour mixture and pour sauce over fish.

A sweet and sour fish dish. The black vinegar gives the fish a wonderful taste and aroma. *Illustrated on page 107.*

Crispy Prawn Fritters

600 gms (21 oz) large prawns
Oil for deep-frying

Seasoning Ingredients
1/2 teaspoon bicarbonate of soda
1/2 teaspoon salt
1 teaspoon sugar
1/2 an egg white
1 tablespoon cornflour
1 dessertspoon cooking oil

Batter Ingredients
120 gms (4 1/4 oz) self-raising flour
240 gms (8 1/2 oz) rice flour
1 1/2 teaspoons baking powder
1/2 teaspoon sugar
1/2 teaspoon salt
1 1/2 cups water
1/2 teaspoon Tabasco sauce

Sweet Sour Chilli Sauce (combined)
4 tablespoons chilli sauce
1 tablespoon tomato sauce
Juice of 5 small limes
2 tablespoons plum sauce
2 tablespoons sugar
1 dessertspoon A1 sauce
1/4 teaspoon salt
1 clove garlic, ground

Shell prawns and remove tails. De-vein and dry with a piece of kitchen paper or tea towel. Mix well with seasoning ingredients. Leave to marinate for 30 minutes.

To make batter, sift both kinds of flour and baking powder into a mixing bowl, add sugar, and salt. Make a well in the centre and gradually blend in water until batter is smooth. It should be slightly thick. Stir in Tabasco sauce.

Heat oil for deep-frying in a wok. Dip seasoned prawns in thick batter and deep-fry in hot oil until golden brown.

Drain on absorbent paper and arrange prawns on a serving dish.

Serve hot with sweet sour chilli sauce.

Seasoning the prawns with egg, cornflour, and oil is called "velveting," meaning to make it smoother. The prawns should be eaten as soon as they are cooked, although the rice flour in the batter will help to keep the prawns crispy for a while.

Butter Prawns with Toasted Coconut

500 gms (17 1/2 oz) large prawns, feelers trimmed
^{1} teaspoon salt
1/2 teaspoon pepper
Oil for deep-frying
90 gms (3 oz) butter
60 gms (2 oz) pan-toasted coconut, blended in electric blender
2 teaspoons sugar
10 chilli padi, finely sliced
Spring onion and coriander leaves, chopped
Juice of 1 small lime

Omelette

2 eggs, beaten
1 teaspoon light soya sauce
1/4 teaspoon salt
1/2 teaspoon pepper

Season prawns with 1/2 teaspoon salt and pepper for 30 minutes.

Make a thin omelette with the omelette ingredients and when it has cooled, chop finely. Set aside.

Heat oil for deep-frying and fry seasoned prawns until just cooked. Drain from oil.

Heat butter over low heat and put in toasted coconut, sugar, 1/2 teaspoon salt and chilli padi. Toss well until fragrant and add finely chopped omelette, spring onion, coriander leaves and lime juice.

Put in pre-fried prawns and toss until well-coated with omelette mixture. Serve hot.

Illustrated on page 108.

Paper Wrapped Prawns

8 king prawns, cleaned and towelled dry
8 grease-proof paper bags, folded to fit size of prawns
1/2 tablespoon cooking oil
Oil for deep-frying
Cucumber and tomato slices for garnishing

Seasoning Ingredients

1 tablespoon oyster sauce
1/2 tablespoon light soya sauce
1/2 tablespoon of brandy or Chinese rice wine
1 teaspoon ginger juice
1 teaspoon sesame oil
1/2 teaspoon sugar
1/2 teaspoon salt
1/2 teaspoon pepper
1/2 tablespoon cornflour
2–3 cloves garlic, minced
1 stalk spring onion, chopped
1 sprig coriander leaves, chopped

Trim prawn feelers and snip off the sharp points on the heads. Leave the shells intact. Remove entrails by piercing end of tails with a skewer. Lift and pull entrails out from the tail ends. Make a small slit in the back of the prawns with a sharp knife to allow seasonings to penetrate.

Marinate prawns with seasoning ingredients for at least 2 hours.

Grease the inside of the paper bags with a little cooking oil and push prawns into the bags, tail end first. Fold and staple the end.

Heat oil for deep-frying until hot and deep-fry packages for approximately 3 minutes or until prawns are cooked.

Drain in a colander and serve hot, garnished with cucumber and tomato slices.

Wrapped in paper and deep-fried the goodness of the prawns and the marinade is sealed in and retained. Finger bowls or wet towels are a nice idea to clean sticky fingers.

Prawn Balls

300 gms (10½ oz) medium-sized prawns, shelled and de-veined
1 loaf day-old white bread, cut into small 1 cm (⅓ in) cubes
Oil for deep-frying
Chilli sauce

Seasoning Ingredients
1 teaspoon light soya sauce
½ teaspoon sesame oil
¼ teaspoon salt
¼ teaspoon pepper
¼ teaspoon sugar
½ an egg white
1 teaspoon cornflour

Minced Ingredients
1 stalk spring onion
1 sprig coriander leaves
2 fresh water chestnuts

Dry prawns with a tea towel and marinate with seasoning ingredients. Stir in minced ingredients and refrigerate for 30 minutes.

Drop teaspoonfuls of seasoned prawn mixture onto bread cubes and form into bread-coated balls. Makes 24.

Deep-fry in hot oil over low heat until golden in colour.

Drain and serve with chilli sauce.

Ideal finger food for a cocktail party. Do not use fresh bread as it will absorb and retain too much oil when fried.

Vegetarian King Prawn Fritters

250 gms (8¾ oz), approximately ½ a small Chinese turnip (*sar kok*)
1 medium-sized carrot
4 dried Chinese mushrooms, soaked and shredded
1 piece firm white beancurd (*tau kwa*), cut into ½ cm (¼ in) thick pieces
1 large piece dried beancurd sheet, cut into 12 cm (4¾ in) squares and wiped with damp cloth
Oil for deep-frying
2 teaspoons tapioca flour mixed with 2 tablespoons water
Chilli sauce

Seasoning Ingredients
1 teaspoon salt
1 teaspoon sugar
¼ teaspoon pepper
1 teaspoon vegetarian oyster sauce
1 teaspoon Chinese rice wine
1 teaspoon sesame oil
1 teaspoon light soya sauce

Batter
120 gms (4¼ oz) self-raising flour
¾–1 cup water
½ teaspoon salt
¼ teaspoon pepper

Cut turnip and carrot into ½ x 10 cm (¼ x 4 in) strips. Boil carrot for 3–5 minutes. Drain well. Boil Chinese turnips for 1–2 minutes. Drain well.

Marinate carrot, Chinese turnip and mushrooms with seasoning ingredients for at least 30 minutes.

Deep-fry the beancurd strips in hot oil until light golden brown. Drain and set aside.

Spread tapioca paste on the edges of a small square piece of beancurd sheet. Place 2 strips each of turnip, carrot, mushrooms and fried beancurd diagonally across, a little off the centre. Roll up tightly like a Swiss roll, so they resemble prawns. Seal the ends with tapioca paste. Makes 20.

Just before deep-frying, dip into prepared batter. Deep-fry in hot oil until golden.

Serve with chilli sauce.

Vegetarian food need not be boring. The end result of this recipe looks like real prawns but without the cholesterol.

Fried Spicy Crispy Cuttlefish

600 gms (21 oz) small-sized cuttlefish
1/2 teaspoon pepper
1 tablespoon chilli or cooking oil

Sauce Ingredients (combined)
1 tablespoon sugar
1 tablespoon oyster sauce
3/4 tablespoon thick soya sauce
1/2 teaspoon pepper

Clean cuttlefish thoroughly and remove eyes and ink sacs. Cut the cuttlefish into 1 cm (1/3 in) circles and split the heads into two. If the tentacles are too long, trim into 5 cm (2 in) lengths. Place cuttlefish in a colander to drain well. Season with pepper for 30 minutes.

Heat oil in a wok until hot and deep-fry cuttlefish for 2 minutes or until just cooked. Drain from oil and allow to cool thoroughly.

Reheat oil in the same wok and fry cuttlefish over low–medium heat until golden brown and crisp. While frying, cover the wok as the water content in the cuttlefish could make the oil splatter violently. Stir occasionally to give cuttlefish an even colour. Drain from oil and allow to cool.

Heat wok with chilli or cooking oil until hot. Pour in combined sauce ingredients and immediately add the cuttlefish. Stir-fry quickly to coat thoroughly with sauce.

Dish out and serve immediately.

To make chilli oil, see recipe on page 20. If hard pressed for time, fried cuttlefish can be kept in an air-tight container until required. Stored in the refrigerator it will remain crispy for up to a week.

Vegetarian Crab Meat Balls

350 gms (12 1/2 oz) peeled yam, cut into small pieces
1 tablespoon non-glutinous rice flour (*tang meen fun*)
2 pieces 30 x 10 cm (12 x 4) dried beancurd sheets, wiped with a slightly damp towel
2 teaspoons tapioca flour mixed with 2 tablespoons water
Oil for deep-frying
Lettuce leaves
Chilli sauce

Seasoning Ingredients
1 teaspoon sugar
1/4 teaspoon pepper
3/4 teaspoon salt
1 tablespoon cooking oil

Minced Ingredients
50 gms (1 3/4 oz) carrot
3 dried Chinese mushrooms, soaked
1 red chilli
1 stalk spring onion
2 sprigs coriander leaves

Steam yam over rapidly boiling water for 15 minutes or until soft. Mash with a potato masher while still hot until fine.

Mix in non-glutinous flour and seasoning ingredients. Stir in minced ingredients and mix well. Divide equally into 2 portions.

Spread out the beancurd sheets and spread yam mixture lengthwise. Spread tapioca paste along the edges and roll up like a Swiss roll. Cut each roll into 9–10 slices with a greased knife.

Heat oil for deep-frying until hot. Deep-fry vegetarian meatballs until golden in colour, stirring with a perforated ladle.

Drain and arrange on a serving dish. Garnish with lettuce and serve with chilli sauce.

Illustrated on page 109. Check the quality of the yam by slicing a small piece off the tip. A good quality yam will leave a powdery residue on the knife.

Vegetarian Roast Goose

5 pieces thick dried beancurd sheets (*foo peh*)
Satay sticks
1 teaspoon honey mixed with 2 teaspoons water
Oil for deep-frying

Sauce Ingredients
1 piece preserved beancurd cube (*lam yee*) mixed in 1 cup water
1 tablespoon sugar
1 teaspoon light soya sauce
1 teaspoon pepper
1 teaspoon sesame oil

Wipe beancurd sheets carefully with a slightly damp cloth.

Combine the sauce ingredients. Brush each of the beancurd sheets with the sauce. Fold each sheet into three overlapping layers, brushing with more sauce on the surface to obtain a rectangle package approximately 12½ x 7½ cm (5 x 3 in).

Take a folded beancurd rectangle and thread with a sharp satay stick or skewer to hold the multiple layers together and to prevent it from unfolding when fried.

Steam over rapidly boiling water for 45 minutes. Cool and brush surface with honey mixture. Leave overnight in the refrigerator.

The next day, heat a wok with deep-frying oil until hot. Reduce heat and deep-fry each package separately until golden brown. Carefully remove the skewers and cut into serving size pieces.

Serve hot. Sufficient for 8 with 2 other dishes.

The Chinese try to make vegetarian food more interesting by imitating the texture of the meat. Although it is not that close there is a resemblance in appearance.

Dried Radish Omelette

3 eggs
1 stalk spring onion, chopped
45 gms (1½ oz) dried radish (*choy poh*), soaked for 10 minutes and finely chopped
2 tablespoons cooking oil
2 cloves garlic, minced

Seasoning Ingredients
1 teaspoon light soya sauce
½ teaspoon sugar
½ teaspoon sesame oil
¼ teaspoon pepper

Beat eggs well with a fork and add seasoning ingredients and spring onion. Mix well and set aside.

Drain the soaked radish and mince finely.

Heat a flat pan or wok with 1 tablespoon of the oil and stir-fry garlic and radish for 1–2 minutes over low heat. Remove and stir into egg mixture.

Heat pan or wok again with remaining oil until hot. Pour in the egg mixture and cook over low heat until slightly brown. Turn over and cook other side until slightly brown.

One of the dishes commonly served with porridge, but it goes well with rice too.

Egg Fu Yong

180 gms (6 1/3) shelled prawns, diced
2 teaspoons light soya sauce
1/2 teaspoon pepper
3 large eggs
1/4 teaspoon sugar
1/4 teaspoon salt
4 tablespoons cooking oil
3 dried Chinese mushrooms, soaked and shredded
2 slices ham or chicken, shredded
1 stalk spring onion, chopped
60 gms (2 oz) beansprouts, tailed
1 tablespoon frozen green peas

Sauce Ingredients (combined)
1/2 cup fresh chicken stock
1 teaspoon light soya sauce
1/4 teaspoon salt
1/4 teaspoon sugar
1/4 teaspoon pepper
1 teaspoon cornflour

Season prawns with 1 teaspoon soya sauce and 1/4 teaspoon pepper and set aside.

Break eggs into a separate bowl and add remaining soya sauce, remaining pepper, salt and sugar. Whisk with a fork until well combined.

Heat a flat pan or wok with 1 tablespoon of the oil until hot and stir-fry mushrooms for 1 minute. Add prawns and fry until they change colour. Remove and combine with beaten eggs, ham, spring onion and beansprouts. Mix well.

Reheat pan with 2 tablespoons oil until hot. Reduce heat and pour in 2–3 tablespoons of the egg mixture. Turn and cook egg pancake on the other side. Repeat procedure with the rest of the egg mixture, adding extra oil to pan if necessary. Arrange on serving dish.

Heat pan with 1 tablespoon of oil until hot and pour in combined sauce ingredients. Bring to the boil, add peas and simmer for 1 minute until sauce thickens.

Pour over eggs and serve.

Fu yong is the name of a flower belonging to the lotus family. The leaves are used as medicine. Egg Fu Yong is bright and colourful, just like the flower

Pan-Fried Gingers in Egg Batter

2 long purple brinjals with green stems
1/4 teaspoon sugar
1/4 teaspoon salt
1/4 teaspoon pepper
3 tablespoons cooking oil
Tomato and cucumber slices for garnishing

Egg Mixture (combined)
2 large eggs, beaten with a fork
1/4 teaspoon pepper
1/4 teaspoon salt
1 teaspoon sesame oil

Chopped Ingredients
1 red chilli, seeded
1 stalk spring onion
2 sprigs coriander leaves

Rinse the brinjals and place them whole into an oven or oven toaster. Grill, turning occasionally, until soft (about 8–10 minutes). Allow to cool and carefully peel off the skin, leaving the green stem ends intact.

Carefully lift the peeled brinjals and place on a plate. Using a fork, lightly press and flatten the brinjals. Season with sugar, salt and pepper.

Heat 3 tablespoons oil in a shallow saucepan. Holding the stem end of the brinjals, dip into egg mixture and carefully lower onto heated oil. Then pour half of the remaining egg mixture over the brinjals. Sprinkle half of the combined chopped ingredients on the brinjals.

After the brinjals turn golden brown, turn them over and pour in remaining egg mixture and chopped ingredients. Cook until golden.

Transfer to serving dish and garnish with tomato and cucumber slices.

STEAMED DISHES

Steamed Pork with Dried Shrimp Paste

300 gms (10½ oz) belly pork, skinned and cut into strips
1 teaspoon cornflour
1 teaspoon sugar
½ teaspoon pepper
½ teaspoon light soya sauce
5 cm (2 in) knob of ginger, shredded
3 cloves garlic, chopped
2 red chillies, chopped
5 cm (2 in) square piece dried shrimp paste (*belacan*)

Marinate pork with cornflour, sugar, pepper and light soya sauce. Spread shredded ginger, garlic and chillies over the surface and leave for 20 minutes.

Put dried shrimp paste in a dry wok and fry over low heat until dry and crumbly. Sprinkle the dried shrimp paste over the pork mixture.

Place dish in a steamer over rapidly boiling water and steam for 20 minutes.

Not a 100% Chinese dish, but an ingenious combination of Chinese and Malay food to turn out a very appetising dish with rice. Chicken can be used instead of pork.

Steamed Pork with Saltfish

180 gms (6⅓ oz) belly pork, skinned and coarsely minced
5 slices ginger, shredded
1 red chilli, sliced
Juice of 1 small lime
45 gms (1½ oz) saltfish (threadfin), thinly sliced

Seasoning Ingredients
¼ teaspoon pepper
½ teaspoon sugar
1 teaspoon sesame oil
½ teaspoon light soya sauce
1 teaspoon cornflour

Season pork with seasoning ingredients in a heat-proof dish. Mix in ginger, chilli and lime juice and leave for 30 minutes.

Spread saltfish on top of pork mixture and steam over rapidly boiling water for 15 minutes.

This slightly hot and sour dish is very appetising and the addition of saltfish means you will need to serve lots of rice with this dish. Pork can be substituted with chicken.

Steamed Pork with Pickled Vegetable

180 gms (6⅓ oz) minced lean pork with a little fat or belly pork
60 gms (2 oz) pickled vegetable (*tung choy*), minced
1 red chilli, minced
1 sprig coriander leaves for garnishing

Seasoning Ingredients
½ teaspoon sugar
¼ teaspoon pepper
1 teaspoon light soya sauce
2 teaspoons cornflour
2 tablespoons water

Mix minced pork together with *tung choy* and red chilli in a shallow heat-proof dish. Stir in seasoning ingredients and leave for 15 minutes.

Steam over rapidly boiling water for 12–15 minutes.

Serve garnished with coriander leaves.

A dish typically served with porridge but just as good with rice. Chicken can be used instead of pork.

Steamed Meat Balls Rolled in Omelette Strips

2 eggs
1/4 teaspoon salt
1/4 teaspoon pepper
500 gms (17 1/2 oz) minced pork or chicken
200 gms (7 oz) minced prawns
2 tablespoons cooking oil
1 teaspoon salt
8–9 small bunches Shanghai white cabbage (*siew pak choy*), kept whole
1 teaspoon Chinese rice wine

Seasoning Ingredients
1/2 teaspoon salt
1/2 teaspoon pepper
1/2 teaspoon sugar
1/2 teaspoon sesame oil
1 teaspoon light soya sauce
1 teaspoon fresh ginger juice
1 tablespoon cornflour

Finely Chopped Ingredients
3 water chestnuts
2 dried Chinese mushrooms, soaked
1 red chilli
1 stalk spring onion

Sauce Ingredients (combined)
3/4 cup fresh chicken stock
1/3 teaspoon salt
1/4 teaspoon pepper
1 teaspoon cornflour

Beat eggs with salt and pepper. Lightly grease a heated wok and make thin omelettes with egg mixture. Cool and cut into thin strips.

Combine minced pork or chicken and prawns and stir in seasoning ingredients. Lift mixture with the hand and throw forcefully into a bowl continuously for 1 minute. This procedure makes the meat paste firm and smooth.

Stir finely chopped ingredients into mixture and refrigerate for 30 minutes.

Shape mixture into golf-sized balls with slightly wet hands. Roll and coat the meat balls with omelette strips. Place on a greased oven-proof dish and steam over rapidly boiling water for 10 minutes.

Drain liquid from dish and use with chicken stock to make 3/4 cup of required stock for the sauce.

Bring a saucepan of water to the boil. Add 1 tablespoon of oil and salt. Blanch the cabbage for 1–2 minutes. Drain and arrange around the meat balls.

Heat a wok until hot with 1 tablespoon of oil and add rice wine. Immediately pour in combined sauce ingredients and bring to the boil. When sauce thickens, pour over the meat balls and vegetables.

This tasty meat ball dish is a popular Dim Sum dish.

Steamed Meat Balls with Hair Vegetable

500 gms (17½ oz) minced lean pork with a little fat
60 gms (2 oz) carrots, finely minced
3 water chestnuts, minced
2 slices ham, minced
8 gms (¼ oz) hair vegetable (*fatt choy*), soaked and chopped
1 stalk spring onion, chopped
1 red chilli, seeded and chopped

Seasoning Ingredients
1 egg
½ teaspoon salt
½ teaspoon sugar
½ teaspoon pepper
½ teaspoon sesame oil
1 teaspoon light soya sauce
1 teaspoon Chinese rice wine
1 tablespoon cornflour

Combine minced pork, carrots and water chestnuts with ham, hair vegetable, spring onion and chilli.

Throw mixture against a board or bowl continuously for 1 minute to improve the texture of the meat.

Form mixture into golf-sized balls and arrange on a greased heat-proof dish.

Steam over rapidly boiling water for 12–15 minutes.

Serve with chilli sauce, red vinegar dip or ginger vinegar dip.

The pork and ham can be substituted with chicken. Red vinegar dip is Chinese red rice vinegar used directly from the bottle. To make ginger vinegar dip, heat 2 tablespoons of white or red vinegar gently and stir in 1 teaspoon of sugar until it dissolves. Pour over 5 thin slices of ginger which have been finely shredded and leave overnight before using as a dip.

Steamed Pork with Yam (*Kao Yok*)

600 gms (21 oz) belly pork
2 teaspoons light soya sauce
Pinch of pepper
Oil for deep-frying
½ a medium-sized yam, cut into 4 x 6 cm (1½ x 2⅓ in) slices

Sauce Ingredients
1 cube preserved beancurd (*lam yee*), mashed with a spoon
1 teaspoon five spice powder
½ teaspoon sugar
1 tablespoon light soya sauce
½ tablespoon thick soya sauce

Bring a wok or saucepan of water to the boil and blanch the pork for 5 minutes. Drain well and prick the skin and the meat with a fork to enable seasonings to penetrate.

Marinate pork with light soya sauce and pepper for 30 minutes.

Heat oil in the wok until hot and deep-fry yam slices until lightly browned. Drain from oil and set aside.

Put in the seasoned pork and deep-fry until lightly browned. Remove from oil and let the pork cool. Cut into 1 cm (⅓ in) thick slices.

In a heat-proof dish or bowl, arrange the pork alternating with yam in a circle to fill the dish. Pour the combined sauce ingredients over the pork and yam.

Place in a steamer over rapidly boiling water and steam for 1¼ hours until pork is very tender.

A famous and popular Cantonese dish. If well made, the tender pork will practically melt in the mouth.

Steamed Pork Leg with Szechuan Vegetable

1 pork leg, $^4/_5$–1 kg ($^1/_3$–$^1/_2$ lb), de-boned
1 tablespoon light soya sauce
$^1/_2$ teaspoon pepper
$^1/_2$ teaspoon salt
1 tablespoon thick soya sauce
Oil for deep-frying
1 piece (60 gms, 2 oz) Szechuan vegetable (*char choy*), soaked for 30 minutes and shredded
3 slices ginger
2 red chillies, seeded and sliced
2 teaspoons cornflour mixed with 1 tablespoon pork stock
2 stalks spring onion, chopped

Sauce Ingredients

1 tablespoon fermented black beans, soaked in water for 10 minutes and drained
1 tablespoon light soya sauce
2 tablespoons Chinese rice wine
$^1/_2$ tablespoon sugar

Marinate pork leg with light soya sauce, salt and pepper for 30 minutes. Put pork leg into a large saucepan and add enough water to cover pork. Bring to the boil and simmer over low heat for 1–1$^1/_2$ hours.

Drain pork leg and wipe dry with kitchen paper. Rub with 1 tablespoon thick soya sauce. Reserve the pork stock for thickening solution.

Heat oil in a wok for deep-frying until hot and deep-fry the pork leg for 5 minutes or until the skin is dark brown. Remove and after cooling for a little while cut into thick slices and arrange on a heat-proof dish.

Spread the Szechuan vegetable, ginger and chillies on top of the pork. Pour combined sauce ingredients down the side of the dish.

Steam over rapidly boiling water for 1 hour until pork is completely tender.

Carefully strain liquid from dish into a saucepan and bring to the boil. Thicken with cornflour mixture and pour over pork.

Serve sprinkled with spring onions.

This procedure requires some effort but the result is well worth the trouble. Choose the meatier hind legs for this recipe.

Steamed Pork Ribs with Preserved Black Beans

300 gms (10$^1/_2$ oz) pork ribs, cut into 4 cm (1$^1/_2$ in) pieces
2 teaspoons preserved black beans, soaked in water for 10 minutes, rinsed and drained
2 small pickled sour plums
1 red chilli, minced
2 cloves garlic, minced
1 stalk spring onion, chopped

Seasoning Ingredients

1 teaspoon sugar
$^1/_4$ teaspoon pepper
$^1/_2$ teaspoon light soya sauce
1 teaspoon cornflour

Marinate pork ribs with seasoning ingredients and mix in the black beans, sour plums, chilli and garlic. Leave to stand for 2 hours.

Mix well again just before steaming and place over rapidly boiling water for 40 minutes until pork ribs are tender.

Serve sprinkled with chopped onions.

A very popular Dim Sum dish that can also be served as a main course with rice.

Steamed Boneless Chicken with Ham

2 chicken thighs, cleaned and de-boned
1 tablespoon cooking oil
1 teaspoon salt
1 teaspoon sugar
2–3 whole stalks mustard green, washed
120 gms (4¼ oz) ham slices, cut into 2 x 4 cm (¾ x 1½ in) pieces
½ tablespoon cornflour mixed with 1 tablespoon water

Seasoning Ingredients

1 teaspoon salt
½ teaspoon sugar
2 teaspoons light soya sauce
½ teaspoon sesame oil
¼ teaspoon pepper
2 tablespoons water
1 tablespoon cornflour
1 tablespoon cooking oil

Sauce Ingredients (combined)

1 cup fresh chicken stock or water
½ teaspoon salt
½ teaspoon sugar
1 teaspoon light soya sauce
1 teaspoon oyster sauce
½ teaspoon sesame oil
¼ teaspoon pepper

Using the blunt edge of a cleaver, lightly pound chicken. Marinate with seasoning ingredients and leave for 30 minutes.

Put marinated chicken on a clean board and cut each piece into 2 lengthwise and then into 2½ cm (1 in) slices. Brush a little oil onto a heat-proof dish and arrange chicken neatly in 4 rows.

Place in steamer and steam chicken over rapidly boiling water for 12 minutes.

Meanwhile bring water to boil in a saucepan. Put in oil, salt and sugar. Put in mustard green and boil until just cooked. Drain immediately.

Remove chicken from steamer and carefully pour the gravy on the dish into combined sauce ingredients. Arrange mustard green around the edge of the chicken and place ham strips on top of each piece of chicken.

In a clean saucepan, bring sauce ingredients to the boil. Thicken with cornflour mixture, then pour gravy over ham and chicken.

The aroma of ham goes well with steamed chicken. Mustard green can be substituted with kale but use only the tender shoots.

Steamed Chicken with Mushrooms on Lotus Leaf

2 whole chicken thighs or 6 chicken wings, cut into 2 cm (¾ in) pieces
4 dried Chinese mushrooms, soaked and halved
1 small piece cloud ear fungus, soaked, hard centre trimmed off, cut into 1 cm (⅓ in) pieces
8 slices ginger, shredded
1 red chilli, seeded and sliced
2 stalks spring onion, chopped
1 fresh lotus leaf, washed and wiped dry
1 teaspoon cooking oil
1 tablespoon fried shallot crisps

Seasoning Ingredients

2 teaspoons light soya sauce
1 teaspoon Chinese rice wine
1 teaspoon sesame oil
½ teaspoon sugar
½ teaspoon pepper
½ teaspoon salt
2 teaspoons cornflour
1 tablespoon cooking oil

Marinate chicken, mushrooms and cloud ear fungus with seasoning ingredients, ginger, chilli and spring onion. Set aside for 30 minutes.

Trim lotus leaf to fit a heat-proof dish. Brush with oil and line the dish. Put in marinated ingredients.

Steam over rapidly boiling water for 15 minutes.

Serve sprinkled with shallot crisps.

If fresh lotus leaf is not available, substitute with dried lotus leaf. Trim the leaf to fit the dish and soak in water until soft. *Illustrated on page 110.*

Steamed Chicken with Chinese Broccoli

2 whole chicken thighs or 1/2 a chicken, cleaned
1 tablespoon fresh ginger juice
1 1/4 teaspoons salt
2 tablespoons sesame oil
1 tablespoon cooking oil
2–3 stalks Chinese broccoli (*kai lan*), tough stems discarded and remaining stems cut in 2
2 sprigs coriander leaves

Sauce Ingredients (combined)

1 tablespoon cooking oil
1/2 tablespoon sesame oil
1 shallot, sliced
1 1/2 tablespoons oyster sauce
1 1/2 tablespoons light soya sauce

Place chicken on a heat-proof dish and marinate with ginger juice and 1 teaspoon salt for 30 minutes.

Steam chicken over rapidly boiling water for 20 minutes or until just cooked through.

Remove from the steamer and rub with sesame oil while still hot. Cool and cut into serving size pieces and arrange neatly on a serving dish.

Heat cooking oil in a wok and add 1/4 teaspoon salt. Add water and bring to the boil. Blanch the Chinese broccoli for 2 minutes, then remove and plunge into cold water. Drain well and arrange around the chicken.

To make the sauce, reheat a clean wok with 1 tablespoon cooking oil and 1/2 tablespoon sesame oil and lightly brown shallots. Turn off the flame and stir in oyster and light soya sauces.

Pour sauce over chicken and vegetable and garnish with coriander leaves.

A good wholesome meal that is ideal if you are hard pressed for time.

Steamed Chicken Wings with Chinese Mushrooms

12 chicken wings, cut into two sections at the joints, cleaned and drained
2–3 dried Chinese mushrooms, soaked and shredded
2 red chillies, seeded and sliced
1 sprig coriander leaves, chopped
1 stalk spring onion, chopped

Seasoning Ingredients

1 tablespoon light soya sauce
1 tablespoon oyster sauce
2 teaspoons cornflour
1 teaspoon sugar
1 teaspoon thick soya sauce
1/2 teaspoon salt
1/4 teaspoon pepper
2 1/2 cm (1 in) piece ginger, minced

Marinate chicken wings with seasoning ingredients for 1 hour.

Place on a heat-proof dish and sprinkle with mushrooms and chillies

Steam over rapidly boiling water for 12 minutes.

Serve hot garnished with coriander leaves and spring onion.

Perfect for people on the go, this dish is quick and easy to prepare. Soak the mushrooms and marinate the chicken before you go out. When you come home you'll have dinner on the table within 12 minutes.

Steamed Stuffed Chicken Wings

10 chicken wings, wing tips discarded, cleaned and drained
3/4 teaspoon salt
1 tablespoon cooking oil
2–3 stalks mustard green, cut into 2
1 stalk spring onion, chopped
1 sprig coriander leaves, chopped

Stuffing Ingredients (shredded)
2 dried Chinese mushrooms, soaked
2 water chestnuts
60 gms (2 oz) ham
1 piece dried scallop, steamed

Seasoning Ingredients
1/4 teaspoon salt
1/4 teaspoon pepper
1/4 teaspoon sugar
1/2 teaspoon sesame oil

Sauce Ingredients (combined)
1 cup fresh chicken stock
1/2 teaspoon salt
1/4 teaspoon pepper
1/2 teaspoon sugar
1 teaspoon oyster sauce
1 teaspoon light soya sauce
1/2 teaspoon thick soya sauce
1/2 teaspoon sesame oil
2 teaspoons cornflour

Season chicken wings with 1/2 teaspoon salt and leave for 15 minutes.

Bring a saucepan of water to the boil and scald the chicken wings for 5 minutes.

Drain, cool and cut each wing into 2 at the joints. De-bone each section carefully. Set aside the saucepan of boiled water for scalding the mustard green.

Season shredded stuffing ingredients with seasoning ingredients. Divide into 20 portions and carefully stuff each de-boned wing. Arrange on a heat-proof dish and steam over rapidly boiling water for 15 minutes.

Bring the saucepan of water to the boil again. Add oil and 1/4 teaspoon salt and blanch the mustard green for 2 minutes. Drain and arrange around the chicken.

Put combined sauce ingredients in the wok and bring to the boil. Stir until sauce thickens and pour over chicken wings and mustard green.

Serve garnished with spring onion and coriander leaves.

The stuffing can be varied by substituting the water chestnuts, ham and dried scallop with 60 gms (2 oz) bamboo shoots, 1 Chinese sausage (sliced) and 60 gms (2 oz) canned abalone.

Steamed Chicken with Oyster Sauce

1 whole chicken thigh and drumstick, cut into 1 1/4 cm (1/2 in) pieces
4 dried Chinese mushrooms, soaked and quartered
2 tablespoons cooking oil
4 shallots, sliced

Seasoning Ingredients
1 clove garlic, sliced
1 1/4 cm piece ginger, shredded
1 red chilli, sliced
1/2 tablespoon preserved soya bean paste
1 tablespoon oyster sauce
2 teaspoons sesame oil
1 teaspoon Chinese rice wine
1 teaspoon sugar
1/4 teaspoon salt
1 teaspoon cornflour
1 egg white, beaten

Marinate chicken and mushrooms with seasoning ingredients in a heat-proof dish for 30 minutes.

Heat oil in a wok and stir-fry shallots until lightly browned. Stir shallot crisps and oil into chicken and mushroom mixture.

Steam over rapidly boiling water for 20 minutes.

Serve this dish with rice and a vegetable for a nutritious and wholesome meal.

Steamed Pomfret with Mushrooms

1 Chinese pomfret (*tau tai cheong*)
or white pomfret (*pak cheong*),
approximately 600–720 gms (21–25 oz)
1 1/2 tablespoons cooking oil
2 tablespoons fresh chicken stock or water
3 dried Chinese mushrooms,
soaked and shredded
4 cm (1 1/2 in) ginger, shredded
1 red chilli, cut into strips
2 stalks spring onion,
cut into 4 cm (1 1/2 in) lengths
2 sprigs coriander leaves,
cut into 4 cm (1 1/2 in) lengths
1 tablespoon fried shallot crisps

Seasoning Ingredients

1 teaspoon salt
1 teaspoon sugar
1 teaspoon light soya sauce
1 teaspoon sesame oil

Clean fish and trim the fins and tail. Make 2 diagonal cuts across each side of the body and marinate with seasoning ingredients for 20–30 minutes.

Just before steaming fish, combine oil and stock and pour over fish. Spread shredded mushrooms, ginger and chilli on the surface of the fish.

Steam over rapidly boiling water for 15 minutes.

Serve hot, garnished with spring onion, coriander leaves and shallot crisps.

The Chinese are always in favour of steaming fish with a smooth texture, like the pomfret, to retain its natural flavour. Timing is essential in steaming so as not to spoil the texture, and the fish must be absolutely fresh. The garoupa and sea bass are also popular.

Steamed Fish with Pickled Sour Plums

1 fish (pomfret, threadfin or garoupa),
approximately 600–720 gms (21–25 oz)
1 1/2 teaspoons salt
1 teaspoon pepper
120 gms (4 1/4 oz) salted green stems (*harm choy*),
soaked for 30 minutes and shredded
4 dried Chinese mushrooms,
soaked until soft and shredded
90 gms (3 oz) pork or chicken, cut into strips
4 cm (1 1/2 in) ginger, shredded
2 red chillies, seeded and cut into strips
2 pickled sour plums (*sheen mui*)
1 teaspoon sesame oil
1/2 cup water
3 tablespoons cooking oil
3–4 shallots, sliced
2 stalks spring onion, cut into 5 cm (2 in) lengths
2 sprigs coriander leaves,
cut into 5 cm (2 in) lengths

Clean fish thoroughly and rub with salt and pepper. Place on a heat-proof dish.

Spread salted green stems, mushrooms, chicken or pork, ginger and chillies over fish.

Lightly squeeze sour plums over the fish and place beside fish. Add sesame oil and water and place in a steamer over rapidly boiling water. Steam for 15 minutes.

Meanwhile, heat oil in a wok until hot and fry shallots until lightly browned. When fish is cooked, pour oil and shallots over fish.

Serve garnished with spring onion and coriander leaves.

This is the popular Teochew style of steaming fish. The result is a soupy dish with a tangy flavour. Illustrated on page 111.

Steamed Garlic Fish

1 pomfret, approximately
600–750 gms (21–26½ oz)
2 tablespoons oil
4–6 dried Chinese mushrooms, soaked and finely chopped
1 red chilli, seeded and finely minced
6–8 cloves garlic, finely sliced
1 stalk spring onion, chopped
2 sprigs coriander leaves, chopped
300 gms (10½ oz) rice vermicelli (*mai fun*), scalded

Seasoning Ingredients
1 teaspoon salt
½ teaspoon sugar
¼ teaspoon pepper

Sauce Ingredients (combined)
1 cup chicken stock
2½ tablespoons light soya sauce
½ tablespoon thick soya sauce
1 teaspoon sesame oil

Marinate fish with seasoning ingredients for 15–30 minutes.

Heat oil in frying pan and stir-fry minced mushrooms for 1 minute until fragrant. Put in chilli and half the garlic, and stir-fry until golden brown.

Dish out into combined sauce ingredients. Stir in remaining garlic and pour over fish.

Steam over rapidly boiling water for 12–15 minutes.

Garnish with spring onion and coriander leaves and serve with scalded *mai fun* or rice.

One of my favourite steamed fish dishes which has never failed to earn compliments from my guests. The natural flavour of the fish is enhanced by the mushrooms and garlic. You will not be able to resist drinking the delicious gravy as a soup.

Steamed Fish Bladders Topped with Prawns

75 gms (2⅔ oz) dried fish bladders
Oil for deep-frying
1 teaspoon alkaline water
1 kg prawns (2⅕ lbs), shelled and minced
2 egg whites
½ teaspoon salt
¼ teaspoon pepper
Crab roe or minced carrot
1 tablespoon cooking oil
1 dessertspoon Chinese rice wine
240 gms (8½ oz) crab meat
8–10 button mushrooms, sliced
10 snow peas or 90 gms (3 oz) peas
2 sprigs coriander leaves

Sauce Ingredients (combined)
1 cup fresh chicken stock
½ teaspoon salt
¼ teaspoon pepper
1 teaspoon cornflour

Dry fish bladders in the sun for 1 hour and deep-fry until puffy. Soak in a basin of water until soft. As fish bladders are light, it is necessary to weigh them down.

Drain and cut into matchbox-sized pieces. Add alkaline water and mix well, then wash thoroughly with water. Squeeze dry and leave aside. Hard pieces, if any, should be discarded.

Season prawns with 1 egg white, salt and pepper and beat with a spoon until mixture is sticky.

Spread a spoonful of minced prawns over each piece of fish bladder. Top with a little crab roe. If this is not available, substitute with a little minced carrot.

Steam fish bladders in a steamer for 12 minutes.

Heat 1 tablespoon oil in a wok, add rice wine, then put in crab meat, mushrooms, snow peas or peas and stir-fry for 1–2 minutes. Add sauce ingredients and bring to the boil. As soon as it thickens, spoon half of the sauce over fish bladders.

Stir 1 beaten egg white into remaining gravy and when it boils again, pour over fish bladders.

Garnish with coriander leaves and serve hot.

Fish bladder does not come cheap and although bland in taste it has a unique texture ideal for soups. This dish can be served as a Dim Sum or main course.

Steamed Cuttlefish Rings

4 large cuttlefish, remove heads, entrails and side flaps
6 salted duck egg yolks
3 pieces Japanese dried seaweed sheets (*nori*), 22 x 19 cm ($8\frac{2}{3}$ x $7\frac{1}{2}$ in)
4 pointed wooden cocktail sticks
2 tablespoons Japanese soya sauce
2 teaspoons Japanese horseradish (*wasabi*)
2 tablespoons light soya sauce
10 chilli padi, chopped

Rinse the cuttlefish and pat dry with kitchen paper.

Lightly grease a plastic sheet and place 3 duck egg yolks in the centre. Roll out into a neat rectangle to fit $\frac{1}{3}$ of a *nori* sheet. Turn flattened yolk onto one end of a *nori* sheet and remove plastic sheet.

Cut 1 piece of *nori* sheet into two and place one half on top of egg yolk. Roll up from the egg side like Swiss roll and cut into two. Repeat with remaining 3 duck egg yolks.

Stuff each cuttlefish with a duck egg roll. Secure the open end with a small cocktail stick.

Place on a bamboo or wire rack and steam over rapidly boiling water for 10 minutes.

When cool, slice each cuttlefish into 4 or 5 pieces. Serve with Japanese soya sauce and *wasabi* or light soya sauce and *chilli padi* dip.

A combination of Chinese and Japanese ideal for buffet entertaining. The dish can be prepared well ahead and stored uncut in the refrigerator until required.

Steamed Oysters

8 fresh large oysters
3 tablespoons cooking oil
2 shallots, sliced
2 teaspoons fermented black beans, soaked 10 minutes, rinsed, drained and chopped
1 tablespoon oyster sauce
$2\frac{1}{2}$ cm (1 in) piece ginger, finely chopped
1 red chilli, sliced
1 green chilli, sliced
1 spring onion, finely chopped

Scrub oysters under running tap water to remove the sand. Discard dead oysters that are open and remain open when tapped. Insert an oyster knife into the hinge between the shells and cut through the ligament. Prise the shells apart carefully by twisting with the knife to separate them. Cut the oyster free from the shells and leave in the bigger shell. Discard the other shell. Rinse off any pieces of broken shell. Arrange the shells with the oysters on a large heat-proof dish and set aside.

Heat oil in a wok and lightly brown shallots. Drain from the oil and set aside.

Stir-fry fermented black beans over low heat for 1 minute. Turn off the heat and stir in the oyster sauce.

Spoon the fermented black beans and oyster sauce mixture on each of the oysters and sprinkle with ginger and red and green chillies.

Steam oysters over rapidly boiling water for 12 minutes.

Sprinkle with shallot crisps and spring onion and serve hot.

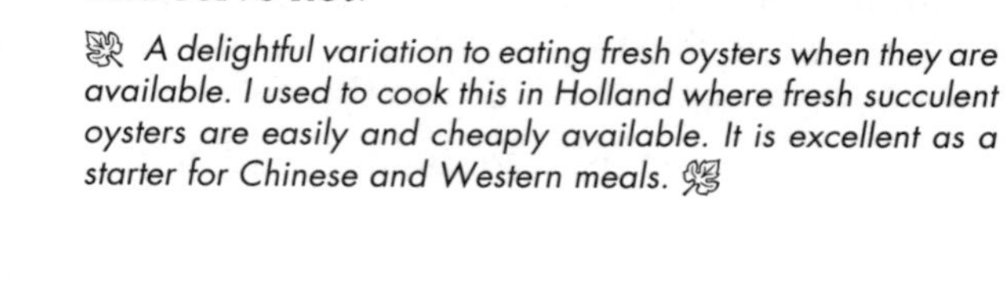

A delightful variation to eating fresh oysters when they are available. I used to cook this in Holland where fresh succulent oysters are easily and cheaply available. It is excellent as a starter for Chinese and Western meals.

Steamed Prawns and Asparagus Rolls

300 gms (10½ oz) small prawns, shelled and rinsed, minced
150 gms (5¼ oz) fat and lean pork or chicken, minced
60 gms (2 oz) carrot, finely diced and scalded in boiling water for 5 minutes
2 water chestnuts, finely diced
1 red chilli, chopped
1 stalk spring onion, chopped
12 large or 24 small fresh asparagus tips approximately 10 cm (4 in) long
2 eggs, made into thin omelettes, finely shredded or chopped ham
1 tablespoon cooking oil
1 teaspoon Chinese rice wine

Seasoning Ingredients

½ teaspoon salt
½ teaspoon sugar
¼ teaspoon pepper
1 teaspoon light soya sauce
½ teaspoon Chinese rice wine
¼ teaspoon sesame oil
2 teaspoons cooking oil, to be added last

Sauce Ingredients

½ cup fresh chicken stock
1 teaspoon light soya sauce
¼ teaspoon thick soya sauce
½ teaspoon salt
¼ teaspoon pepper
¼ teaspoon sugar
1 teaspoon cornflour

Combine prawns and pork or chicken with carrots, water chestnuts, chilli and onion. Add seasoning and mix well. Stir in the oil.

Throw mixture against a chopping board or into a bowl continuously for 1 minute to improve the texture of the mixture. Refrigerate for 30 minutes.

Divide the mixture into 12 portions. With lightly greased hands, wrap meat mixture around the asparagus. Allow the ends to protrude a little. Roll and coat with omelette strips or for variation top with finely chopped ham.

Arrange asparagus roll on a greased heat-proof dish and steam over rapidly boiling water for 8 minutes.

Meanwhile, heat oil in a wok and when hot add wine. Add combined sauce ingredients and stir until sauce thickens.

Pour over steamed asparagus rolls and serve.

The thicker type of asparagus is preferred for this dish because it has more flavour. Illustrated on page 112.

Steamed Prawns with Garlic Sauce

300 gms (10½ oz) large–medium-sized prawns with shells
1 tablespoon cooking oil
6 cloves garlic, minced
1 red chilli, minced
2 stalks spring onion, chopped

Seasoning Ingredients

½ tablespoon fresh ginger juice
1 tablespoon Chinese rice wine
1 tablespoon light soya sauce
½ teaspoon sesame oil
¼ teaspoon salt
¼ teaspoon pepper
½ teaspoon sugar
1 tablespoon cooking oil

Trim the heads and feelers of the prawns. Devein and make a small slit with a sharp knife on the underside of each prawn to allow the marinade to penetrate. Season with the seasoning ingredients on a heat-proof dish and leave aside for 15 minutes.

Steam prawns over rapidly boiling water for 8–10 minutes.

Heat 1 tablespoon of the oil in a wok until hot and lightly brown garlic. Turn off the heat, stir in the chilli and spring onions. Pour garlic sauce over the prawns and serve.

This is quick to prepare and perfect for family dining. Serve with vegetables and rice.

Steamed Prawn Wrapped in Wantan Skin

300 gms (10½ oz) shelled prawns, coarsely minced
200 gms (7 oz) fat and lean pork or chicken, finely minced
5 water chestnuts, chopped
1 tablespoon chopped spring onion
1 tablespoon chopped coriander leaves
24 medium-sized prawns, shelled, de-veined with tails left on
¼ teaspoon pepper
¼ teaspoon sugar
¼ teaspoon salt
48–50 *wantan* skins
1 egg white, beaten
Chilli sauce

Seasoning Ingredients

½ tablespoon Chinese rice wine
½ tablespoon sesame oil
1 tablespoon cornflour
1 teaspoon sugar
¾ teaspoon salt
½ teaspoon pepper

Mix chopped prawns and pork or chicken with water chestnuts, spring onion and coriander, and stir in seasoning ingredients. Leave for 30 minutes.

Season the whole prawns with pepper, sugar and salt for 15 minutes.

Put 1 teaspoon of minced mixture in the centre of the wantan skin. Place a prawn on top of the filling. Brush one side of another piece of wantan with a little egg white and place it on top of the prawn with the brushed side down. Wrap the two skins around the filling and prawn, and let the tail of the prawn stick out. Repeat procedure to obtain 24–25 wrappings.

Place the wrappings on lightly greased bamboo baskets and steamed over rapidly boiling water for 10 minutes.

Remove and serve with chilli sauce.

This dish is a delight to the eye as well as to the palate. Wantan skins keep well in an air-tight container in the refrigerator for up to a week.

Steamed Stuffed Cucumbers

1 large cucumber, skinned and cut into 3 cm (1¼ in) rounds
½ teaspoon salt
90 gms (3 oz) pork or chicken, minced
60 gms (2 oz) prawns, minced
1 dried Chinese mushroom, soaked and finely chopped
1 red chilli, seeded and finely chopped
1 tablespoon cornflour for dusting cucumber
1 teaspoon cornflour mixed with 1 tablespoon chicken stock or water

Seasoning Ingredients

½ teaspoon salt
¼ teaspoon sugar
¼ teaspoon pepper
1 teaspoon light soya sauce
½ teaspoon sesame oil
1 teaspoon cornflour

Scoop out the centre of the cucumber rounds. Rub with salt and place on a heat-proof serving dish.

Combine minced pork or chicken and prawns with mushrooms, chillies and seasoning ingredients. Mix well.

Dust the inside of the hollowed cucumber pieces with cornflour and stuff them with the meat mixture.

Steam over rapidly boiling water for 25–30 minutes.

Remove from steamer and drain gravy from the dish into a saucepan and bring to the boil.

Thicken with cornflour mixture and pour over the cucumber pieces.

A great vegetable dish with rice. For more 'crunch' add 1 or 2 fresh minced water chestnuts to stuffing mixture.

Steamed Stuffed Cabbage

10 large pieces cabbage, rinsed
1 teaspoon salt
1/2 tablespoon plain flour mixed with 1 tablespoon water
1 tablespoon cooking oil
1 teaspoon Chinese rice wine
1 sprig coriander leaves

Minced Ingredients (combined)
150 gms (5 1/4 oz) pork or chicken
120 gms (4 1/4 oz) prawns
5 water chestnuts
2 dried Chinese mushrooms
1 stalk spring onion

Seasoning Ingredients
1/2 teaspoon salt
1/2 teaspoon pepper
1/2 teaspoon sesame oil
1 teaspoon light soya sauce
1 teaspoon cornflour

Sauce Ingredients (combined)
1/2 cup fresh chicken stock
1/2 teaspoon salt
1/2 teaspoon pepper
1/2 teaspoon sugar
1/2 teaspoon sesame oil
1 teaspoon light soya sauce
1 teaspoon Chinese rice wine
1 teaspoon cornflour

Boil cabbage leaves in a large saucepan of boiling water with salt for 5–6 minutes until soft. Drain and set aside to cool.

Marinate combined minced ingredients with seasoning ingredients and leave for 10 minutes.

Divide meat mixture into 10 portions. Place each portion in the centre of a cabbage leaf and wrap like a spring roll. Seal the edges with a little flour paste.

Arrange cabbage rolls on a heat-proof dish and brush with oil. Place over rapidly boiling water and steam for 12 minutes.

Remove from steamer and drain gravy from the dish and add to combined sauce ingredients.

Heat oil in a wok until hot and sprinkle in rice wine. Pour in sauce ingredients and bring to the boil. Simmer over low heat for 2 minutes and pour over cabbage.

Serve garnished with coriander leaves.

Wrapping is easier once the cabbage has been blanched and softened.

Steamed Mushrooms with Shanghai White Cabbage

10–12 dried Chinese mushrooms, soaked until soft
5 tablespoons cooking oil
1/2 tablespoon sesame oil
1/2 cup water
300 gms (10 1/2 oz) Shanghai white cabbage (*siew pak choy*)
1 teaspoon salt
2 shallots, sliced
2 cloves garlic, minced
1/2 teaspoon sugar
1 tablespoon light soya sauce

Seasoning Ingredients
1/4 teaspoon salt
1/4 teaspoon pepper
1/2 teaspoon salt
1/2 teaspoon light soya sauce
1/2 teaspoon oyster sauce
1/2 teaspoon Chinese rice wine
1 clove garlic, smashed

Lightly squeeze out the water from the soaked mushrooms and marinate with seasoning ingredients for at least 1 hour or overnight in the refrigerator.

Place seasoned mushrooms in a heat-proof dish and stir in combined 2 tablespoons cooking oil, sesame oil, and water.

Steam over rapidly boiling water for 30 minutes.

If using large bunches of Shanghai white cabbage, halve them lengthwise. Scald in boiling water with salt and 1 tablespoon of the oil for 1–2 minutes. Drain and arrange around the mushrooms.

Heat remaining 2 tablespoons of the oil in a wok until hot and lightly brown shallots and garlic. Add sugar and light soya sauce and immediately pour over vegetables.

Illustrated on page 137. First grade dried Chinese mushrooms should be used for this dish. Choose large ones with a light brownish-black colour and a highly cracked surface.

Steamed Mushrooms with Shanghai White Cabbage
Page 136

Steamed Mushrooms with Prawn Filling
Page 145

Steamed Ginger Brinjals
Page 145

Steamed Herbal Winter Melon Soup
Page 152

Steamed White Fungus and Rock Sugar in Coconut
Page 153

Gingko Nut and Water Chestnut Desset
Page 153

Braised Pork Ribs with Sea Cucumbers
Page 157

Braised Pot Pourri
Page 158

Steamed Mushrooms with Prawn Filling

3 tablespoons cooking oil
12 dried Chinese mushrooms, soaked until soft and drained
300 gms (10½ oz) prawns, shelled, de-veined and minced
2 water chestnuts, minced
1 Chinese sausage, sliced, optional
12 green peas
½ an egg white, beaten

Sauce Ingredients 'A' (combined)

1 cup fresh chicken stock
½ teaspoon salt
½ teaspoon pepper
½ teaspoon sugar
1 teaspoon sesame oil
1 teaspoon oyster sauce

Seasoning Ingredients

¼ teaspoon salt
¼ teaspoon pepper
¼ teaspoon sugar
1 teaspoon cornflour
½ teaspoon sesame oil
½ an egg white, lightly beaten, to be added last (reserve ½ for the sauce)

Sauce Ingredients 'B' (combined)

¾ cup of reserved stock
1 teaspoon Chinese rice wine
¼ teaspoon salt
¼ teaspoon pepper
¼ teaspoon sugar
1 teaspoon cornflour

Heat wok with oil until hot and stir-fry mushrooms for 1–2 minutes. Add combined sauce ingredients 'A' and simmer for 5 minutes over low heat.

Drain the mushrooms from the stock and allow to cool. Reserve the stock for making the sauce.

Combine minced prawns with water chestnuts and stir in seasoning ingredients. Add the beaten egg white and beat with a spoon until mixture is sticky.

Stuff mushrooms with the prawn mixture and press a green pea and 1 or 2 slices of sausage on each of the stuffed mushrooms. Steam over rapidly boiling water for 10 minutes.

Remove from steamer and carefully pour liquid into combined sauce ingredients 'B'. Bring gravy to the boil. Reduce heat and simmer for 2–3 minutes. Add the beaten egg white and pour over the mushrooms.

A popular Dim Sum dish. Illustrated on page 138. The filling can be varied by using crab meat, scallops, etc.

Steamed Ginger Brinjals

3 brinjals or eggplants, pared, halved or quartered and cut into 10 cm (4 in) lengths
½ teaspoon salt
2 tablespoons cooking oil
3 cloves garlic, finely chopped
3 shallots, finely chopped
4 slices ginger, finely chopped
1 red chilli, chopped
1 stalk spring onion, chopped
1 sprig coriander leaves, chopped

Seasoning Ingredients

1½ tablespoons light soya sauce
1 teaspoon dark soya sauce
1 teaspoon sesame oil
½ teaspoon sugar

Soak the cut brinjals in water with salt for 5 minutes. Rinse and drain well.

Arrange on a heat-proof dish and steam over rapidly boiling water for 15 minutes until brinjals are soft. Drain off the liquid from the dish.

Heat wok with 2 tablespoons oil until hot and lightly brown garlic, shallots and ginger. Put in combined seasonings and stir in chilli, spring onion and coriander leaves.

Remove from heat and quickly pour over steamed brinjals.

If you are always having unexpected guests for lunch or dinner, this is one dish that can be prepared in a jiffy. It is simple and yet deliciously tasty. I have served this dish many times and have never failed to win approving compliments. Illustrated on page 139.

Steamed Beancurd with Minced Prawns

1 roll Japanese soft beancurd, cut into 10 slices
300 gms shelled prawns, de-veined and minced
2 water chestnuts, minced
1 red chilli, seeded, finely minced
1 stalk spring onion, finely minced
2 teaspoons cornflour
2 stalks spring onion, chopped

Seasoning Ingredients 'A'
1/4 teaspoon salt
1/4 teaspoon pepper
1/2 teaspoon Chinese rice wine
1/2 teaspoon sesame oil

Seasoning Ingredients 'B'
1/2 teaspoon salt
1/2 teaspoon pepper
1/2 teaspoon sugar
1 teaspoon fresh ginger juice
1/2 teaspoon sesame oil
1 teaspoon cornflour

Sauce Ingredients (combined)
3 tablespoons fresh chicken stock
1/4 teaspoon sugar
1/4 teaspoon salt
Pinch of pepper
1/2 teaspoon sesame oil
1/2 teaspoon Chinese rice wine
1/2 teaspoon light soya sauce
1 teaspoon cornflour
1 tablespoon oil, to be added last

Arrange cut beancurd on a heat-proof dish and scoop out a hole in the centre of each piece with a teaspoon or knife.

Sprinkle seasoning ingredients 'A' on the beancurd.

Mix the minced prawns with minced water chestnuts, chilli and spring onion and stir in seasoning ingredients 'B'.

Dust the centre of the beancurd with cornflour then fill and stuff with minced prawn mixture.

Steam beancurd over rapidly boiling water for 10 minutes.

Pour liquid from beancurd dish into combined sauce ingredients and bring to the boil in a saucepan.

Add the oil and simmer for 1–2 minutes.

Pour sauce over the beancurd and serve garnished with spring onion.

Japanese beancurd is extremely soft and great care should be taken when removing it from the cylindrical package. Snip off the protruding tapered end with scissors and carefully place the roll on a cutting board. Using a sharp knife slice through the centre portion then carefully squeeze it into a basin of water. Slice the half-roll of beancurd by supporting it with your palm under the water.

Steamed Spicy Stuffed Beancurd

1 roll Japanese soft beancurd, cut into 10 slices
2 teaspoons cornflour
100 gms (3½ oz) lean pork with a little fat or chicken, minced
3 water chestnuts, finely chopped
2 slices ginger, finely chopped
1 red chilli, finely chopped
1 stalk spring onion, finely chopped
1 tablespoon cooking oil
1 teaspoon Chinese rice wine

Seasoning Ingredients

¼ teaspoon salt
¼ teaspoon pepper
½ teaspoon sugar
1 teaspoon sesame oil
1 teaspoon cornflour
2 teaspoons cooking oil, to be added last

Sauce Ingredients (combined)

½ cup fresh chicken stock
¼ teaspoon pepper
¼ teaspoon sugar
½ teaspoon salt
½ teaspoon Chinese rice wine
½ teaspoon sesame oil
1 teaspoon cornflour

Place beancurd on a heat-proof dish and carefully scoop out a small hole in the centre with a small teaspoon or knife.

Dust hollow centre with a little cornflour.

Mix minced pork or chicken with seasoning ingredients and stir in water chestnuts, ginger, chilli and spring onion.

Stuff each piece of beancurd with mixture.

Steam over rapidly boiling water for 10 minutes.

Carefully drain liquid from dish into the combined sauce ingredients.

Heat wok with 1 tablespoon oil and sprinkle in wine.

Pour in the combined sauce ingredients and bring to the boil.

Reduce heat and simmer for 1 minute.

Pour sauce over stuffed beancurd and serve.

A little pork fat will make the stuffing smoother.

Butterfly Prawns on Beancurd

12 medium-sized prawns, shelled with tails left on
150 gms (5¼ oz) lean pork with a little fat or chicken, minced
150 gms (5¼ oz) small prawns, shelled, minced
2 large squares soft beancurd, cut into 12 pieces
1 tablespoon cooking oil
1 teaspoon cornflour mixed with 1 tablespoon chicken stock or water

Seasoning Ingredients 'A'

¼ teaspoon salt
¼ teaspoon pepper
¼ teaspoon sugar
½ teaspoon cornflour

Seasoning Ingredients 'B'

1 teaspoon sesame oil
½ teaspoon light soya sauce
½ teaspoon Chinese rice wine
½ teaspoon salt
¼ teaspoon pepper
1 teaspoon cornflour

Finely Chopped Ingredients

2 water chestnuts
1 red chilli
1 stalk spring onion
1 sprig coriander leaves

Sauce Ingredients (combined)

½ cup fresh chicken stock
1 teaspoon light soya sauce
1 teaspoon Chinese rice wine
1 teaspoon oyster sauce
½ teaspoon sugar
¼ teaspoon salt
¼ teaspoon pepper

De-vein prawns. Using a sharp knife, carefully slit prawns from the head to the tail end but do not cut right through.

Dry the prawns with a tea towel and season with the seasoning ingredients 'A' and set aside.

Marinate minced pork or chicken and prawns with seasoning ingredients 'B' and stir in finely chopped ingredients. Leave for 30 minutes.

Using a 2½ cm (1 in) round biscuit cutter, carefully stamp out the centre portion of each beancurd, or use a knife to hollow out the centre. Carefully lift and arrange hollowed beancurd on a heat-proof dish.

Fill the hollowed beancurd with minced meat and prawn mixture using a teaspoon. Spread a whole prawn, split side down, on the surface of the meat and prawn mixture. Curl and spread the tail end to the centre of the prawn. To do this easily ensure that the inner portion of the tail shell is removed.

Steam beancurd over rapidly boiling water for 8 minutes.

Remove dish from the steamer and carefully pour the liquid into the combined sauce ingredients.

Heat 1 tablespoon of oil in the wok until hot and add the combined sauce ingredients. When it comes to the boil, thicken with cornflour mixture.

Pour over steamed beancurd and serve hot.

The large square beancurds are very soft. If you are preparing this dish for guests buy an extra piece, just in case. The centre portions of the beancurd can be stored in the refrigerator immersed in a bowl of water. Use them to make Beancurd with Crab Meat Sauce, or Braised Fried Beancurd with Dried Sole, or Hot Sour Soup.

Steamed Beancurd with Chicken and Mushroom Sauce

1 square or 1 large round cake of soft beancurd, rinsed
150 gms (5¼ oz) chicken fillet, diced
1 tablespoon cooking oil
2 shallots, sliced
1 clove garlic, minced
2 dried Chinese mushrooms, soaked and diced
3 water chestnuts, skinned and diced
4 young corns, diced
1 tablespoon green peas
1 teaspoon cornflour mixed
with 1 tablespoon chicken stock or water
1 stalk spring onion, chopped
1 red chilli, seeded, chopped

Seasoning Ingredients 'A'
¼ teaspoon salt
¼ teaspoon pepper
½ teaspoon Chinese rice wine
½ teaspoon sesame oil
½ tablespoon of cooking oil

Seasoning Ingredients 'B'
¼ teaspoon salt
¼ teaspoon pepper
¼ teaspoon sugar
½ teaspoon cornflour

Sauce Ingredients (combined)
¾ cup fresh chicken stock
¼ teaspoon salt
¼ teaspoon pepper
½ teaspoon sugar
1 teaspoon Chinese rice wine
1 teaspoon sesame oil
1 teaspoon light soya sauce
1 teaspoon oyster sauce

Marinate beancurd with seasoning ingredients 'A' for 15 minutes in a heat-proof dish.

Marinate chicken with seasoning ingredients 'B' and leave aside for 15 minutes.

Place beancurd in a steamer over rapidly boiling water and steam for 10 minutes.

Heat a wok with oil and lightly brown shallots and garlic. Put in dried mushrooms and stir-fry for 1 minute. Add chicken and toss until meat changes colour. Put in water chestnuts, young corn and green peas and stir-fry for 30 seconds.

Pour in combined sauce ingredients and bring to the boil. Reduce the flame and simmer for 2–3 minutes.

Thicken with cornflour mixture and sprinkle in spring onion and chilli.

Pour sauce over hot beancurd and serve with rice.

If you like more vegetables with this dish, scald some tender mustard greens with a little oil and arrange around the beancurd.

Steamed Eggs with Prawns

2 tablespoons cooking oil
3 shallots, sliced
3 large eggs
1½ cups water
120 gms (4¼ oz) shelled prawns, chopped
1 tablespoon reserved oil from frying shallots
1 stalk spring onion, chopped

Seasoning Ingredients
1 teaspoon salt
¼ teaspoon sugar
¼ teaspoon pepper

Heat 2 tablespoons oil in a wok and lightly brown shallots. Drain and set shallot crisps aside. Reserve the oil.

Beat eggs gently. Do not create any froth. Stir in seasoning ingredients and water. Add prawns and pour into a heat-proof dish.

Steam over rapidly boiling water for 12 minutes until the egg custard is just set.

Pour in 1 tablespoon of the reserved oil.

Serve sprinkled with spring onion and shallot crisps.

To vary the dish, use chopped barbecued pork (char siew) or minced pork. The recipe appears simple but it requires skill to obtain a perfect custard with a smooth surface and texture. The amount of water to egg is important, and timing of steaming and control of heat are crucial. The Japanese are very good at making this dish called chawan mushi.

Steamed Three-Variety Eggs

3 large chicken eggs
1/2 teaspoon salt
1/4 teaspoon pepper
2 teaspoons light soya sauce
1 1/2 cups water
2 salted duck egg yolks, cut into 8 each
1 century egg, diced
1 tablespoon cooked oil
1 stalk spring onion, chopped

Gently beat the eggs. Do not create any froth. Stir in salt, pepper, soya sauce, water, the duck egg yolks and the century egg.

Pour into a heat-proof dish and steam over rapidly boiling water for 12 minutes.

Sprinkle oil over the egg custard and serve garnished with spring onion.

A delightfully smooth egg custard, delicious when served with porridge or rice.

Steamed Chicken Glutinous Rice (*Lor Ma Kai*)

1 1/2 kg (3 1/3 lbs) chicken
1 kg (2 1/5 lbs) glutinous rice
8 tablespoons cooking oil
60 gms (2 oz) dried Chinese mushrooms, soaked and cut into strips
8 shallots, sliced
2 teaspoons salt
1 teaspoon thick soya sauce
1 heaping teaspoon five spice powder
4 cups water
2 red chillies, seeded and sliced
2 stalks spring onion, chopped
4 sprigs coriander leaves, cut into 2 1/2 cm (1 in) lengths
Chilli sauce

Seasoning Ingredients
4 tablespoons oyster sauce
2 teaspoons rice wine
1 teaspoon thick soya sauce
2 teaspoons light soya sauce
2 teaspoons ginger juice
1 teaspoon sesame oil
1 teaspoon sugar
1/2 teaspoon pepper
1 heaping teaspoon cornflour

De-bone chicken and cut into 1 1/2 cm (1/2 in) thick slices. Season with seasoning ingredients for at least 1 hour.

Wash and drain glutinous rice and steam for 45 minutes.

Heat oil in a wok and fry mushrooms for 1–2 minutes. Drain from oil and leave aside.

Lightly brown shallots and put in glutinous rice, salt, thick soya sauce and five spice powder and fry for 1 minute. Add water, mix well and simmer gently, covered, for 5–10 minutes. Remove from heat.

Grease 12 medium rice bowls and put in some fried mushrooms and seasoned chicken at the bottom of each bowl. Fill with glutinous rice and press with the back of a spoon to fill 3/4 of rice bowl.

Steam over rapidly boiling water for 45 minutes.

To serve, turn steamed glutinous rice onto a small dish. Garnish with chillies, spring onions and coriander leaves and serve hot with chilli sauce.

A popular dish served for Dim Sum and breakfast.

Double Steamed Chicken with Herbs

1 small chicken, skinned and cut into 6 portions
15 gms (1/2 oz) sliced ginseng (*pow sum*)
1/4 teaspoon salt

Lightly crush each portion of chicken with a pestle and mortar, and set aside.

In a double boiling saucepan bring water to the boil. Place a Chinese rice bowl in the top compartment of the double boiling saucepan. Put ginseng and salt in the bowl.

Place a pair of disposable wooden chopsticks across the bowl in a criss-cross manner, ensuring that they will not slip into the bowl. Carefully place chicken on top of the chopsticks.

Cover the saucepan and double boil the chicken over medium heat for 3–3 1/2 hours. Make sure the water in the bottom compartment does not boil dry by adding boiling water constantly.

When steaming is completed, remove and discard the chicken as it will be tasteless. There should be a whole bowl of herbal chicken essence enough for 1.

This chicken essence is very nutritious and if taken regularly, once or twice a week will restore a person in fragile health (say my grandmother and mother). Chinese herbs, like all food, are considered either heating (yang), cooling (yin) or neutral. The terms heating and cooling are not related to the temperature or spiciness of the food. Rather, they refer to the effect the food has on the system and its yin-yang balance. Pow sum is cooling and therefore adds yin to a person who feels heaty.

Double Boiled Chicken with White Fungus Soup

1/2 a medium-sized chicken, skinned and cut into 4 pieces
30 gms (1 oz) canned Yunnan or smoked ham, diced into 2 cm (3/4 in) cubes
5 cups chicken stock, oil skimmed off
4 slices ginger
1 piece white or silver fungus, soaked, hard centre discarded and cut into 2 cm (3/4 in) pieces
1 teaspoon salt
1/2 tablespoon rock sugar

Place chicken and ham in a double boiler and add chicken stock, ginger, white fungus, salt and rock sugar. Cover and double boil for 1 1/2 hours.

Remove the ham and continue to double boil for another 1 1/2 hours.

Transfer all ingredients and soup into 4 individual soup bowls and serve hot.

A nutritious soup valued for its healthy properties. The white or silver fungus is expensive but it is said to be good for clearing out the respiratory system. If using an electric crock-pot, slow cook on high for 3 1/2 hours.

Double Boiled Winter Melon and Ham Soup

500 gms (17 1/2 oz) winter melon, peeled, seeds and fibrous material removed
45 gms (1 1/2 oz) canned Yunnan ham or smoked ham, cut into 1/2 cm (1/4 in) strips
2 slices ginger
4 cups fresh chicken stock
1 teaspoon salt
1/4 teaspoon black pepper
1/2 tablespoon Chinese rice wine

Cut the winter melon into 5 x 2 1/2 cm (2 x 1 in) pieces.

Put into a double boiler together with remaining ingredients and double boil for 20–30 minutes until melon becomes transparent and tender.

Steamed Herbal Winter Melon Soup

1 winter melon,
approximately 1½–2 kg (3 ⅓–4 ½ lbs), washed
1 chicken drumstick, skinned and cut into strips
1 teaspoon salt
½ tablespoon rock sugar
6 Chinese dried red dates, rinsed, seeded and slit to release flavour
1 dessertspoon dried long ngan, rinsed
3 cups fresh chicken stock
1 teaspoon salt

Herbs
2 pieces *pak kee*
6 slices ginseng (*yong sam*)
1 teaspoon *kei chi*

Slice off the top stem end of the winter melon and use as a lid. Decorate the rim of the melon with a zig-zag cut all around. Scoop out the seeds and pith and rinse the melon with boiling water.

Season the chicken with salt for 15 minutes. Blanch in boiling water for 1 minute.

Place chicken in the melon with rock sugar, red dates, dried long ngan and herbs. Stand the melon on a shallow bowl to hold it steady and upright.

Bring chicken stock with salt added to the boil and pour into melon. The stock level should come up to almost the rim of the melon.

Cover with the melon lid. Place in a steamer over gently boiling water and steam for 1–1¼ hours.

Serve hot, using the melon as a soup tureen.

Illustrated on page 140. The herbs in this soup are renowned for their healing powers. Pak kee is meant to be good for blood circulation and fatigue. Ginseng renews vigour and boosts blood circulation. Kei chi is essential for good vision and red dates are a good cure for anaemics.

Steamed Black Chicken in Coconut

1 large old coconut
1 small black chicken, skinned
1 teaspoon salt
1 tablespoon Chinese rice wine
4 dried Chinese red dates, rinsed, seeded and slit to release flavour

Saw off the top small section of the coconut and keep as a lid. Drain off the coconut water and rinse the inside. Do not remove the flesh. Stand the coconut on a bowl and fill the bowl with water to cover half the coconut. This will prevent the coconut from cracking during steaming.

Rub the outside of the chicken with salt and the inside with the wine. Leave for 15 minutes.

Put the chicken into the coconut together with the red dates. Do not add water. Cover the coconut with the coconut lid.

Place the bowl with the coconut into a steamer and steam over gently boiling water for 5 hours.

Serve the soup from the coconut or transfer to a soup bowl.

The coconut flesh gives a sweet and fragrant taste to this nutritious soup. If coconut is not available, place the chicken and the rest of the ingredients with 1 cup fresh chicken stock in a deep Chinese steam bowl, approximately 12 ½ cm (5 in) in diameter. Put a 2½ cm (1 in) high wire rack in a large pot or a wok. Place the covered bowl on the rack. Fill the pot or wok with enough water to submerge ⅓ of the bowl. Steam over gently boiling water for 5 hours.

Steamed White Fungus and Rock Sugar in Coconut

20 gms (2/3 oz) dried lotus seeds, approximately 20, soaked for 30 minutes
10 gms (1/3 oz) white fungus, approximately 1/2 a medium-sized piece, soaked for 10 minutes
1 large old coconut
60 gms (2 oz) rock sugar

Skin and split lotus seeds into two halves. Remove the bitter centres and leave aside.

Cut the softened white fungus into small florets and discard the hard centre and set aside.

Saw off a small top section of the coconut and keep as lid. Discard coconut water and rinse. Do not remove the flesh. Stand coconut on a bowl and fill the bowl with enough water to cover half of the coconut. This is to ensure that the coconut will not crack during steaming.

Place all ingredients together with rock sugar into the coconut and fill to the brim with water. Cover with the coconut lid.

Place in a steamer and steam over medium heat for 3 1/2 hours.

Carefully remove the coconut and place on a small basket lined with serviette or table napkins and serve hot.

Serves 2 as a drink for dessert or any time. Steaming in a coconut gives the soup a sweet taste and a hint of coconut in the flavour and fragrance. *Illustrated on page 141.*

Gingko Nut and Water Chestnut Dessert

6 cups water
300 gms (10 1/2 oz) rock sugar
180 gms (6 1/3 oz) gingko nuts, shelled and bitter centres removed
22 water chestnuts, skinned and diced into 1/2 cm (1/4 in) cubes
2 egg whites, lightly beaten
3 tablespoons sweet potato flour
1 tablespoon cornflour
1/2 cup water

In a large saucepan, bring water and rock sugar to a slow boil. When the sugar dissolves, put in the gingko nuts. Boil over low heat for 10 minutes, then add the water chestnuts. Simmer for another 10 minutes.

Combine the sweet potato flour, cornflour and water, and strain the mixture.

Slowly drizzle and stir the egg white into the soup. Repeat with the flour solution. When it boils again, remove from heat.

Serve hot or cold.

Illustrated on page 142.

Steamed Dried Beancurd Sticks and Gingko Nuts

2 dried beancurd sticks, soaked to soften and cut into 2½ cm (1 in) lengths
20 shelled gingko nuts, halved and bitter core removed
60 gms (2 oz) rock sugar
1 egg, beaten (optional)

Place softened beancurd sticks, gingko nuts and rock sugar into a Chinese steam bowl, approximately 12½ cm (5 in) in diameter. Fill to the brim with water. Cover the steam bowl with the lid.

Put a round wire rack, approximately 2½ cm (1 in) in height, into a large pot or wok and place the steam bowl on the rack. Fill the pot or wok with enough water to submerge ⅓ of the bowl.

Steam over rapidly boiling water for 1½ hours.

Remove the lid and stir in beaten egg. Serve hot.

A sweet dessert drink for 2. Gingko nuts are believed to be good for bladder disorders, asthma and coughs. Once the nuts have been cracked, soak them in water for a few minutes until the brown skin can be rubbed off.

Double Steamed Hasma

1 tablespoon dried hasma (*shuet kak*), soaked overnight
10 dried Chinese red dates, slit and seeded to release flavour
½ tablespoon ginseng *(pow sum)*
4 cups water
2 tablespoons rock sugar

Rinse the soaked hasma and place into a double boiling saucepan together with the remaining ingredients.

Steam for 4 hours, constantly topping the bottom compartment with boiling water.

If a double boiler is not available, place all ingredients into an electric crock-pot and cook on high for 4 hours.

Discard red dates and ginseng and serve either hot or cold.

Hasma is the gland of a snow frog. It is translucent and jelly-like and perfect for soups. It is believed to balance the system and to enhance the complexion.

BRAISED AND STEWED

DISHES

Braised Shin of Beef

360 gms (12 2/3 oz) shin of beef, chopped into thick slices
2 tablespoons cooking oil
8 slices ginger
2 cloves garlic, crushed
2 shallots, sliced
30 gms (1 oz) dried lily buds, soaked to soften and knotted individually
45 gms (1 1/2 oz) cloud ear fungus, soaked and shredded
12 red dates, seeded
12 shelled chestnuts, optional
1 tablespoon cornflour mixed with 2 tablespoons water

Seasoning Ingredients
1/2 teaspoon bicarbonate of soda
1/2 teaspoon salt
1/2 teaspoon pepper
1/2 tablespoon light soya sauce
2 teaspoons cornflour

Sauce Ingredients (combined)
1 1/2 cupS fresh beef stock
1/2 teaspoon salt
1 teaspoon sugar
1/4 teaspoon pepper
1/2 tablespoon yellow bean paste
1/2 tablespoon light soya sauce

Marinate beef with seasoning ingredients and leave for 1 hour.

Heat wok with the cooking oil until hot and add the beef. Stir-fry briskly for 4–5 minutes. Put in the ginger, garlic and shallots and stir-fry until fragrant. Add the lily buds, cloud ear fungus, red dates and chestnuts and mix well.

Pour in combined sauce ingredients and bring to the boil.

Transfer to a large earthen pot or heavy saucepan and simmer covered for 20–30 minutes. If an electric crock-pot is used, cook for 1 hour or until the meat is tender.

Thicken with cornflour mixture and serve in the earthen pot or on a serving dish.

Dried lily buds are commonly used in braised dishes with meat. Tied in the middle with a single knot they add texture and crunch. Soak in hot water for about 30 minutes to soften.

Oxtail and Vegetable Stew

1 oxtail, approximately 1 kg (2 1/5 lbs)
2 tablespoons cooking oil
2 onions, chopped
2 cloves garlic, crushed
2 tablespoons plain flour
1 carrot, roll cut into wedges
1 leek, approximately 150 gms (5 1/4 oz), white part only, sliced
10 new potatoes, boiled and skinned
2 medium tomatoes, quartered

Seasoning Ingredients
1/2 teaspoon salt
1/2 teaspoon sugar
1 teaspoon pepper
2 teaspoons light soya sauce
1 teaspoon dark soya sauce

Sauce Ingredients (combined)
5 cups beef stock
3 cloves
4 cm (1 1/2 in) cinnamon
1/4 piece nutmeg
1 teaspoon salt
2 teaspoons light soya sauce
1 teaspoon dark soya sauce

Wash the oxtail and wipe dry. Slice off the surplus fat and cut into sections between the bones. Marinate with seasoning ingredients.

Heat oil in a saucepan until hot and stir-fry the onion and garlic until fragrant. Coat the oxtail sections with flour and add to the pan. Fry until pale golden. Add the carrot and stir-fry for 1 minute.

Put in the combined sauce ingredients, bring to the boil and simmer for about 2 hours. Add the remaining vegetables, leek, potatoes and tomatoes, and continue to simmer for another 1/2 hour or until the meat is tender.

Transfer to serving dish and serve hot.

Braising tenderises the oxtail and allows it to absorb all the fragrances and flavours from the spices and seasonings. Using fresh beef or chicken stock made from bones and bits of leftover meat is preferable to stock cubes. Fresh stock is the essential base to a rich and flavourful oxtail soup.

Stewed Beef with Soya Bean Paste

600 gms (21 oz) stewing beef
(brisket or silverside),
cut into 2½ cm (1 in) cubes
2 tablespoons cooking oil
5 cloves garlic, minced
1 tablespoon preserved soya bean paste
(*tau cheong*)
4 cm piece ginger, shredded
2 small star anise
1¼ cm (½ in) piece cinnamon
1 stalk spring onion
2 sprigs coriander leaves
1 red chilli, cut into strips

Sauce Ingredients (combined)
3½ cups fresh beef stock
1 tablespoon light soya sauce
1 teaspoon thick soya sauce
2 teaspoons sugar
½ teaspoon pepper

Heat cooking oil in a pot until hot and stir-fry garlic, soya bean paste and ginger until fragrant. Put in star anise and cinnamon and stir-fry for 30 seconds. Add the beef and toss until it changes colour.

Pour in combined sauce ingredients. Bring to the boil, reduce heat to low and simmer for 1½–2 hours until meat is tender.

Transfer to serving dish and garnish with spring onion, coriander leaves and chilli.

This is a hearty meal made with a less expensive cut of beef. The combination of soya bean paste and spices is easily absorbed by the beef and diminishes the "beefy" flavour.

Braised Pork Ribs with Sea Cucumbers

600 gms (21 oz) pork ribs,
cut into 4 cm (1½ in) pieces
4 tablespoons cooking oil
4 cloves garlic, minced
3 shallots, sliced
6 white peppercorns
1 medium-sized dried squid, rinsed
and cut into strips with a pair of scissors
6 dried Chinese mushrooms, soaked to soften
1 kg (2⅕ lbs) sea cucumbers, rinsed
and cut into 2 x 5 cm (¾ x 2 in) pieces
3 cups water

Seasoning Ingredients
1½ tablespoons light soya sauce
1 tablespoon thick soya sauce
1 tablespoon oyster sauce

Wash the pork ribs and trim off the excess fat. Drain well.

Heat oil in a wok until hot and stir-fry garlic, shallots and peppercorns for 1 minute until fragrant. Add the pork ribs, dry squid, mushrooms and sea cucumbers, and stir-fry for 5 minutes until fragrant. Add the seasoning ingredients and stir-fry briskly for 5 minutes longer.

Pour in water and bring to the boil. Lower heat and simmer for 1½ hours or until ribs are tender.

Chicken drumsticks or pig's trotters can be used as a substitute for ribs. Sea cucumbers may not be much to look at but they are a highly prized ingredient. On their own they taste bland and gelatinous, but they readily absorb flavours from other ingredients like mushrooms and meat. *Illustrated on page 143.*

Braised Pot Pourri

800 gms (28 oz) pork ribs,
cut into 5 cm (2 in) lengths
500 gms (17½ oz) belly pork,
skinned and cut into slices
(½ cm, ¼ in thick and 5 cm, 2 in long)
4 pieces Chinese sausages, sliced slantingly
1 tablespoon cooking oil
24 cloves garlic, skinned and kept whole
2 shallots, sliced
8–10 dried Chinese mushrooms,
soaked and halved
20 pieces cloud ear fungus (*wan yee*), soaked
1 tablespoon Chinese rice wine
8–10 pairs pre-fried chicken feet
3 pieces sea cucumber,
rinsed and cut into 5 cm (2 in) pieces
2 teaspoons cornflour mixed
with 2 tablespoons water
2 stalks spring onion, chopped
2 sprigs coriander leaves, chopped

Seasoning Ingredients 'A'
1 tablespoon light soya sauce
½ tablespoon thick soya sauce
1 tablespoon oyster sauce
½ teaspoon salt
¼ teaspoon pepper
1 teaspoon sugar

Seasoning Ingredients 'B'
½ tablespoon light soya sauce
1 teaspoon thick soya sauce
1 teaspoon sugar
½ teaspoon salt
¼ teaspoon pepper

Sauce Ingredients (combined)
2 cups fresh chicken stock or water
½ tablespoon light soya sauce
1 teaspoon thick soya sauce
½ teaspoon salt
¼ teaspoon pepper
1 teaspoon sugar

Marinate ribs with seasoning ingredients 'A' and belly pork with seasoning ingredients 'B' for at least 30 minutes.

Heat a saucepan without oil until hot. Stir-fry pork belly for about 5 minutes until liquid evaporates. Remove pork and set aside.

Put in sausages and stir-fry until lightly browned and fragrant, about 3 minutes. Dish out and set aside.

Reheat a clean saucepan with 1 tablespoon oil and lightly brown garlic and shallots. Add dried mushrooms and toss for 1 minute. Put in the cloud ear fungus and stir-fry for a few seconds. Drizzle in Chinese rice wine. Add pork ribs, chicken feet and fry for 2 minutes.

Pour in sauce ingredients and bring to the boil. Put in sea cucumber and fried belly pork. Reduce heat and simmer for 30–45 minutes or until ribs are tender and sauce is thickened.

Put in Chinese sausages. Thicken with cornflour mixture. Lastly stir in spring onion and coriander leaves.

A rich stew that goes well with rice. It tastes even better the next day after reheating. Illustrated on page 144.

Stewed Garlic Pork Ribs

600 gms (21 oz) pork ribs,
cut into 7 cm (2¾ in) pieces
Oil for deep-frying
2½ cups water
16 cloves garlic
3 lengths (10 cm, 4 in) of wild sugar cane
(*chook cheh*), bruised or ½ tablespoon rock sugar

Seasoning Ingredients
½ teaspoon salt
½ teaspoon five spice powder
¼ teaspoon thick soya sauce
1 teaspoon white or cider vinegar
½ tablespoon light soya sauce
½ tablespoon Chinese rice wine
2 tablespoons cornflour

Wash and trim off excess fat from the pork ribs. Marinate with seasoning ingredients for 2 hours or overnight in the refrigerator.

Heat oil in a wok for deep-frying and fry pork ribs for 2 minutes. Remove and drain.

Put pork ribs, water, garlic and sugar cane in a pot and bring to the boil.

Reduce heat and simmer for 45–60 minutes or until meat is just tender.

Choose straight, meaty ribs and keep the bones for soup. Deep-frying seals in the juices and accentuates the fragrance of the ribs.

Braised Pork Ribs in Black Bean Sauce

600 gms (21 oz) pork ribs,
cut into 4 cm (1$^1/_2$ in) pieces
2 tablespoons cooking oil
5 cloves garlic, minced
5 slices ginger, minced
2 red chillies, seeded and chopped
1 tablespoon fermented black beans, rinsed, soaked for 10 minutes and chopped finely
1 leek, white part only,
cut into 1$^1/_4$ cm ($^1/_2$ in) diagonal slices, optional
2 cups water or enough to cover pork ribs
2 stalks spring onions,
cut into 2$^1/_2$ cm (1 in) lengths
$^1/_2$ tablespoon cornflour mixed
with 1 tablespoon water

Seasoning Ingredients

2 tablespoons light soya sauce
$^1/_2$ thick soya sauce
1 tablespoon Chinese rice wine
$^1/_4$ teaspoon pepper
2 teaspoons sugar

Wash pork ribs and trim off the excess fat.

Heat oil in a wok until hot and sauté pork ribs for 2 minutes. Remove the meat leaving the oil in the wok. Add the garlic, ginger and chillies and stir-fry for 30 seconds. Put in fermented black beans and stir-fry for 30 seconds. Add leek and toss well for 1 minute.

Return pork ribs to wok and mix well. Pour in water and add the seasoning ingredients.

Bring to the boil, reduce heat and simmer for approximately 1 hour until pork ribs are tender and sauce reduced.

Add spring onion and thicken sauce with cornflour mixture.

The black beans make this dish salty. Depending on your taste, you may not require table salt.

Braised Pork with Potatoes

600 gms (21 oz) pork loin or belly pork, sliced
1 tablespoon light soya sauce
$^1/_2$ teaspoon pepper
3 tablespoons cooking oil
4 slices ginger
2 cloves garlic, sliced
1 leek, white part only, sliced diagonally
2 tablespoons Chinese rice wine
3 medium-sized potatoes,
cut into 2$^1/_2$ cm (1 in) cubes
and deep-fried until golden brown
2 red chillies, seeded and sliced
1 sprig coriander leaves

Sauce Ingredients (combined)

1 cup water
2 tablespoons light soya sauce
1 dessertspoon sugar
$^1/_2$ teaspoon pepper
$^1/_4$ teaspoon salt

Marinate pork with soya sauce and pepper and leave for 30 minutes.

Heat cooking oil in a pot and lightly brown ginger and garlic. Add leek and stir-fry for 30 seconds. Put in pork and toss until meat changes colour. Add the rice wine and stir-fry for 30 seconds.

Pour in combined sauce ingredients, cover and bring to the boil. Reduce heat and simmer for 30 minutes or until meat is tender.

Add the potatoes and red chillies and cook for another 5 minutes.

Serve hot garnished with coriander leaves.

Potatoes are not a common ingredient in Chinese cooking, but they are sometimes used in braised dishes, where they take on the flavour of the ginger and garlic and taste delicious.

Braised Pork with Beancurd and Eggs

600 gms (21 oz) belly pork,
cut into 2 x 4 cm (3/4 x 1 1/2 in) pieces
4 tablespoons cooking oil
3 flat squares soft beancurd,
cut into 4 cm (1 1/2 in) squares
6 cloves garlic, sliced
2 tablespoons sugar
8 hard boiled eggs, shelled

Sauce Ingredients (combined)
2 cups fresh chicken or pork bone stock
2 tablespoons light soya sauce
2 tablespoons thick soya sauce
1/2 teaspoon salt
1/4 teaspoon pepper

Heat 2 tablespoons of cooking oil and fry beancurd cubes on both sides until lightly browned. Remove and leave aside.

Heat remaining oil in a wok and add garlic and sugar. Cook until sugar turns into a light caramel. Quickly add combined sauce ingredients and bring to the boil.

Put in the pork and simmer over low heat for 25 minutes.

Add eggs and leave to simmer for another 10 minutes. Finally, add the fried beancurd and let it simmer for 5 minutes more.

Serve hot.

Chicken can be used instead of pork if you prefer.

Stewed Pork

600 gms (21 oz) belly pork,
cut into 2 x 5 cm (3/4 x 2 in) pieces
1 whole pod garlic
1 cup water

Seasoning Ingredients
2 teaspoons thick soya sauce
2 dessertspoons light soya sauce
1 dessertspoon sugar
1 teaspoon salt
1/2 teaspoon pepper

Marinate pork with seasoning ingredients for at least an hour.

Heat a saucepan without oil until hot and stir-fry pork and garlic for about 5 minutes until the liquid evaporates. Add water and simmer for 45 minutes or until pork is tender.

A rich stew with tender, garlic-flavoured meat. If a darker sauce is preferred, add 1 extra teaspoon thick soya sauce. Chicken meat can be used instead of pork.

Pork and Eggs in Soya Sauce

600 gms (21 oz) belly pork,
cut into 2 x 5 cm (3/4 x 2 in) pieces
2 whole pods garlic, keep the skin on,
rinsed and lightly crushed
2 tablespoons light soya sauce
2 tablespoons thick soya sauce
1 tablespoon sugar
1 teaspoon salt
1 star anise
2 cm (3/4 in) piece cinnamon
2 1/2 cups water
1/4 teaspoon five spice powder
6 hard boiled eggs, shelled

Heat a pot until hot (do not add oil) and put in pork. Stir-fry for 3 minutes. When the fat oozes out, grease the pan with it. Add garlic and toss for 2 minutes or until fragrant.

Reduce heat and stir in light and thick soya sauce, sugar, salt, star anise and cinnamon. Stir-fry quickly to mix well until meat is evenly coated.

Pour in the water and add five spice powder. Bring to the boil. Reduce heat and simmer, covered, for 20 minutes.

Add the eggs and continue to simmer for 10–15 minutes until meat is tender.

If a spicy sauce is preferred, add 2 whole red chillies to the water. Frying the pork (or chicken) in a greaseless pot or pan reduces water content and accentuates the aroma.

Pig Trotters in Chinese Black Vinegar

2 pig trotters, cleaned
and cut into 5 cm (2 in) pieces
3 tablespoons cooking oil
5 dessertspoons soya bean paste,
ground separately
5 dessertspoons Chinese black vinegar
2 teaspoons sugar
6 cups water or enough to cover trotters
1 teaspoon thick soya sauce

Ground Ingredients

15 shallots
15 cloves garlic
6 red chillies

Boil a large saucepan of water and scald trotters for 5 minutes. Drain.

Heat a saucepan or a deep claypot with oil until hot and stir-fry ground ingredients until fragrant. Add the ground soya bean paste and continue to stir-fry until aromatic. Put in trotters and fry for another 3 minutes. If necessary, sprinkle with a little water to prevent burning. Add vinegar, sugar and enough water to cover trotters.

Cover the pot and bring to the boil. Reduce heat and allow to simmer for 1½ hours until trotters are tender, stirring occasionally to prevent sticking. When the trotters are tender, stir in thick soya sauce.

Be sure to buy the hind legs as they are meatier and can better withstand the long simmering.

Braised Trotters with Mushrooms and Chestnuts

1 whole pig trotters, about 1⅕ kg (2½ lbs)
Oil for deep-frying
10 shelled chestnuts, rinsed
1 tablespoon cooking oil
10 dried Chinese mushrooms, soaked until soft
2 cloves garlic, finely ground
1 whole pod garlic, lightly crushed
½ cup water

Seasoning Ingredients

1 teaspoon salt
2 teaspoons light soya sauce
2 teaspoons thick soya sauce
1 teaspoon pepper
1 teaspoon sugar

Wash trotter and drain well. Make a lengthwise slit with a very sharp knife to cut just through the skin. This is to ensure that the marinating ingredients get into the meat. Pierce the lean part of the meat with a fork. Marinate the trotter with seasoning ingredients for at least 4 hours, preferably overnight.

Steam the trotter together with the marinade over boiling water for 2 hours.

Deep-fry chestnuts for 1 minute in hot oil. Drain.

Heat 1 tablespoon of cooking oil in a wok and fry mushrooms and garlic until fragrant. Place this and the fried chestnuts at the bottom of a crock-pot large enough to put the whole trotter in.

Put in ½ cup water and place trotter into the pot. Cook for 1–1½ hours until trotter is soft and tender.

If a thicker gravy is required, blend 1 teaspoon cornflour with a little water and add to sauce 15 minutes before turning off the slow cooker. The multiple steps may seem tedious but they are necessary to transform the tough trotters into an appealing, smoothly textured dish. The Hokkiens excel at making this dish and there are many delicious versions.

Braised Chicken with Chestnuts

600 gms (21 oz) chicken,
cut into bite-sized pieces
240 gms (8½ oz) shelled dried chestnuts
Oil for deep-frying
2 tablespoons cooking oil
4 slices ginger, shredded
2 cloves garlic, minced
1 shallot, sliced
2 teaspoons cornflour mixed
with 1 tablespoon chicken stock or water
2 stalks spring onion, chopped

Seasoning Ingredients
2 teaspoons light soya sauce
½ teaspoon thick soya sauce
1 teaspoon sesame oil
1 teaspoon Chinese rice wine
½ teaspoon sugar
½ teaspoon pepper
1 teaspoon cornflour

Sauce Ingredients (combined)
1¼ cups fresh chicken stock
½ tablespoon light soya sauce
½ tablespoon Chinese rice wine
½ teaspoon thick soya sauce
½ teaspoon sugar
¼ teaspoon pepper
¼ teaspoon salt

Marinate chicken with seasoning ingredients for 20 minutes. Boil the chestnuts in water for 5 minutes. Drain.

Heat a wok with oil and deep-dry chestnuts for 2–3 minutes. Remove chestnuts from oil and set aside. Put in chicken and deep-fry for 5 minutes until lightly browned. Drain from oil.

Reheat a clean wok with 2 tablespoons oil and lightly brown ginger, garlic and shallot. Return chicken and chestnuts to the wok and toss well.

Add combined sauce ingredients and bring to the boil. Lower the flame and simmer for 20–25 minutes until chicken is tender.

Thicken with cornflour mixture and serve garnished with spring onion.

Use fresh chestnuts if they are available, otherwise use the large dried variety.

Braised Soya Sauce Chicken

4 whole chicken thighs and drumsticks
2 sprigs of coriander for garnishing

Seasoning Ingredients
1 tablespoon light soya sauce
½ tablespoon Chinese rice wine
½ teaspoon salt
½ teaspoon pepper

Sauce Ingredients (combined)
2 cups water
4 tablespoons light soya sauce
1 teaspoon thick soya sauce
1 teaspoon sesame oil
1 teaspoon sugar
2–5 cm (1–2 in) piece ginger, smashed
4–5 stalks white part of spring onion
4 petals or ½ piece star anise
2 cm (¾ in) cinnamon
5 cm (2 in) piece dried orange peel

Marinate chicken thighs with seasoning ingredients for at least 30 minutes.

Combine sauce ingredients in saucepan and bring to the boil. Put in seasoned chicken. When sauce boils again, reduce heat and simmer over medium–low heat for 20 minutes. Leave to soak in sauce for 30 minutes.

Chop the chicken and arrange on a serving dish. Pour 2–3 tablespoons sauce over the chicken.

Garnish with coriander leaves.

Two of the most popular Chinese classics are white-cut chicken and soya sauce chicken. Braised and steeped in a lightly spiced soya sauce, the plain chicken is packed with fragrance. It makes a simple but satisfying meal with rice.

Ginger Chicken in Earthen Pot

1 chicken, approximately 1 kg (2¹/₅ lbs), cut into bite-sized pieces
Oil for deep-frying
4 small squares firm beancurd (*tau kwa*), sliced into 1 x 2¹/₂ cm (¹/₃ x 1 in) slices
2 tablespoons cooking oil
6 slices ginger
4 cloves garlic, sliced
4 shallots, sliced
5 dried Chinese mushrooms, soaked until soft and halved
120 gms (4¹/₄ oz) carrots, sliced
90 gms (3 oz) canned bamboo shoots, sliced
240 gms (8¹/₂ oz) Tientsin cabbage, cut into 5 cm (2 in) lengths
2 red chillies, sliced
6 stalks spring onion, cut into 2¹/₂ cm (1 in) lengths

Seasoning Ingredients

1 teaspoon salt
1 teaspoon sugar
1 teaspoon thick soya sauce
2 teaspoons light soya sauce
1 tablespoon cornflour

Sauce Ingredients (combined)

2¹/₂ cups fresh chicken stock
¹/₂ teaspoon salt
1 teaspoon sugar
¹/₂ teaspoon pepper
1 tablespoon light soya sauce
1 tablespoon oyster sauce
1 teaspoon thick soya sauce
1 teaspoon sesame oil

Marinate chicken with seasoning ingredients for 20 minutes.

Heat oil in a wok until hot and deep-fry beancurd slices until golden brown. Remove and set aside. Deep-fry chicken for 5 minutes. Drain and place in an earthen pot.

Reheat a clean wok with 2 tablespoons of oil and lightly brown ginger, garlic, and shallots. Put in mushrooms and stir-fry until fragrant. Add carrots, bamboo shoots and Tientsin cabbage and fry for 3–5 minutes. Put in sauce ingredients and bring to the boil.

Pour over chicken in claypot, add the chillies and when it boils again, reduce heat, cover and simmer for 25 minutes or until chicken is tender.

Add beancurd and spring onion and simmer for another 5–10 minutes.

Thicken sauce with cornflour mixture and serve.

Illustrated on page 169. Food cooked in an earthen pot has a special aroma and the pot retains heat well allowing the food to remain hot longer.

Claypot Chicken with Salted Fish

600 gms (21 oz) chicken, cut into bite-sized pieces
1 teaspoon Chinese rice wine
1 teaspoon light soya sauce
4 tablespoons cooking oil
15 gms (¹/₂ oz) salted fish, thinly sliced
4 cm (1¹/₂ in) ginger, sliced
2 shallots, sliced
8 dried Chinese mushrooms, soaked and halved
3 stalks spring onion, cut into 2¹/₂ cm (1 in) lengths
1 teaspoon cornflour mixed with 1 tablespoon water

Sauce Ingredients (combined)

³/₄ cup fresh chicken stock
¹/₂ tablespoon Chinese rice wine
¹/₂ teaspoon thick soya sauce
1 teaspoon light soya sauce
1 teaspoon oyster sauce
1 teaspoon sugar
¹/₂ teaspoon pepper
¹/₄ teaspoon salt

Season chicken with Chinese rice wine and light soya sauce for 20 minutes.

Heat wok with 2 tablespoons oil and fry the salted fish until light brown and crisp. Remove and discard oil.

Heat an earthen pot or wok with 2 tablespoons of oil and lightly brown ginger and shallots. Add the mushrooms and stir-fry for 1–2 minutes. Put in chicken and stir-fry for 3–5 minutes.

Add combined sauce ingredients and bring to the boil. Cover and simmer chicken for 15 minutes until tender. Sprinkle in the salted fish and spring onion and simmer for 3 minutes. Thicken sauce with cornflour mixture.

Saltfish fans will love this dish.

Orange Chicken Wings

8–10 chicken wings
1 tablespoon oil
3 slices ginger
12 shallots, keep whole
1 teaspoon tarragon vinegar
1/2 cup orange juice
2 sprigs spring onion, cut into 3 cm (1 1/4 in) lengths, finely shredded and soaked in cold water
Cucumber and orange slices

Seasoning Ingredients

1 teaspoon dark soya sauce
1 teaspoon salt
1/4 teaspoon pepper

Sauce Ingredients (combined)

3/4 cup water
1 teaspoon chicken stock granules
1 teaspoon light soya sauce
1 teaspoon sesame oil
2 teaspoons oyster sauce
1 teaspoon sugar

Discard the chicken wing tips. Make 2 slits on the underside of the wings to allow marinade to penetrate. Season wings with seasoning ingredients for at least 1 hour.

Heat oil until hot and fry ginger and shallost until lightly browned. Add chicken wings and cook until they change colour. Stir in vinegar.

Add orange juice and combined sauce ingredients. Bring to the boil. Cover and simmer for 15–20 minutes until sauce thickens and chicken is tender. If necessary, thicken with 1 teaspoon cornflour mixed with 1 teaspoon water.

Arrange chicken wings on serving dish and pour over the sauce. Garnish with cucumber and orange slices.

Use dark purple shallots, known as Indian shallots, for this dish. They are more pungent and will help to thicken the sauce.

Braised Chicken Wings with Oyster Sauce

10–12 chicken wings, with wing tips cut off.
1/2 tablespoon light soya sauce
1/2 teaspoon pepper
3 tablespoons cooking oil
8–10 slices ginger
2 cloves garlic, sliced
5–6 stalks spring onion, whites cut into 2 1/2 cm (1 in) lengths, greens chopped for garnishing
2 pieces dried scallop, steamed and shredded
1/2 tablespoon Chinese rice wine
1 teaspoon cornflour mixed with 1 tablespoon chicken stock or water
8 stalks flowering mustard green, washed with tough stems discarded
1/2 teaspoon salt

Sauce Ingredients (combined)

1 1/4 cups fresh chicken stock
1/2 tablespoon oyster sauce
1/2 tablespoon Chinese rice wine
1 teaspoon light soya sauce
1/2 teaspoon thick soya sauce
1/2 teaspoon sugar
1/4 teaspoon salt
1/4 teaspoon pepper

Marinate chicken wings with light soya sauce and pepper and leave for 30 minutes.

Heat wok with 2 tablespoons cooking oil until hot and stir–fry ginger, garlic and spring onion until fragrant. Add scallops and stir-fry for 1–2 minutes. Put in chicken wings and toss until they change colour. Sprinkle in the rice wine and stir-fry briskly until well-mixed.

Pour in combined sauce ingredients and bring to the boil. Cover and cook over low heat for 15 minutes until chicken is tender. Thicken with cornflour mixture.

Scald mustard green in boiling water with 1 tablespoon oil and 1/2 teaspoon salt for 1–2 minutes. Drain and arrange around the sides of a serving dish. Place sauce-covered chicken wings in the centre.

Garnish with chopped spring onion and serve.

The Chinese prefer chicken wings to breasts because of their smooth texture. The dried scallops, although expensive, enhance the sweetness of the sauce.

Braised Chicken Feet

20 chicken feet, claws cut off and chopped in 2
Oil for deep-frying
2 tablespoons cooking oil
2 shallots, sliced
3 cloves garlic, minced
2 segments of 1 star anise
1/2 teaspoon Szechuan peppercorns
6 dried Chinese mushrooms, soaked until soft
2 teaspoons cornflour mixed
with 1 tablespoon chicken stock or water

Seasoning Ingredients
1 teaspoon pepper
1 tablespoon light soya sauce
1 teaspoon thick soya sauce

Sauce Ingredients (combined)
1 1/2 cups fresh chicken stock
1 tablespoon thick soya sauce
2 teaspoons light soya sauce
1 teaspoon salt
1 teaspoon sugar
1/2 teaspoon pepper
1/4 teaspoon five spice powder

Marinate chicken feet with seasoning ingredients for at least 1 hour.

Heat wok with enough oil for deep-frying until hot. Put in chicken feet and cover the wok to prevent oil splattering. Deep-fry the chicken feet for 5 minutes or until golden brown. Drain from oil and soak in cold water for 1/2 hour. Drain.

Heat wok with 2 tablespoons of oil and lightly brown shallots and garlic. Add star anise and peppercorns and return chicken feet to the wok. Toss briefly for 2 minutes.

Put chicken mixture into an electric crock-pot and add combined sauce ingredients. Cook on high for 1 hour.

Add the mushrooms and continue to slow cook, stirring occasionally, for 1 1/2 hours or until chicken feet are tender.

Thicken sauce with cornflour mixture.

This is a Szechuan method of braising chicken feet. Some people are put off by chicken feet but they are really quite clean. Chicken feet are covered by a skin which is removed before cooking.

Braised Chicken with Sea Cucumber

600–800 gms (21–28 oz) sea cucumber, rinsed, sliced and drained
8 cm (3 in) piece ginger, sliced
1 tablespoon Chinese rice wine
3 tablespoons oil
1 whole pod garlic, minced
10 dried Chinese mushrooms, soaked to soften
12 chicken feet
12 medium dried oysters, soaked for 5 minutes
10 gms (1/3 oz) black sea moss (*fatt choy*), soaked to soften and drained
3 whole chicken thighs, each cut into 4 pieces
2 tablespoons oyster sauce

Sauce Ingredients (combined)
2 1/2 cups chicken stock
1 1/2 tablespoons light soya sauce
1 1/2 tablespoons thick soya sauce
1 teaspoon salt
1 teaspoon sugar
1/2 teaspoon pepper

Heat a saucepan without oil and put in sea cucumber and ginger. Stir-fry until most of the water has evaporated (about 5 minutes). Add rice wine and toss briefly. Dish out the sea cucumber and discard the ginger. Set aside.

Heat a deep saucepan with oil and lightly brown garlic. Put in the Chinese mushrooms and stir-fry for 2 minutes. Add chicken feet and cook for a further 1–2 minutes. Put in the dried oysters and black sea moss.

Return sea cucumber to saucepan and pour in combined sauce ingredients. Bring to the boil and simmer for about 45 minutes.

Add chicken thighs and oyster sauce and cook for 15–20 minutes, until meat is tender.

Transfer to serving dish and serve hot.

Teochew Duck

1 duck, clean weight
approximately 1½ kg (3⅓ lbs)
1 dessertspoon salt
1 dessertspoon five spice powder
120 gms (4¼ oz) galangal, sliced
Oil for deep-frying
2 tablespoons sugar
2 tablespoons thick soya sauce
5 cups water or enough to cover
more than half the duck
1 tablespoon light soya sauce
6 hard boiled eggs, shelled
Coriander leaves for garnishing

Rub the inside and outside of the duck with salt and five spice powder. Stuff duck with the galangal slices, keeping 3 slices aside. Let the duck stand for at least 2 hours.

Heat deep-frying oil in a deep wok until hot and fry duck for 5 minutes until lightly browned. Remove duck and drain well. Pour off oil, leaving 2 tablespoons in the wok and add sugar and 3 galangal slices. When the oil turns dark golden, turn off heat. Add thick soya sauce. Return duck to wok and coat the whole duck with sauce.

Pour in water to cover more than half of the duck. Put in light soya sauce and hard boiled eggs. Bring to the boil, cover and simmer for about 20 minutes. Remove eggs and set aside.

Turn the duck and continue simmering over low heat for about 1½–2 hours, until duck is tender and sauce is thick. Turn the duck occasionally while simmering.

Before serving, cut duck into serving size pieces and halve the eggs. Place around the duck and pour sauce over. Serve garnished with coriander leaves.

The Teochews are famous for braised dishes and this dish is one of their best. It can be served cold or hot and goes well with rice or porridge. Do not replace galangal with ginger as it is far too pungent for this dish. Illustrated on page 170.

Claypot Ginger Duck

2¾ kg (6 lbs) duck, skinned, feet and neck
removed, chopped into bite-sized pieces
210 gms (7½ oz) young ginger, sliced
2 tablespoons cooking oil
7 cloves garlic, finely minced
1 piece fermented beancurd (*lam yee*)
2 tablespoons hot soya bean garlic paste
1 tablespoon sugar
1 tablespoon thick soya sauce
3½ cups water
2 teaspoons cornflour mixed
with 2 tablespoons water
1 tablespoon chopped coriander leaves
1 tablespoon chopped spring onion

Heat claypot (about 25 cm, 10 in diameter) without oil and fry ginger pieces until fragrant. Add the cooking oil and cook ginger for a minute. Put in garlic and brown lightly. Add fermented beancurd and hot soya bean garlic paste and stir-fry until fragrant.

Add duck and cook for 2 minutes. Put in sugar and thick soya sauce. Toss to mix well.

Add water and bring to the boil. Reduce heat and simmer, covered, for 1–1¼ hours, until duck is tender and sauce is reduced. Stir frequently during simmering.

Thicken with cornflour mixture and stir in chopped spring onion and coriander leaves.

Be sure to use young ginger instead of old ginger so the flavour is not compromised.

Braised Fish with Black Bean Sauce

1 kg ($2^1/_5$ lbs) whole fish
(garoupa, threadfin, red snapper)
Oil for deep-frying
2 shallots, sliced
2 cloves garlic, minced
5 slices ginger, minced
1 tablespoon fermented black beans, soaked in water for 10 minutes, drained and minced
2 red chillies, chopped
2 teaspoons cornflour mixed with 2 tablespoons water
2 stalks spring onion, chopped

Seasoning Ingredients

$^1/_2$ teaspoon salt
$^1/_2$ teaspoon pepper
2 teaspoons light soya sauce
1 tablespoon Chinese rice wine
1 beaten egg white
1 tablespoon cornflour, to be added just before frying fish

Sauce Ingredients (combined)

1 cup fresh anchovy stock
2 teaspoons light soya sauce
$^1/_2$ teaspoon thick soya sauce
2 teaspoons Chinese rice wine
1 teaspoon black vinegar
$1^1/_2$ teaspoons sugar
$^1/_4$ teaspoon salt
$^1/_4$ teaspoon pepper

Clean and scale the fish. Cut two deep slits $2^1/_4$ cm (1 in) apart across each side of the body. Season fish with seasoning ingredients for at least 30 minutes. Just before deep-frying fish coat with cornflour.

Heat oil in a wok for deep-frying until hot. Fry the fish for 2–3 minutes on each side. Remove and drain from oil.

Reheat a clean wok with 2 tablespoons of the oil and stir-fry shallots, garlic and ginger until fragrant. Add the fermented black beans and stir-fry until aromatic. Put in chillies and sauce ingredients.

Return fish to the wok and reduce heat a little. Cover the wok and allow to simmer for 3–5 minutes, or until fish is cooked. Remove the fish carefully and place on a serving dish.

Thicken the sauce with cornflour mixture and add spring onion. Pour sauce over fish and serve hot.

If a crispier skin is preferred, deep-fry the fish a little longer until it is thoroughly cooked.

Braised Fish with Hot Bean Paste

600 gms (21 oz) fish (carp, garoupa, threadfin or red snapper)
Oil for deep-frying
2 teaspoons cornflour mixed with 2 tablespoons water
10 slices ginger, minced
3 cloves garlic, minced
2 shallots, minced
1 dessertspoon hot bean paste
2 stalks spring onion, chopped

Seasoning Ingredients

2 tablespoons Chinese rice wine
$^1/_2$ tablespoon light soya sauce
$^1/_2$ teaspoon pepper

Sauce Ingredients (combined)

1 cup anchovy or fresh chicken stock
2 tablespoons Chinese rice wine
2 teaspoons light soya sauce
1 teaspoon sugar
$^1/_4$ teaspoon pepper
1 teaspoon cornflour

Clean and scale the fish. Score two vertical cuts $2^1/_2$ cm (1 in) apart across each side of the body. Marinate with seasoning ingredients and leave for 15–20 minutes.

Heat a wok with oil for deep-frying until hot. Coat the fish with cornflour mixture and slip into hot oil. Deep-fry for about 3 minutes on each side. Remove and set aside.

Reheat a clean wok with 2 tablespoons of the oil and lightly brown ginger, garlic and shallots. Add the hot bean paste and stir-fry for 1 minute or until aromatic.

Add combined sauce ingredients and when it begins to boil, put in the fish. Cover and simmer for 3–5 minutes until fish is cooked.

Sprinkle in spring onion, dish out carefully and serve hot.

Deep-frying the fish with a coating of cornflour keeps the fish tender and moist.

Braised Fish Head (*Hoong Siew Yee Tau*)

1 fish head (garoupa, red snapper or threadfin), approximately 1 kg (2¹/₅ lbs)
1 tablespoon ginger juice
½ tablespoon light soya sauce
100 gms (3½ oz) belly pork or chicken, shredded
¼ teaspoon salt
¼ teaspoon pepper
Oil for deep-frying
3 tablespoons cornflour
5 slices ginger, shredded
3 cloves garlic, sliced
1 shallot, sliced
4 dried Chinese mushrooms, soaked until soft and halved
120 gms (4¼ oz) carrots, sliced and parboiled
6 pieces young corn, cut into 2
½ a green pepper, cubed
½ tablespoon Chinese rice wine
1 teaspoon cornflour mixed with 1 tablespoon water
1 egg white, lightly beaten
1 stalk spring onion, cut into 2½ cm (1 in) lengths
1 sprig coriander leaves, cut into 2½ cm (1 in) lengths
1 red chilli, cut into strips

Sauce Ingredients (combined)

1 cup fresh anchovy or chicken stock
1 tablespoon light soya sauce
1 teaspoon thick soya sauce
1 teaspoon Chinese rice wine
1 teaspoon sesame oil
1 teaspoon sugar
1 teaspoon pepper
½ teaspoon salt

Clean fish head and cut into 2. Season with ginger juice and light soya sauce for 30 minutes. Marinate shredded pork or chicken with salt and pepper.

Heat a wok with deep-frying oil until hot. Coat the fish with the cornflour and deep-fry for 3–5 minutes. Remove and drain from oil.

Reheat a clean wok with 3 tablespoons of the oil and lightly brown shredded ginger, garlic and shallots. Add the mushrooms and stir-fry for 1 minute until fragrant.

Put in meat shreds and when the meat changes colour add the carrots, young corn and green pepper and stir-fry for 1 minute. Sprinkle in wine.

Pour in combined sauce ingredients. Bring to the boil and put in the fish head.

Reduce the heat, cover the wok and simmer for 5 minutes. Remove the fish head and arrange on a serving dish.

Thicken the sauce with cornflour mixture and beaten egg white. Stir in spring onion, coriander leaves and chilli and pour sauce over fish head.

A famous Cantonese dish. This is one of the best ways to prepare fish head. A claypot can also be used for an even richer flavour.

Ginger Chicken in Earthen Pot
Page 163

Teochew Duck
Page 166

Claypot Fish Head
Page 177

Braised Stuffed Hairy Marrow
Page 178

Mixed Vegetable Stew
Page 182

Roast Pork Ribs
Page 186

Herbal Beggar's Chicken
Page 187

Oyster Grilled Prawns
Page 191

Claypot Fish Head

1 fish head (garoupa, threadfin, red snapper), about 800 gms (28 oz), chopped into large pieces
1/2 tablespoon Chinese rice wine
1/2 tablespoon light soya sauce
1/2 tablespoon ginger juice
1/2 teaspoon pepper
Oil for deep-frying
1 square soft beancurd, cut into 2 1/2 cm (1 in) cubes
3 tablespoons cooking oil
2 1/2 cm (1 in) piece ginger
1 onion, cut into 6 wedges
4 dried Chinese mushrooms
6–8 button mushrooms, canned
2 red chillies, sliced
2 stalks spring onion, cut into 2 1/2 cm (1 in) sections
1/2 tablespoon cornflour mixed with 1 tablespoon water
6–8 leaves lettuce, washed

Batter

1 egg, beaten
2 tablespoons cornflour
2 tablespoons water

Sauce Ingredients

1 cup chicken stock
1 tablespoon oyster sauce
1/2 tablespoon light soya sauce
2 teaspoons Chinese rice wine
1 teaspoon sesame oil
1 teaspoon sugar
1/2 teaspoon pepper

Clean fish head and marinate with rice wine, soya sauce, ginger juice and pepper for 30 minutes.

Heat wok with oil for deep-frying until hot. Coat fish head with batter and deep-fry fish head for 5–8 minutes on each side until golden brown and cooked. Set aside.

Put in beancurd and deep-fry for 2 minutes. Drain from oil and leave aside.

Heat claypot with 3 tablespoons cooking oil and sauté ginger and onion until fragrant.

Put in mushrooms and stir-fry for 1 minute. Add button mushrooms and chillies and toss briskly.

Pour in combined sauce ingredients and bring to the boil.

Put in fish head and beancurd. Reduce heat a little, cover and simmer for 5–8 minutes. Add spring onion and thicken with cornflour mixture.

Arrange lettuce leaves around sides of claypot and serve immediately.

The larger garoupa, threadfin and red snapper are prized for their meaty heads and smooth texture. Well prepared they are a gourmet's delight. Illustrated on page 171.

Braised Stuffed Hairy Marrow

1 hairy marrow,
approximately 250 gms (8 3/4 oz)
Cornflour for dusting
Oil for deep-frying
2 teaspoons oyster sauce
1/2 teaspoon sesame oil
2 teaspoons cornflour mixed
with 1 tablespoon chicken stock or water

Minced Ingredients
150 gms (5 1/4 oz) shelled small prawns
15 gms (1/2 oz) lean pork or chicken
2 water chestnuts
1 stalk spring onion

Seasoning Ingredients
1/2 teaspoon salt
1/2 teaspoon sugar
1/2 teaspoon pepper
1 teaspoon light soya sauce
1 teaspoon sesame oil
2 teaspoons cornflour

Sauce Ingredients
1 1/2 cups fresh chicken or pork bone stock
1/2 teaspoon salt
1/4 teaspoon pepper
1/2 teaspoon sugar

Lightly pare the hairy marrow leaving some of the green skin to give more colour. Slice off both the ends and keep aside. Scoop out the pulp from the centre with a small spoon or a sharp knife. Dust the inside with cornflour and set aside.

Combine the minced ingredients with the seasoning ingredients and mix thoroughly.

Stuff the marrow with this mixture. Put back the sliced ends and secure with toothpicks or cocktail sticks.

Heat oil for deep-frying in a wok until hot. Deep-fry stuffed marrow for 3–4 minutes until just soft. Remove and drain.

Pour off the oil from the wok and add sauce ingredients. When it begins to boil, carefully put in marrow. Cover, reduce heat and simmer for 10–12 minutes or until the marrow is very tender.

Carefully remove the marrow and slice the into 2 1/2 cm (1 in) slices with a sharp knife. Arrange on a serving dish.

Add oyster sauce, sesame oil and cornflour mixture to sauce and stir until thickened.

Pour hot sauce over the marrow and serve.

This is a vegetable dish that reheats well and can be prepared well in advance. Illustrated on page 172.

Braised Tientsin Cabbage with Dried Scallops

600 gms (21 oz) Tientsin cabbage, each leaf halved lengthways and cut into 7½ cm (3 in) pieces
Pinch of bicarbonate of soda
4 medium-sized dried scallops (approximately 30 gms, 1 oz), rinsed
4 tablespoons cooking oil
1½ cups fresh chicken stock or enough to cover cabbage
¼ teaspoon each of salt, pepper and sugar
4 slices ginger, shredded
2 cloves garlic, minced
2 shallots, sliced
½ tablespoon Chinese rice wine
1 teaspoon cornflour mixed with 1 tablespoon chicken stock or water

Sauce Ingredients (combined)
1 cup fresh chicken stock
1 teaspoon light soya sauce
1 teaspoon oyster sauce
1 teaspoon Chinese rice wine
½ teaspoon sugar
¼ teaspoon pepper

Blanch cabbage in a saucepan of boiling water with a pinch of bicarbonate of soda for 1 minute. Drain and set aside.

Place the dried scallops in a small heat-proof dish and steam over rapidly boiling water for 15 minutes. Cool and shred with fingers.

Heat a wok with 2 tablespoons of oil until hot and stir-fry cabbage for 1–2 minutes. Add the fresh chicken stock, which should cover the vegetables, salt, pepper and sugar. Bring to the boil, cover the wok, reduce heat and simmer for 10 minutes.

Drain the vegetables and arrange on a serving dish. Discard the boiled vegetable stock.

Reheat a clean wok with 2 remaining tablespoons of oil and lightly brown ginger, garlic and shallots. Add the shredded scallops and stir-fry briefly. Sprinkle in wine and toss to mix well.

Pour in sauce ingredients and bring to the boil. Reduce heat and simmer for 3–5 minutes.

Thicken with cornflour mixture and pour over vegetables.

Blanching the vegetable in boiling water with a pinch of bicarbonate of soda helps to retain the colour of the vegetable and rid it of its slightly bitter taste.

Braised Tientsin Cabbage with Chestnuts

120 gms (4¼ oz) shelled chestnuts
300 gms (10½ oz) Tientsin cabbage, each leaf halved lengthways and cut into 7½ cm (3 in) pieces
Pinch of bicarbonate of soda
4 tablespoons cooking oil
¾ cup fresh chicken stock
3 slices ginger, shredded
1 shallot, sliced
1 clove garlic, minced
2 teaspoons cornflour mixed with 2 tablespoons chicken stock or water

Seasoning Ingredients
¼ teaspoon salt
¼ teaspoon pepper
½ tablespoon light soya sauce

Sauce Ingredients (combined)
½ cup fresh chicken stock
½ tablespoon Chinese rice wine
½ teaspoon sugar
¼ teaspoon salt
¼ teaspoon pepper

Boil chestnuts in a saucepan of water for 15 minutes. Drain.

Put a pinch of bicarbonate of soda into the boiling water and blanch the cabbage for 1–2 minutes. Drain and set aside.

Heat a wok with 3 tablespoons of oil until hot and fry the chestnuts for 2–3 minutes. Remove chestnuts, leaving oil in the wok. Add the cabbage and stir-fry for 2 minutes. Drain and discard the oil.

Place chestnuts and cabbage in the wok and add the fresh chicken stock and seasoning ingredients. Bring to the boil, lower the heat and simmer for 10 minutes. Drain and discard the stock.

Reheat a clean wok with remaining 1 tablespoon of oil and lightly brown ginger, shallots and garlic. Pour in combined sauce ingredients and bring to the boil. Return cabbage and chestnut to the wok.

Thicken with cornflour mixture and serve hot with rice.

If a darker sauce is preferred, add ½ teaspoon thick soya sauce to sauce ingredients. If you dislike doing last minute cooking, this is one dish that can be prepared way ahead of time and still looks appetising heated just before serving.

Braised Straw Mushrooms with Crab Meat Sauce

500 gms (1½ 12 oz cans) canned or fresh straw mushrooms, rinsed
2 tablespoons cooking oil
4 teaspoons Chinese rice wine
120 gms (4¼ oz) cooked crab meat, from 1 large-sized crab
2 egg whites, lightly beaten
2 teaspoons sweet potato flour mixed with 3 tablespoons chicken stock or water

Sauce Ingredients 'A'
1 cup fresh chicken stock
½ teaspoon salt
1 teaspoon sugar

Sauce Ingredients 'B'
½ cup fresh chicken stock
¼ teaspoon salt
¼ teaspoon pepper
½ teaspoon sesame oil

Scald straw mushrooms in boiling water for 1 minute, then drain.

Heat wok with 1 tablespoon of oil until hot. Add 2 teaspoons wine then sauce ingredients 'A' and bring to the boil. Put in mushrooms, reduce heat and simmer for 5 minutes.

Remove from heat and allow mushrooms to soak in the stock until cooled. Drain and place mushrooms on a deep serving dish.

Reheat wok with 1 tablespoon of oil until hot and add 2 teaspoons wine. Immediately add combined sauce ingredients 'B' and bring to the boil. Stir in crab meat then the egg white.

Thicken sauce with sweet potato flour mixture and pour over mushrooms. Serve hot.

Use fresh crab meat for this dish. Canned crab meat does not have the same sweetness.

Claypot Mushrooms and Mixed Vegetables

3 squares (300 gms, 10½ oz) firm beancurd (*tau kwa*), cut into 2 cm (⅔ in) cubes
Oil for deep-frying
1 tablespoon cooking oil
2 tablespoons hot soya bean garlic paste
2 large pieces (approximately 10 gms, ⅓ oz) wood ear fungus (*mok yee*), soaked and trimmed
12 pieces cloud ear fungus (*wan yee*), soaked and trimmed
150 gms (5¼ oz) fresh shiitake mushrooms, rinsed, soaked and trimmed
100 gms (3½ oz) white part of leek, sliced diagonally ½ cm (¼ in) thick
100 gms (3½ oz) sweet peas
100 gms (3½ oz) red capsicum, seeded, cut into 1½ cm (¾ in) thick diamond slices
1 red chilli, seeded and cut into 1½ cm (¾ in) thick diamond slices
2 tablespoons chopped coriander leaves
2 tablespoons chopped spring onion
2 teaspoons cornflour mixed with 2 tablespoons water
1 teaspoon sesame oil

Sauce Ingredients (combined)
1¼ cups fresh chicken stock
2 tablespoons light soya sauce
3 tablespoons Hoisin sauce

Deep-fry beancurd in hot oil until lightly browned. Drain from oil and set aside.

Heat a claypot (about 25 cm, 10 in diameter) with 1 tablespoon oil and stir-fry the hot soya bean garlic paste for 30 seconds. Put in wood ear fungus and cloud ear fungus and cook for 3 minutes. Add the shiitake mushrooms and stir-fry for 2 minutes. Put in leek and toss briefly. Pour in combined sauce ingredients and bring to the boil.

Add sweet peas, red capsicum, chilli and beancurd. When it boils again, stir in half of the coriander leaves and spring onion.

Thicken with cornflour mixture and lastly stir in sesame oil.

Sprinkle with remaining coriander leaves and spring onion and serve hot.

A healthy dish of colourful vegetables with an excellent sauce. Fresh champignons can be used but fresh shiitake mushrooms give the dish a richer flavour.

Mixed Vegetable Stew

4 tablespoons cooking oil
$^1/_2$ teaspoon salt
90 gms (3 oz) carrots, cut into 2 cm ($^3/_4$ in) cubes
3 leaves Tientsin cabbage,
halved and cut into 4 cm (1$^1/_2$ oz) lengths
90 gms (3 oz) canned bamboo shoots, sliced
5 dried Chinese mushrooms, soaked and halved
90 gms (3 oz) canned straw mushrooms
90 gms (3 oz) canned button mushrooms
or fresh champignons
120 gms (4$^1/_4$ oz) broccoli,
cut into small florets
1 shallot, sliced
2 cloves garlic, minced
15 gms ($^1/_2$ oz) cloud ear fungus,
soaked in warm water until soft
15 gms ($^1/_2$ oz) white fungus,
cut into 2$^1/_2$ cm (1 in) pieces,
hard centres discarded
2 teaspoons sweet potato flour or cornflour
mixed with 2 tablespoons chicken stock or water

Sauce Ingredients (combined)
1 cup fresh chicken or pork bone stock
1 teaspoon salt
$^1/_2$ teaspoon sugar
$^1/_2$ teaspoon pepper
$^1/_2$ teaspoon Chinese rice wine
1 teaspoon light soya sauce
1 teaspoon oyster sauce

Boil a large saucepan of water and add 2 tablespoons of the cooking oil and $^1/_2$ teaspoon salt. Blanch carrot, cabbage and bamboo shoots for 1–2 minutes. Drain and set aside. Blanch dried Chinese, straw and button mushrooms for 1 minute. Drain and set aside. Blanch broccoli for 1 minute and set aside.

Heat wok with 2 tablespoons of the oil until hot and lightly brown shallot and garlic. Put in carrots, cabbage and bamboo shoots and stir-fry for 1 minute. Add the mushrooms and stir-fry for another minute. Put in cloud ear and white fungus and toss briefly.

Pour in combined sauce ingredients and bring to the boil. Reduce heat, add the broccoli, cover the wok and simmer for 5 minutes.

Thicken with sweet potato flour mixture and stir until the sauce is thick and clear.

Transfer to serving dish and serve hot.

Illustrated on page 173. Substitute bamboo shoots with water chestnuts for a crunchier texture.

Braised Dried Beancurd with Dried Chinese Mushrooms

8–10 dried Chinese mushrooms, soaked until soft
3 tablespoons cooking oil
2 slices ginger, shredded
1 shallot, sliced
90 gms (3 oz) broccoli, cut into small florets and rinsed
250 gms (8¾ oz) dried beancurd cubes (*taufu pok*)
1 teaspoon cornflour mixed with 1 tablespoon chicken stock or water
1 teaspoon sesame oil
1 red chilli, sliced, optional
1 stalk spring onion, chopped

Seasoning Ingredients
¼ teaspoon salt
¼ teaspoon sugar
¼ teaspoon pepper
1 teaspoon light soya sauce

Sauce Ingredients (combined)
1¼ cups fresh chicken stock
½ tablespoon thick soya sauce
2 teaspoons light soya sauce
½ teaspoon sugar
¼ teaspoon salt
¼ teaspoon pepper

Season mushrooms with seasoning ingredients for 15 minutes.

Heat 1½ tablespoons of the oil in a wok until hot and stir-fry ginger and shallots until fragrant, then add the mushrooms and fry for another 1–2 minutes. Remove and set aside. Stir-fry the broccoli for 1 minute, remove and set aside.

Reheat remaining oil in the wok and toss beancurd cubes until crisp and light brown in colour.

Add the combined sauce ingredients and mushrooms and bring to the boil. Reduce heat and simmer for 10 minutes. Add the broccoli and simmer for 2 minutes longer.

Thicken with cornflour mixture and lastly sprinkle in sesame oil, red chillies and spring onion.

On the 1st and 15th days of the Chinese lunar month, the devout eat vegetarian. If cooking strictly vegetarian, mushrooms make an equally tasty stock in any recipe.

Braised Fried Beancurd with Dried Sole

2 rolls soft beancurd (Japanese), cut into 18–20 pieces
Oil for deep-frying
1 egg, beaten
4 tablespoons plain flour
1 tablespoon cooking oil
3 slices ginger, finely shredded
1 shallot, sliced
½ tablespoon roasted dried sole (*peen yee*) or dried prawns, finely ground
1 red chilli, seeded and sliced
1 sprig coriander leaves, chopped

Seasoning Ingredients
¼ teaspoon salt
¼ teaspoon pepper
½ teaspoon Chinese rice wine
½ teaspoon sesame oil

Sauce Ingredients
3 tablespoons fresh chicken stock
¼ teaspoon salt
¼ teaspoon sugar
Dash of pepper
½ teaspoon sesame oil
½ teaspoon light soya sauce
½ teaspoon thick soya sauce

Marinate beancurd with seasoning ingredients, taking care not to break the pieces. Leave for 15 minutes and drain.

Heat a wok with deep-frying oil until hot. Carefully dip beancurd in beaten egg and coat with plain flour. Deep-fry beancurd until golden brown. Drain and arrange on serving dish.

Reheat a clean wok with 1 tablespoon oil and sauté ginger and shallots until fragrant.

Add sauce ingredients and return beancurd to the wok. Put in dried sole or dried prawns, reduce heat and simmer, covered, for 2 minutes. Remove cover and sprinkle in chilli and coriander leaves.

Transfer to serving dish and serve hot.

If crispier fried beancurd is preferred, do not return fried beancurd to the wok. Simmer the sauce for 3 minutes instead of 2 minutes and then pour over the beancurd.

Braised Fresh Egg Noodles (*Mun Sang Meen*)

150 gms (5¼ oz) chicken or pork, shredded
120 gms (4¼ oz) shelled small prawns
120 gms (4¼ oz) small–medium cuttlefish, cut into 1¼ cm ½ in) pieces
1½ teaspoons salt
1½ teaspoons sesame oil
1 teaspoon pepper
300 gms (10½ oz) fresh egg noodles (*wantan meen*)
3 tablespoons cooking oil
1 teaspoon sesame oil
3 cloves garlic, minced
2 shallots, sliced
1 leaf Tientsin cabbage, shredded
2–3 stalks mustard green, cut into 5 cm (2 in) lengths
1 tablespoon sweet potato flour mixed with 1 tablespoon chicken stock or water
2 red chillies, seeded and sliced
2 stalks spring onion, chopped

Sauce Ingredients (combined)
2 cups fresh chicken stock
½ tablespoon light soya sauce
½ teaspoon salt
¼ teaspoon pepper

Season meat, prawns and cuttlefish separately with ½ teaspoon each of the salt, sesame oil and a dash of pepper. Leave for 15 minutes.

Bring a saucepan of water to a rapid boil and scald noodles for under a minute. Drain with a wire-mesh noodle ladle and tip noodles into a basin of cold water for 10–15 seconds.

Re-scald noodles in the boiling water again for a few seconds. Drain well and place in a deep serving dish. Mix in 1 tablespoon oil and sesame oil. Leave aside.

Heat the 2 tablespoons of oil in a wok until hot and lightly brown garlic and shallots. Put in meat and stir-fry over high heat for 1 minute. Add cuttlefish and prawns and stir-fry until it changes colour. Remove ingredients to a dish and set aside.

Pour combined sauce ingredients into the wok and bring to a rapid boil. Add cabbage and mustard green, stems first. When it boils again, return meat mixture to the wok. Simmer over low heat for 5–8 minutes.

Stir in the sweet potato flour mixture until sauce thickens. Sprinkle in red chillies and spring onion and mix well.

Pour hot sauce over the noodles and serve immediately.

A lovely noodle dish ideal for light lunches. Be sure not to overcook the noodles or they will turn soggy.

ROASTED, GRILLED AND SMOKED

DISHES

Roast Pork Ribs

1 1/5 kg (2 2/3 lbs) pork ribs, kept in whole panels about 10–12 cm (4–5 in) long
4 cloves garlic, finely chopped
2 thin slices ginger
1 piece star anise
1 tablespoon maltose

Seasoning Ingredients

120 gms (4 1/4 oz) coarse sugar
3 tablespoons light soya sauce
1 teaspoon thick soya sauce
2 tablespoons oyster sauce
1 1/2 tablespoons Hoisin sauce
1 1/2 tablespoons plum sauce
1 tablespoon Chinese rice wine
1/2 teaspoon ginger powder
1 teaspoon five spice powder
1 tablespoon sesame oil
1/4 teaspoon pepper
2 teaspoons meat tenderiser
1/4 teaspoon red colouring

Rinse the panels of ribs. Dry well with kitchen paper.

Mix seasoning ingredients in a bowl. Put in the garlic, ginger, and star anise, and mix well. Pour the mixture over the ribs and marinate for at least 8–10 hours (preferably overnight) in the refrigerator.

Preheat oven to 220°C (400°F) for 15 minutes. Place ribs on a wire rack and roast for at least 1 hour, basting ribs with marinade occasionally and turning ribs over every 15 minutes.

Pour remaining marinade into a small saucepan and add the maltose. Stir over low heat until maltose dissolves.

Pour mixture over ribs and grill on each side for 3–5 minutes, or until well roasted.

This dish can be prepared well ahead of time. Measure the seasoning ingredients as accurately as possible—you'll be rewarded with succulent pork ribs. *Illustrated on page 174.*

Roast Pork (*Char Siew*)

600 gms (21 oz) belly pork or lean and fat pork

Seasoning Ingredients

2 1/2 teaspoons salt
4 tablespoons sugar
1 tablespoon light soya sauce
1/2 tablespoon thick soya sauce
1 tablespoon malt (*mak ngah tong)* mixed with 2 1/2 tablespoons hot water into a syrup
1/2 tablespoon red colouring, optional

Wash pork and dry with a clean towel. Cut into 2 pieces lengthways. Marinate with seasoning ingredients for 5 hours, or preferably overnight in the refrigerator.

Place marinated meat in a preheated turbo broiler or closed grill (175°C, 350°F). Pour half of the marinade over the meat and cook for 12–15 minutes. Turn meat over and pour remaining marinade over meat and cook for a further 12–15 minutes or until cooked through.

Cut into slices and serve with rice or noodles.

Char siew can also be made with chicken. Use de-boned whole chicken legs and follow the same procedure.

Chicken Wings Baked in Foil

6 chicken wings

Seasoning Ingredients

1/2 teaspoon salt
1/2 teaspoon sugar
1/2 teaspoon pepper
1 clove garlic, ground
1 teaspoon ginger juice
1 1/2 teaspoons light soya sauce
1 1/2 teaspoons thick soya sauce
1 1/2 teaspoons mustard
1 1/2 teaspoons cornflour
1 tablespoon cooking oil

Marinate chicken wings with seasoning ingredients for 2 hours.

Wrap in lightly greased tin foil. Place in an oven toaster and bake for 15 minutes.

A quick and simple dish to prepare but very tasty. For variation, replace mustard with oyster sauce.

Herbal Beggar's Chicken

1 whole chicken, approximately 1 1/2 kg (3 1/3 lbs), cleaned and well drained
1 1/2 kg (3 1/3 lbs) plain flour
1 teaspoon salt
3 1/2 cups water
2 sheets tracing paper and cling wrap

Seasoning Ingredients 'A'

1/2 teaspoon salt
1/4 teaspoon pepper
1/2 tablespoon Chinese rice wine
1/2 tablespoon sesame oil

Seasoning Ingredients 'B'

1/2 tablespoon sugar
1/2 teaspoon rock salt
1/4 teaspoon pepper
1 tablespoon light soya sauce
1/2 tablespoon thick soya sauce
1/2 tablespoon Chinese rice wine
1 teaspoon sesame oil
2 teaspoons shallot oil

Herbs (rinsed, combined and steamed for 10–15 minutes)

10 gms (1/3 oz) *tong kwai*
15 gms (1/2 oz) *kei chi*
20 gms (2/3 oz) *yok chok*
20 gms (2/3 oz) *tong sum*
3 pieces *pak kee*
6 red dates, slit and seeds removed
1 tablespoon Chinese rice wine
3 tablespoons fresh chicken stock

Rub seasoning ingredients 'A' on the outside of the chicken and seasoning ingredients 'B' on the inside of the chicken. Stuff chicken with herbs and leave to marinate for 3 hours in the refrigerator.

Put flour into a basin and mix with salt and water to form a stiff, pliable dough. Roll out into a rectangle, big enough to wrap chicken.

Wrap the chicken with 1 layer of greased wax paper and cover with cling wrap or oven bag. Wrap with another layer of wax paper.

Cover the whole chicken with flour paste. Place chicken in a roasting pan and bake in preheated oven at 190°C (375°F) for 3 hours.

Crack open flour paste, remove paper and wrap and serve hot.

There must be many stories of the origin of this dish. In one story, during a time of civil unrest, a Qing Dynasty emperor was forced to flee the palace to escape his enemies. Tired and famished, he came upon a beggar preparing his dinner—a stolen chicken which he had covered in mud and baked over a fire. It was so delicious that it became the emperor's favourite dish and ended up on the imperial table. The use of dough instead of mud does not in any way reduce the quality of this lovely dish. *Illustrated on page 175.*

Mustard Chicken

4 whole legs of chicken, dried with kitchen towel
Lettuce
Cucumber slices

Seasoning Ingredients

1 teaspoon salt
1/2 teaspoon pepper
1 teaspoon chilli powder
4 tablespoons prepared mustard
4 tablespoons lime juice
50 gms (1 3/4 oz) sugar
1 tablespoon Worcestershire sauce
1 teaspoon light soya sauce
1/4 teaspoon thick soya sauce
2 tablespoons shallot oil

Score chicken to allow marinade to penetrate. Season chicken with seasoning ingredients and leave for at least 5 hours.

Preheat turbo-broiler or grill to 180°C (350°F). Place chicken in turbo-broiler or grill and spoon 1/4 of marinade over the chicken. Grill for 12–15 minutes. Spoon 1/4 of marinade halfway through grilling.

Turn over chicken and repeat marinading procedure.

Chop chicken into bite-sized pieces and arrange on serving plate. Garnish with lettuce and cucumber slices and serve hot.

The mustard adds a lovely tangy taste to the marinade.

Smoked Szechuan Chicken

1 whole chicken, approximately 1 1/2 kg (3 1/3 lbs), cleaned and drained well
1 tablespoon rice wine
3 thick slices ginger
2 stalks spring onion, cut into 3 cm (1 1/4 in) sections
Oil for deep-frying

Seasoning Ingredients (finely ground)
2 tablespoons salt
1/2 teaspoon roasted Szechuan peppercorn powder
1 teaspoon roasted cinnamon powder
2 star anise, roasted

For Smoking
1 1/3 rice measuring cups rice
1 tablespoon tea leaves
2 tablespoons sugar

Dip
1 tablespoon roasted peppercorns mixed with 2 tablespoons salt

Split chicken by cutting through the breast. Wash and drip dry. Make a deep slit to the bone along the centre of the drumsticks to enable the seasonings to penetrate.

Rub inside and outside of the chicken with 3/4 of the seasonings. Rub in wine and place ginger and spring onion inside chicken. Leave aside for 3 hours.

Bring a saucepan of water to the boil. Scald chicken until skin changes colour by first ladling the water over the chicken and then by dipping the chicken in the water for a few seconds. Drain well and wipe chicken with a dry cloth.

Spread smoking ingredients into an old wok. Place a rack over the mixture and spread chicken out on the rack, skin side down. Cover and if necessary line the rim of the cover with damp tea towels to prevent smoke from escaping.

Smoke chicken over low heat for 15 minutes. Turn chicken over half-way through smoking. To ensure even smoking, turn and tilt the wok so the smoke covers the chicken. After smoking chicken should take on an even golden colour.

Remove chicken and place on a heat-proof plate. Steam over rapidly boiling water for 20–25 minutes.

Heat oil for deep-frying in a wok until hot. Place chicken on a large perforated ladle and scoop hot oil over to brown the skin. Let oil heat until smoking hot and drop chicken into wok. Deep-fry for a few minutes until crispy and evenly browned.

Chop into pieces. Garnish and serve with dip.

Smoking is a long process and it is best done outdoors. The seasoning for this dish can be finely blended in a pepper mill. Only 3/4 of the amount is sufficient to marinate the chicken. Store the remainder in an air-tight container.

Salt Baked Chicken

1 whole chicken, approximately 1 1/2 kg (3 1/3 lbs)
1 teaspoon thick soya sauce
2 stalks spring onion, coarsely chopped
3 slices *tong kwai* or 2 whole star anise
5 kg (11 lbs) coarse salt
3 large sheets mulberry paper or white absorbent wrapping paper, 70 cm (27 1/2 in) squares

Seasoning Ingredients
1 teaspoon salt
2 teaspoons ginger juice
1 tablespoon brandy or Chinese rice or rose wine

Ginger and Spring Onion Dip
4 tablespoons shallot or cooked oil
1 teaspoon salt
6 slices ginger, minced
2 stalks spring onion, minced

Clean the chicken and rub the outside with the thick soya sauce. Rub the inside with seasoning ingredients and stuff the chicken with spring onion and *tong kwai*. Seal the cavity with a small sharp skewer or metal pin. Set aside.

Heat the wok with the coarse salt for 20–25 minutes until very hot stirring constantly. Cover the wok.

Wrap the chicken with the 3 layers of mulberry paper, one sheet at a time. Oil the top sheet with a little cooking oil.

Make a well in the centre of the heated salt and place chicken in it. Cover the wrapped chicken completely with salt. Leave the chicken to cook, covered, on moderate heat for 10 minutes, and remove.

Reheat the salt until very hot, stirring constantly to be sure the salt is evenly heated. Return chicken to the wok with the other side down. Cover with salt and cook for another 10–15 minutes over low heat.

Remove mulberry paper wrappings from chicken and discard stuffing. Cut into bite-sized pieces and serve hot with ginger and spring onion dip.

To prepare the ginger and spring onion dip, warm the shallot oil and add salt. Remove from heat and stir well. Pour over minced ginger and spring onion.

Use an old wok to prepare this dish as the salt causes the wok to rust. Salt baked chicken tastes best when made with free range (kampung) chicken. A Hakka speciality, the Chinese believe this dish is nutritious and good for the health.

Smoked Duck

1 whole duck, approximately 2 kg ($4^1/_2$ lbs), cleaned and drained well
Oil for deep-frying
Salt and pepper
Plum sauce or Hoisin sauce

Seasoning Ingredients

1 tablespoon salt
1 tablespoon Chinese rice wine
2 teaspoons potassium nitrate (*huan*), optional
1 teaspoon roasted Szechuan peppercorns, ground
1 teaspoon pepper
4–5 slices ginger, minced
1 stalk spring onion, minced

Smoking Ingredients

75 gms ($2^3/_4$ oz) Chinese black tea leaves
120 gms ($4^1/_4$ oz) camphor wood chips
180 gms ($6^1/_3$ oz) rice
2 pieces dried orange peel, crumbled

Dry duck thoroughly with a tea towel. Rub the inside and outside of the duck with combined seasoning ingredients. Leave to marinate overnight in the refrigerator. Cover with a plastic cling wrap to prevent the skin from drying out.

Bring a large saucepan of water to the boil and blanch duck for 5 minutes. Lift out the duck and hang out in an airy place to dry for 2 hours.

Place smoking ingredients in a wok over high heat. When smoking, put a wire rack over smoking ingredients. Place duck in a pan and set it on the rack. Cover and smoke over moderate heat for 10 minutes. Turn the duck over and smoke for about 5 minutes more.

Remove duck and transfer to a dish. Put into a steamer and steam over rapidly boiling water for $1^3/_4$–2 hours. Remove and drain well. Wipe moisture from the skin.

Heat wok with oil for deep-frying until very hot and deep-fry duck until the skin is dark brown and crisp, about 10–15 minutes. Ladle the oil over the duck constantly to get even browning.

Drain from oil and chop into bite-sized pieces. Arrange on a serving dish.

Serve with a pepper and salt, plum sauce or Hoisin sauce.

The time and effort invested in the preparation of this dish are rewarded with a tender, succulent duck with crispy skin.

Oyster Grilled Prawns

½ kg (1 lb) large prawns
2½ cm (1 in) piece of ginger, cut into strips
4 red chillies, seeded and chopped
½ tablespoon each of shallot and garlic crisps
2 tablespoons cooking oil
2 screwpine (*pandan*) leaves, cut into 2

Seasoning Ingredients
1 tablespoon oyster sauce
1 dessertspoon chilli sauce
1 dessertspoon sugar
1 teaspoon light soya sauce
¼ teaspoon thick soya sauce
Dash of pepper
Pinch of salt

Wash prawns, leave shell on and trim feelers and legs. Season prawns with seasoning ingredients for 20 minutes.

Grease a piece of tin foil with oil. Place prawns in centre. Sprinkle in ginger strips, red chillies and shallot and garlic crisps. Place screwpine leaves on top. Fold the tin foil into a package.

Place in an electric grill or oven toaster and grill for 12–15 minutes.

Illustrated on page 176. All kinds of seafood can be baked in foil. Sealing the foil allows the prawns to cook in their own steam so they retain their nutrition and aroma.

Baked Brinjals

4 brinjals, sliced slantingly 1 cm (⅓ in) thick without cutting through
1 teaspoon salt
2 tablespoons cooking oil
1 tablespoon preserved soya bean paste (*tau cheong*)
4–5 cloves garlic, minced
2 red chillies or 6 bird chillies, sliced
Juice of 1 small lime

Seasoning Ingredients
1 teaspoon pepper
1 teaspoon light soya sauce
2 tablespoons cooking oil

Immerse the sliced brinjals in water with salt added for 5 minutes. Drain and marinate with seasoning ingredients for 15 minutes.

Brush the brinjals with oil and wrap into a neat package with foil. Bake in preheated oven or oven toaster (205°C, 400°F) for 15 minutes until soft and cooked through.

Heat oil in a wok until hot. Reduce heat and stir-fry soya bean paste and garlic until fragrant. Stir in chillies.

Place brinjal package on a serving plate and sprinkle lime juice over hot brinjals.

Recipe Index

BEEF

PORK

CHICKEN

SEAFOOD

VEGETABLES

BEANCURD

RICE & NOODLES

EGGS

DESSERTS

General Index